BREAKING THE MOULD
HOW THE PDs CHANGED
IRISH POLITICS

STEPHEN COLLINS

Gill & Macmillan

Gill & Macmillan Ltd
Hume Avenue, Park West, Dublin 12
with associated companies throughout the world
www.gillmacmillan.ie

© Stephen Collins 2005
0 7171 3937 9
Index compiled by Helen Litton
Type design by Make Communication
Print origination by Carrigboy Typesetting Services, Co. Cork
Printed and bound by MPG Books, Cornwall

The paper used in this book is made from the wood pulp
of managed forests. For every tree felled, at least one tree
is planted, thereby renewing natural resources.

A CIP catalogue record for this book is available
from the British Library.

5 4 3 2 1

BREAKING THE MOULD
HOW THE PDs CHANGED
IRISH POLITICS

CONTENTS

ACKNOWLEDGMENTS

This book would have been impossible to write, particularly in the time available, were it not for the help and cooperation of a number of those involved in founding the Progressive Democrats. They gave generously of their time and were remarkably frank about the highs and lows of their journey on the political rollercoaster they set in motion twenty years ago.

Party leader and Tánaiste, Mary Harney, and her predecessor, Des O'Malley, made themselves available for lengthy interviews. Michael McDowell, Paul Mackay, Liz O'Donnell, Pat Cox, Mairin Quill and John Dardis did likewise. Among the others who gave me the benefit of their experience with the party were Barra Ó Tuama, Brigid Teefy, Stephen O'Byrnes, Michael Parker, John Higgins, Geraldine Kennedy, Oliver O'Connor and Odran Flynn.

The staff at PD headquarters were unfailingly helpful in providing me with access to the available records. Thanks to Noirin Slattery for sorting through the party archives, to Rachel Lacey and Bernie Connolly for their help and to Iarla Mongey and Susan O'Shea for ensuring that busy politicians were prepared to make time available to talk about events that happened long ago in political terms.

A special word of thanks to a number of people who gave me access to their private records. Paul Mackay, a founder and trustee of the party, gave me the ideal start to the project by going through his detailed diaries for 1985 and 1986, and he also supplied me with his scrapbooks. Niamh Brennan made available her meticulously assembled files, which contain almost all the founding documents of the party, as well as a comprehensive set of newspaper cuttings. Former Labour party minister, Barry Desmond, also let me have his extensive newspaper files on the PDs, as well as contemporary documents.

My thanks to long-time friends and journalistic colleagues, Joseph O'Malley and Gerald Barry, for reading the draft and making valuable suggestions for improving the text.

I would like to thank the staff of the National Archives, the National Library and the Oireachtas Library for their courtesy and cooperation.

Finally, thanks to Fergal Tobin of Gill & Macmillan for commissioning the book and for his encouragement during the project. Thanks also to Deirdre Rennison Kunz and Helen Thompson at Gill & Macmillan for all their help, and to Helen Litton for the index.

INTRODUCTION

On a cold Saturday morning in December, just four days before Christmas Day 1985, a new political party was launched onto a deeply depressing Irish political scene. At a hastily organised press conference, Desmond O'Malley, Mary Harney and Michael McDowell told a group of sceptical journalists about their plans to transform Irish politics. At that stage the country was experiencing a crisis of confidence that evoked the dark days of the 1950s. Garret FitzGerald's government was struggling to get the national debt under control and there was even talk of intervention by the International Monetary Fund. With Fine Gael and Labour at loggerheads over public-spending cuts, their only solution was an ever-increasing tax burden on workers. This had led to an unemployment rate of almost 20 per cent and a return to large-scale emigration. Even more depressingly the alternative was Fianna Fáil, the party that had created the debt in the first place and whose leader, Charles Haughey, blithely denied economic reality. There were real fears that the inevitable return to office of Fianna Fáil at the next election would reduce Ireland to the status of a European Argentina, with Haughey taking the role of Juan Perón.

This was the political background that confronted a little band of optimists who set out, in the winter of 1985, to break the mould of Irish politics. Des O'Malley was easily the best-known of the founders and the success of the new party—provisionally titled the Progressive Democrats—rested almost entirely on his shoulders. One of the foremost politicians of his era, O'Malley had that indefinable charisma that characterises the true political leader. In December 1985, however, many doubted whether he had the temperament or the capacity for the bread-and-butter work of party leadership that would be required to get the new party off the ground.

Earlier in 1985 O'Malley had finally been expelled from Fianna Fáil at the conclusion of a long and bitter struggle with Charles Haughey for the soul of the party founded by Éamon de Valera. By the end he was a marginalised figure in the party that many had believed it was his destiny to lead. Instead, the Fianna Fáil parliamentary party and the grassroots organisation opted decisively for Haughey and his brand of politics, and O'Malley was driven out into what seemed to be an unending political wilderness.

For six months after his expulsion O'Malley dithered about launching the Progressive Democrats. It seemed that he doubted his own capacity to lead a new party; there were many in Irish politics who doubted whether he had it in him. While O'Malley's ability and integrity were widely admired, he was also regarded as impatient, tetchy and uncomfortable with the back-slapping side of politics, which is so important in Ireland—particularly for a party leader.

He was pushed and prodded into forming the new party by Mary Harney, another inveterate anti-Haughey Fianna Fáil TD. She had stayed on in the party after O'Malley's expulsion, but was far more enthusiastic than he was about taking the ultimate step of forming a new political organisation. Harney, who was much younger than O'Malley, was a more easy-going personality, but she nonetheless displayed great political courage in standing up to Haughey's bully boys. Much earlier than her hero, she had come to the conclusion that a new party was the only outlet for the kind of politics they wanted to pursue.

Harney was finally expelled from the Fianna Fáil parliamentary party for voting for the Anglo-Irish Agreement negotiated by Garret FitzGerald in November 1985. Her expulsion provided the catalyst for the formation of the Progressive Democrats, or the PDs, as the party came to be known. Unlike O'Malley, she saw no future for herself as an Independent Fianna Fáil TD, lurking on the margins of politics. Unfettered by O'Malley's dynastic sense of obligation to his Fianna Fáil supporters in Limerick, Harney had no qualms about launching an entirely new party.

Most of the media coverage of the launch concentrated on O'Malley and Harney, but a third figure, no less formidable, if then little-known, was with them that morning. He was Michael McDowell, chairman of the Fine Gael organisation in Taoiseach Garret FitzGerald's own constituency of Dublin South East. A prominent barrister, McDowell gave the PDs credibility because he was the only one of the leading founder members who had neither left Fianna Fáil nor been expelled because of opposition to Haughey. More importantly, McDowell quickly became the intellectual engine of the new party, and his drive and fearlessness in debate were critical in its development.

The fourth person sitting at the top table facing the media was Paul Mackay, who had been a senior figure in Haughey's own constituency organisation in Fianna Fáil. An experienced accountant, Mackay was instrumental in setting up the PDs and in the days before the launch had arranged the bank loan that funded the acquisition of its headquarters at South Frederick Street in Dublin. Mackay and McDowell were the trustees of the new party. Another who was there to witness the launch was Adrian Hardiman, the undisputed rising star of the Law Library, who had been a Fianna Fáil council candidate a year before. A small group of O'Malley supporters from Limerick, led by Brigid Teefy, was also present to back their TD.

O'Malley delivered a short address in which he outlined his reasons for taking such a bold step:

> 'For the last year I have been struck by the strength of feeling through-out the country in favour of breaking the mould of Irish politics and giving Irish voters a new and real alternative. I believe that the old loyalties on which the present parties feed are no longer enough to sustain them.'

Many dismissed the new party as merely an anti-Haughey rump. An *Irish Press* editorial endorsed this view by saying that the PDs appeared to be based on personality rather than principle. However, from the very beginning O'Malley had a clear political agenda that defined the PDs and marked the party out from both Fianna Fáil and Fine Gael. In his first address as leader of the new party he continued:

> 'I believe there is a great consensus in Ireland which favours a peaceful approach to the problem in Northern Ireland; which favours funda-mental tax reform; which favours a clear distinction between Church and State. Irish politics must be transformed. Experience tells me that no such transformation will come from within the existing parties. It must come from outside. There must be a new beginning.'

Haughey dismissed the PDs as being engaged in 'political escapism', and most commentators pointed to the failure of a succession of new parties since the 1940s to break the stranglehold of Fianna Fáil, Fine Gael and Labour on political power. New parties had flared into existence before, some, like Clann na Poblachta, even had a short-term electoral break-through and had made it into government, but all had burned up quickly in the harsh atmosphere of competitive electoral politics.

Against that background the PDs have been a remarkable success and, twenty years on, have proved to be the most enduring small party in the history of independent Ireland. More importantly, the party can justly claim to have had a profound ideological impact on the political agenda of the past two decades. Some—particularly on the left—argue that this impact has been detrimental to the cohesiveness of Irish society, while PD supporters maintain that the party played a pivotal role in transforming Ireland into a prosperous, modern, low-tax economy. One way or another, there is no argument about the fact that the PDs have not only broken the mould of party politics but have played a vital role in shaping Irish society as it faced into the twenty-first century. That is an achievement that would have astonished even the most optimistic well-wishers who crammed into 25 South Frederick Street on the day the PDs was born.

Chapter 1

O'MALLEY LEAVES FIANNA FÁIL

Des O'Malley was expelled from Fianna Fáil in May 1985, at a time of unremitting depression in Irish politics. The party in which he had served as a senior figure had been permeated at the top by a culture of sleaze and fear. By 1985 Charles Haughey—who was elected party leader in 1979—and his cronies had achieved total control over the party. Meanwhile the Fine Gael–Labour coalition government, led by Garret FitzGerald, struggled to deal with the massive national debt run up by Fianna Fáil between 1977 and 1981. When Labour leader, Dick Spring, vetoed serious cuts in public spending, the only option left was a steep hike in taxation, but that simply drove the economy deeper and deeper into recession.

By this stage O'Malley, who had often been referred to by the media and by colleagues in Fianna Fáil as a potential leader of the party and future Taoiseach, had accepted that Haughey and his minions exercised total control over Fianna Fáil. He was dismayed at what was happening to the party he had served as a Cabinet minister and felt increasingly isolated. O'Malley's isolation was compounded by the fact that he had never had an easy relationship with the majority of his Fianna Fáil colleagues, although he had won the unswerving loyalty of a small group. During his heyday in the 1970s he had sometimes exhibited the haughtiness that characterised so many of the Fianna Fáil top brass, accustomed as they were to ruling what they seemed to feel was a one-party State. Although O'Malley, despite his abrasive style, was always regarded as a politician of integrity. He may not have had the free and easy manner of many of his party colleagues, but the voters respected his grittiness and regarded him as an honest man.

O'Malley entered politics in 1968 when his uncle, Donogh, one of the most colourful politicians of his era, died suddenly of a heart attack at the age of just forty-seven. Des, whose father had twice been mayor of Limerick, was approached by the Fianna Fáil hierarchy and invited to run for the vacancy. After checking that Donogh's widow, Hilda, was not interested in running he accepted, and was duly selected at a convention presided over by Haughey. Another senior party figure, Neil Blaney, arrived on the scene to run the election campaign in the traditional, aggressive Fianna Fáil manner. Winning the by-election in Limerick East was crucial for the then Taoiseach, Jack Lynch, who had succeeded Seán Lemass only two years earlier. Lynch presided over a parliamentary party deeply divided between the faction that supported Charles Haughey and that which supported George Colley. Donogh O'Malley had been a friend and a supporter of Haughey and it was therefore widely assumed that his nephew would follow in his footsteps and join the Haughey faction.

When he was duly elected, after a tough campaign, O'Malley proved a bitter disappointment to Haughey and Blaney because he quickly became an unequivocal supporter of Jack Lynch. When the crisis in the North developed in 1968, O'Malley was a strong backer of the Lynch policy of moderation. He regarded the Lynch approach to the North as a continuation of the policy followed by Lemass, and from the beginning he set his face against any cooperation, overt or covert, with republicans and their allies who regarded the use of violence as legitimate.[1]

This determination to give no aid or comfort to the IRA in any circumstances put O'Malley at odds with Haughey and Blaney. After the Fianna Fáil victory in the 1969 general election he was appointed government chief whip by Taoiseach Jack Lynch. It was a rapid promotion for the young TD from Limerick, and he was plunged almost immediately into the maelstrom of the arms crisis. As government chief whip, O'Malley had a ringside seat from which to observe the crisis unfolding. The details of that event have been chronicled elsewhere,[2] but it ended in May 1970 with Haughey being fired from the government in the early hours of the morning, while O'Malley was promoted to Minister for Justice at a critical time in the nation's history. For the first time since the Civil War there were real fears at the highest level in government that the fabric of democracy was under threat.

Throughout the 1970s O'Malley remained a committed supporter of Jack Lynch and became his most trusted lieutenant. In an effort to heal the rift in the party, Lynch brought Haughey back into the Cabinet after the Fianna Fáil landslide election victory in 1977, but it only made things worse. Haughey immediately began plotting to succeed to the leadership and Lynch's government was gradually destabilised. In the autumn of 1979 the Taoiseach decided he would step down in January 1980, but he was persuaded to bring his resignation date forward in the belief that it might help to thwart Haughey's ambitions.

'Jack was not pushed out by Haughey,' says Barra Ó Tuama, a close personal friend of Lynch who acted as an unofficial advisor to the Taoiseach. 'Jack was going to the United States in the autumn of 1979, but before he went he called me and said he was planning to retire the following January. He asked me to go to Dublin and tell George Colley.' Ó Tuama told Lynch that he should tell Colley himself, which the Taoiseach duly did. 'George subsequently asked me if Jack would be prepared to pull back his retirement date to December, so as to wrong-foot Haughey. I put it to Jack and he said he would. That is why he went in December [1979].'

The effort to wrong-foot Haughey failed, but Ó Tuama remains convinced that Colley should have won the ensuing leadership contest. 'I know for a fact that on the night before the vote Colley had the numbers, but people were got at and threatened.'[3]

O'Malley threw himself enthusiastically into the campaign to get George Colley elected leader in succession. Like other senior establishment figures in the party, he was stunned when Haughey emerged triumphant by 44 votes to 38 and found it very difficult to come to terms with the fact that a man who had been fired on suspicion of importing arms for the IRA nine years earlier was now the leader of Fianna Fáil.

Despite the deep distrust between them, Haughey asked O'Malley to serve in his first government and the invitation was accepted. Haughey often remarked that 'you don't have to like people to work with them' and O'Malley shared that philosophy. After losing office in June 1981, Fianna Fáil was back in power just nine months later and O'Malley was again asked to serve despite his involvement in the first heave against Haughey, which had followed the February 1982 election. That heave collapsed ignominiously and O'Malley was annoyed with his co-conspirators for botching the attempt. He was even more annoyed six months later when one of his followers, Charlie McCreevy, put down a motion of No Confidence in Haughey without consulting anyone. McCreevy, who was only five years in the Dáil, had already become a figure of controversy in Irish politics. First elected in on Lynch's coat-tails in 1977, he soon became a strong supporter of Charles Haughey and participated in the plot to destabilise Lynch's leadership. It did not take long before he became disillusioned with Haughey's failure to take decisive action on the economy and he then became a vocal critic of the leader from the backbenches. He established a reputation for himself as a stubborn Kildareman who didn't care what anyone thought about him.

As Haughey's second government—famously tagged with the acronym GUBU by Conor Cruise O'Brien—lurched from crisis to crisis in the summer and autumn of 1982, McCreevy simply walked into the party offices and put down a motion of No Confidence in the leader. If Haughey was taken by surprise at McCreevy's action, O'Malley was even more so.

'I was furious at his behaviour in October 1982, when he put down the motion of No Confidence in Haughey,' says O'Malley. 'I was in Spain on official business as the Department was considering the possible sale of the Great Southern Hotels Group. I was looking at the operation of the Parador Hotels in Spain, which were also State-owned, and I went there with Michael McNulty, the head of Bord Fáilte. In the middle of the night, at about 3.00 am, I got a phone call to say that McCreevy had put down the motion of No Confidence a few hours earlier. Before I went to Spain it had been agreed that nothing of the kind would be done for at least a fortnight. McCreevy's foolish and impetuous action helped Haughey to remain as Fianna Fáil leader for nearly ten years longer than he might have done and the consequences for Ireland were disastrous. Whatever McCreevy did for Ireland as Minister for Finance, he didn't do much for the country in 1982.'[4]

O'Malley had to rush back to Dublin for the vote and felt obliged to resign from the Cabinet as Minister for Industry and Commerce because he had no option but to oppose Haughey. He was livid that a challenge had been instigated when the anti-Haughey faction was totally unprepared for a contest. Martin O'Donoghue, who was Minister for Education, also felt he had no option but to resign, and the two men joined with George Colley in a determined effort to oust Haughey. The attempted heave failed, however, and McCreevy's motion was defeated comfortably by 58 votes to 22. There was pandemonium in Leinster House when the result was announced.

When Haughey's most implacable opponent, Jim Gibbons, appeared in the hall and tried to make his way towards the door, he was surrounded by a crowd of angry Haughey supporters. One of them struck Gibbons and a group of Dáil ushers had to swoop in to protect him and escort him safely to his car. The unruly crowd spilled out into the car park and other anti-Haughey TDs, quickly dubbed the 'Club of 22', received rough treatment. McCreevy was chased across the car park, kicked and jostled and called a 'bastard' and a 'Blueshirt'. Gardaí helped him to get into his car, but the crowd surrounded it, banging on the roof and shouting insults as he drove away through the Kildare Street gates of Leinster House.[5] 'Disgraceful scenes marred the Haughey victory last night when former Minister, Jim Gibbons, was punched outside Leinster House and Charlie McCreevy had to leave under garda protection,' reported the *Irish Independent* political correspondent, Chris Glennon. Gibbons denounced a 'Nazi Fascist element' in Fianna Fáil.[6]

Four months later O'Malley was involved in a final attempt to depose Haughey. The Fianna Fáil government had been ousted by Garret FitzGerald's Fine Gael–Labour coalition in November 1982, amid a welter of rumours about phone-tapping and bugging carried out at the behest of the government. When Haughey lost power the new Minister for Justice, Michael Noonan, investigated the allegations and his findings were sensational. He confirmed publicly, on 20 January 1983, that the phones of political journalists Geraldine Kennedy and Bruce Arnold had been tapped on the instructions of Seán Doherty, Minister for Justice, and that normal procedures had not been followed. Even more surprising was the disclosure that Ray MacSharry had borrowed Garda equipment to secretly record a conversation with Martin O'Donoghue back in October 1982. Fianna Fáil was immediately plunged into another crisis, but this time few gave Haughey a chance of surviving. A special party meeting was called to discuss the implications of the revelations and there was widespread speculation that Haughey would resign; a number of TDs had reportedly gone to him and asked him to step down.

At the meeting, one of the crucial contributions was made by Ray Burke, a swashbuckling figure, who said that Haughey should be allowed to go in his own time and should not be humiliated by being asked to step down immediately. Haughey himself told the meeting that the media would not hound him from office and declared he would make his own decision, in his own time. The impression conveyed to many wavering TDs was that Haughey was prepared to stand down, but wanted to be afforded the dignity of resigning in his own time. His opponents backed off to give him the time he required, but that merely gave Haughey the breathing space he needed to stage a comeback. Part of

Haughey's strategy was to provoke and encourage a squabble between all the pretenders to his office. The race to succeed him began immediately, with Des O'Malley being challenged by Gerry Collins and Michael O'Kennedy and, later, by Brian Lenihan and John Wilson.

When the crucial party meeting began on 7 February, Ben Briscoe proposed the motion requesting Haughey to resign and it was seconded by Colley. Crowds gathered on Kildare Street throughout the day as Fianna Fáil TDs debated the issue from 11.00 am until midnight. Much of the time at the meeting was spent on attacking the media. Charlie McCreevy, who had given a detailed interview to the *Sunday Press* the day before, was the butt of much criticism. This time around there was a secret ballot, but again Haughey won by 40 votes to 33.

The three heaves against Haughey in 1982 and 1983 had been deeply traumatic for the party as a whole, but particularly for the defeated faction. Many of the TDs who had opposed Haughey—and incurred not only his wrath but also the wrath of their party organisations—did not want to hear another word about changing the leadership. They decided, quite deliberately, to keep their heads down and concentrate on personal survival as they watched Garret FitzGerald's government struggle to tackle a deepening economic crisis.

The Fine Gael–Labour coalition elected in November 1982 had a small but decisive Dáil majority, but it was presented with horrendous economic problems. Its ability to tackle those problems was undermined at the very beginning of its term in a particularly damaging way. A few weeks after taking office Alan Dukes, the tall, chain-smoking and extremely bright Minister for Finance, went on radio to say that the Budget deficit for 1983 would have to be cut from £900 million, as per Fianna Fáil's proposed estimates, to £750 million. Dukes faced an immediate public challenge on the issue from the inexperienced Tánaiste and Labour leader, Dick Spring. A prickly young politician who had been catapulted to leadership after less than two years in the Dáil, Spring was in hospital for a very painful operation to remove four metal pins from his back—the result of a car accident a year earlier that had nearly killed him. From his hospital bed, Spring issued a public statement saying that there was no agreement between the two parties in government on the size of the deficit and he telephoned Garret FitzGerald to tell him of his anger at Dukes' interview. Spring expected a furious row with his Taoiseach, but to his surprise found that FitzGerald agreed with him. The Taoiseach had come to the conclusion that Department of Finance officials were being too alarmist.[7]

In his memoirs FitzGerald recalled his thinking thus:

'They seemed to feel that unless the current deficit were reduced to a figure close to £750 million in 1983, external confidence in our economy might wither, and our ability to borrow this sum, plus our capital needs, might thus be prejudiced. Alan Dukes, pitch-forked into the Finance portfolio in the most adverse circumstances conceivable, was in no position to challenge this rather apocalyptic view of his officials.'[8]

Dukes actually went to see Spring in hospital and brought with him a rising young civil servant called Michael Buckley, who would later go on to a hugely successful career in business, ending up as CEO of the biggest public company in Ireland: AIB. As Buckley tried to explain the budgetary position to him, Spring turned to Dukes and said, 'Get that man away from me. He's making me sick.'[9]

As the pressure on the coalition steadily increased, FitzGerald took the extraordinary decision to cross-check his own Finance Department's forecasts with none other than Henry Kissinger, who at that time was running a consultancy service in New York. FitzGerald rang Kissinger in early January and asked him to check the New York financial markets to establish what the reaction would be to an Irish current Budget deficit of £900 million rather than £750 million. On 10 January 1983, the day after Dukes' radio interview, Kissinger rang back to say that the expectation in New York was that the Irish government would be going for a current Budget deficit of around £900 million, which would leave the Exchequer borrowing requirement for the year at 12 per cent of GNP. Happy to receive this advice, the Taoiseach visited his Tánaiste in hospital to tell him the problem had been solved, and it was considered by the Cabinet two days later. A statement issued after the Cabinet meeting said: 'There has been concern on the part of the Taoiseach, the Tánaiste and a number of Ministers of both parties that the figure of £750 million, which the Minister for Finance has mentioned as a target to aim at, should be taken as reflecting a Government decision on a matter that is still under review.' Dukes was then forced to abandon his plans and ultimately come up with a Budget that contained the higher current deficit target of £900 million.[10]

The incident was probably the critical moment in the lifetime of the FitzGerald coalition. It meant that the government settled for a policy of containment with regard to the public finances and opted for extra taxation rather than spending cuts as the core of its budgetary policy. The consequences for the economy were dire and the long-term political fallout for Fine Gael was just as bad. In his subsequent Budgets, Dukes had no option but to raise taxes across the board to prevent the public finances from spiralling out of control. The increasing burden of tax on work accelerated the growth in unemployment and, while welfare payments and services were protected, the impact on the economy was devastating.

Facing a deadlock with his coalition partner over the economy, FitzGerald concentrated much of his energy on trying to devise a solution to the continuing crisis in Northern Ireland. The ruthless campaign of terror waged by the IRA had plunged the North into a mindless cycle of violence during the early 1980s. As a first step towards an agreed political solution to the underlying problem, FitzGerald established the Forum for a New Ireland and invited all the parties on the island of Ireland to attend. Not surprisingly, the forum was boycotted by unionist parties while Sinn Féin was excluded because of its association with the IRA campaign. The Forum became, in effect, a vehicle for devising a broadly agreed, constitutionalist, nationalist position.

Haughey took part, but adopted an old-fashioned, pre-Lemass, Fianna Fáil policy of a unitary Irish State as the only acceptable solution. Eventually he agreed to a form of words that acknowledged the unitary State as 'the particular structure of political unity which the Forum would wish to see established', but which also referred to the federal solution and joint authority as other options to be considered. Immediately on publication of the Forum Report in May 1984, Haughey reversed positions and maintained that only a unitary State would bring peace to the North. FitzGerald, Spring and SDLP leader John Hume were horrified by Haughey's reaction, which almost upstaged the Forum Report itself. There was also some disquiet in Fianna Fáil at the manner in which Haughey had effectively decided party policy without a full debate. Senator Eoin Ryan demanded a meeting of the parliamentary party to discuss the issue, but when it was held, after some delay, there was overwhelming support for the Haughey line. Following the three-hour meeting, O'Malley publicly criticised what he termed the stifling of debate within the party. Haughey reacted immediately and demanded that the whip be withdrawn from O'Malley. On a roll-call vote the motion to withdraw the whip was passed by 56 votes to 16. Dissent within the party had now been effectively crushed. Party press officer P.J. Mara, briefing political correspondents, summed up the new mood in the party with the old Italian Fascist party slogan: '*Uno duce, una voce*'. By way of clarification he added, 'There'll be no more nibbling at my leader's bum.'[11]

Meanwhile O'Malley was isolated as a nominal Fianna Fáil TD without the party whip. He was so marginalised that Fine Gael's John Kelly described him as being reduced to 'sleeping under political bridges'.[12] A final parting of the ways with an increasingly confident Haughey was now inevitable. The breach arose in February 1985 out of O'Malley's refusal to vote with parliamentary colleagues against a Bill to liberalise the family planning laws in February 1985.

'I was expelled from the party organisation because I wouldn't vote against the Family Planning Bill introduced in the Dáil by Barry Desmond. This was an attempt to clear up the stupid and messy situation created by Haughey himself in his 1979 legislation, which made condoms available on prescription only from a pharmacy.'[13]

It was not just his refusal to toe the line in the vote that left his fellow party TDs squirming but the fact that he delivered an electrifying speech to the Dáil that totally undermined their case. Defending the concept of a pluralist State, O'Malley stressed the effect a defeat of the Bill would have on opinion in Northern Ireland and he denounced the partitionist mentality of those who opposed the government's legislation:

'The politics of this would be very easy. The politics would be, to be one of the lads, the safest way in Ireland. But I do not believe that the interests of this State, or our Constitution and of this Republic would be served by putting politics before conscience in regard to this. There is a choice of a kind that can only be answered by saying that I stand by the Republic and accordingly, I will not oppose this Bill.'[14]

The use of the old Civil War catchphrase, 'I stand by the Republic', rubbed salt into the wounds as far as many of his Fianna Fáil colleagues were concerned, but the speech was hailed by TDs of all parties as one of the best in the Dáil chamber for many years. The former minister, who was now just an ordinary member having already lost the party whip, attempted to balance the impact of his speech by abstaining on the vote rather than supporting the government Bill outright. He was hoping that he could still have a future in Fianna Fáil; Haughey thought otherwise. On the night of 26 February, O'Malley was summoned to Mount Street to face

a motion calling for his expulsion. O'Malley's wife, Pat, and a crowd of
supporters from Limerick waited outside Fianna Fáil headquarters on that
cold night as O'Malley was hauled before the party's National Executive for
'conduct unbecoming' a party member. Charles Haughey, who had seen off
three attempts by O'Malley to remove him from the Fianna Fáil leadership,
came to that meeting determined to get rid of his old adversary once and
for all. 'It's him, or me,' Haughey told a number of people who tried to
intercede on O'Malley's behalf. Eighty-two people crammed into the
meeting room in Mount Street for the final showdown. O'Malley, who was
permitted to address the gathering, asked for a secret ballot on the
expulsion motion, but Haughey demanded a unanimous public decision.
On three different occasions during the meeting he interceded to say: 'I
want it to be unanimous for the good of the party and the organisation.'
When a few speakers made it clear that a unanimous vote was out of the
question, Haughey demanded an open roll-call vote. This was a flagrant
violation of the party's own rules, which stipulated that all votes should be
secret; nobody protested. Yet another roll-call vote was taken and the
motion to expel O'Malley was passed by 73 votes to 9.[15]

When the Limerick TD emerged into the glare of the television lights
on the street outside there were scenes that recalled the GUBU days of
three years earlier. As O'Malley supporters, journalists and members of
the party's National Executive jostled around on the street, Haughey left
the building to a few scattered *boos* and a solitary chant of '*Seig Heil, Seig
Heil*' from one protestor. O'Malley himself was one of the calmest people
present and as he kissed his wife in front of the cameras he remarked, 'I
hope that is not conduct unbecoming.'[16] The jocularity could not disguise
the seriousness of the situation for O'Malley, however, and it appeared to
many that night that a brilliant political career had come to an end. At
forty-six years of age he had served as a Cabinet minister or a front-bench
member for fourteen years and had been tipped by many people,
including former Taoiseach Jack Lynch, as a future Taoiseach. On that
night in 1985 it appeared his political future was bleak, even as his
Limerick supporters stoutly maintained that he would be back.

Previous Fianna Fáil ministers who had resigned or been expelled had
vanished into the wilderness. A striking example was Neil Blaney, who
was expelled from Fianna Fáil in 1971 on exactly the same grounds as
O'Malley. Blaney, like O'Malley, had been at the top in Fianna Fáil for
fifteen years, but once he was expelled he never came in from the political
wilderness. There was some irony in the fact that the two men would now

sit together for a while on the Independent benches in the Dáil because they represented the divergent strands of opinion that had dragged Fianna Fáil in opposite directions for twenty years. Yet the party, which emphasised unity and discipline above all other virtues, had expelled them both. The expulsion of O'Malley from Fianna Fáil in February 1985 left Haughey in total control of the party he had taken over five years earlier. His supporters were delighted with the move and claimed that Fianna Fáil was now a unified and cohesive political party for the first time since Haughey became leader in December 1979. 'There is a unity of purpose now that hasn't been there since Charlie took over. We have a united party again,' said Albert Reynolds a few weeks after O'Malley's expulsion.[17]

At this stage O'Malley was not thinking in terms of starting a new political party:

> 'During the years of conflict in Fianna Fáil I never seriously con-
> sidered establishing a new party. I felt Haughey's leadership would
> disintegrate and with a less determined crook that might have been
> the case. Waverers and even opponents of Haughey were frightened
> into supporting him again and again, our hope that there might be a
> disintegration of his leadership proved unfounded. It took several
> years for the realisation of that to become clear. It was only after my
> expulsion that the formation of a new party became a topic of
> conversation and then a realistic objective.'[18]

O'Malley's departure marked the final step in Haughey's take-over of Fianna Fáil. With leading opponents of 1979 dead, expelled or cowed, Haughey had total control of the party, to do with as he willed. The few remaining deputies with doubts about his leadership, like David Andrews, were simply too weary of the struggle to keep fighting him. Doherty was back in the parliamentary party, and MacSharry had won election to the European Parliament and was immediately installed as leader of the Fianna Fáil group in Strasbourg, though he still retained his seat in the Dáil. Albert Reynolds and Pádraig Flynn were leading members of the Opposition front bench. The Haughey faction now commanded Fianna Fáil, while O'Malley and all that he represented had been banished to the political wilderness. With FitzGerald's government fatally undermined by its inability to deal with the economy, it seemed only a matter of time before Fianna Fáil, under Haughey, would win a comfortable overall majority and hold the reins of power, without any strings attached.

Chapter 2 ~

BIRTH PANGS

On the night Des O'Malley was expelled from Fianna Fáil a disillusioned Fine Gael activist, Michael McDowell, was at home watching television. As the event unfolded on RTÉ news McDowell commented to his wife, Niamh, that if the former minister started a new political party, he was sure to get support because the time was right. Niamh replied that if he felt that strongly, he should make his views known to O'Malley.

> 'I had never met O'Malley in my life, but Niamh said that if I really thought there should be a new party, it would only come about if people like me helped him. I said that I would write him a letter. She said, "Do it now." I said, "I'll do it tomorrow." She said, "Do it tonight and I'll post it for you." So I did.'[1]

'Dear Mr O'Malley, I wish to express to you a deepfelt sentiment of admiration, warmth and sympathy with you in your recent battles,' began the letter. McDowell then went on to quote a stirring injunction from Charles de Gaulle he had read not long before: 'Remember this lesson. History does not teach fatalism. There are moments when the will of a handful of free men breaks through determinism and opens up new roads. People get the history they deserve.'

McDowell continued: 'As I see it, you are in a unique position to open up a new road now . . . I write to tell you that I (and many similar people to whom I have spoken) would happily assist you and associate with you in breaking political moulds.' Having explained his Fine Gael background, McDowell went on to predict that sometime in 1986 or 1987 the Fine Gael–Labour coalition would fragment and lose power and he deplored the fact that the people would be faced with a choice of the coalition for another term, or voting for Fianna Fáil. 'I have no hesitation in saying that

I will do anything I can to help you to transform Irish politics (which you can now do) and that I am always available to assist you if called upon.[2]

At that stage Michael McDowell was an up-and-coming young barrister, from a strong Fine Gael family, who had lost the political faith. Intelligent, supremely confident and ideologically opposed to increasing State involvement in the economy, he was appalled at what he regarded as Labour's undue influence in government. McDowell, a grandson of Eoin MacNeill, founder of the Irish Volunteers in 1912 and a senior minister in the first government of the Free State, was a natural member of the Fine Gael élite. As a newly qualified barrister he had worked in party headquarters during the victorious election campaign of 1973. The newly installed Taoiseach, Liam Cosgrave, wrote to him on behalf of the Fine Gael party to express 'our deepest appreciation and best thanks for the magnificent contribution you made to our victory'. He was subsequently an active member in Dublin South East and narrowly failed to get elected to Dublin City Council in 1979. He was personally close to the party's constituency TD, Garret FitzGerald, who became party leader in 1977. As a schoolboy in the 1960s at the Dublin Jesuit private school, Gonzaga College in Dublin, McDowell had become friendly with FitzGerald's son, John, and was a frequent visitor to the family home.

As a young adult he had even spent a summer holiday with the FitzGeralds in France. McDowell became chairman of the Taoiseach's constituency organisation in 1981 and was issued with a special pass to give him access to the Taoiseach's Office in Government Buildings and to his home in Palmerston Road. However, McDowell soon became disillusioned with what he regarded as the political stalemate that was paralysing the Fine Gael–Labour coalition under FitzGerald. During the negotiation of the second of those coalitions he made a speech declaring that nothing could be worse for the country than 'the half-hearted implementation of a compromise between two divergent views as to how the country should be run by a Government divided along ideological lines.'

It was an extraordinary speech because its main focus was on an issue that was to become central to Irish politics for the following two decades: the link between income tax rates and unemployment. 'A new and radical departure is called for; tax on work must be ended if unemployment is to be tackled.' He suggested abolishing tax on work altogether and compensating with taxes on property. Another proposal was that instead of 'subsidising idleness', the State should require people to work in return for long-term State benefit. McDowell forecast that if FitzGerald and Spring agreed a half-hearted compromise programme rather than a radical departure to tackle the roots of unemployment, they would be swept from power four years later.[3] FitzGerald, with the backing of the vast majority of party members, went ahead and negotiated a coalition deal with Labour. McDowell was left to cry in the wilderness, but as time went on he felt entirely vindicated. 'He made a succession of Cassandra-like speeches predicting doom for the party. Friends and colleagues were dismayed and FitzGerald angered,' observed Gerald Barry in the *Sunday Tribune*.[4]

In the Law Library McDowell regularly discussed politics with Michael O'Leary, a former leader of the Labour party who had defected to Fine Gael in 1982. O'Leary, who was first elected as a Labour TD in 1965 and had never lost an election, was charming and unreliable in equal measure. He was intelligent and witty, but had a very low boredom threshold and could be a frustrating colleague to work alongside. At the previous general election O'Leary had performed the remarkable feat of getting elected as a Fine Gael TD just weeks after quitting as Labour leader following a humiliating rejection of his policies at Labour's annual conference. He soon became disillusioned with the coalition, however, particularly as he was excluded from office at the insistence of his former Labour colleagues. On a visit to McDowell's house shortly before Christmas 1984, the two men drew up a list of the seats Fine Gael would lose at the next election. They arrived at the grand total of twenty-one (in the event, when the election came over two years later, it was nineteen), and con-cluded that there was no way of stopping a Fianna Fáil landslide. It was not long after that, in February 1985, that McDowell wrote to O'Malley.[5]

Another person who wrote to O'Malley was Dublin accountant, Paul Mackay. He had been an active member of Fianna Fáil and was party treasurer in Haughey's Dublin North Central constituency. A long-time supporter of George Colley, Mackay refused to be intimidated by Haughey and had the toughness of character to refuse to hand over a list of party donors to him. A bitter internal dispute ensued, but Mackay proved a much tougher nut to crack than Haughey or his supporters had expected. Eventually, he was expelled from the organisation in 1983 and he watched from the sidelines as O'Malley was thrown out of the party.

In a letter dated 29 March Mackay wrote:

'Dear Des, I write to commiserate with you on your recent expulsion from the Fianna Fáil party and to extend my full support and help in

any political initiative you may consider in the future. You are aware of the support you have throughout the country. Several of my friends and acquaintances have assured me that they are more than willing to help you should you decide to pursue the option of establishing a new political grouping. I am assured by them that both time and finance would be made available.[6]

Looking back on that time, Mackay recalls, 'I was fecked out of Fianna Fáil in May of 1983 and I was doing nothing politically. Subsequently, Des O'Malley had his problems and he was fecked out. At that time there was talk about the formation of a new party and I wrote to him saying: "If you are establishing a new party, count me in." At that time Mary Harney was in the background, but I didn't know either of them too well.'[7]

McDowell and Mackay were to play a critical role in the formation of the new party, but at the time they were strangers as far as O'Malley was concerned and he waited some time before responding to their letters.

At that stage, in the spring of 1985, O'Malley was relying on old friends and allies in Fianna Fáil to weigh up the prospects for a new party; Seamus Brennan—the former Fianna Fáil general secretary who had been an anti-Haughey TD since 1981—Mary Harney and David Andrews were chief among them. Brennan was anxious to establish whether the electorate was disposed to respond to a new party led by O'Malley and he discussed the issue with Barra Ó Tuama, the Cork businessman and concert promoter who was a strong supporter of the anti-Haughey faction in Fianna Fáil.

'We discussed the issue a few times and it was suggested that I would go away and organise a poll,' says Ó Tuama. 'We agreed on the questions and Seamus Brennan said that if the results came out positively, he would move to the new party.' Ó Tuama went ahead and commissioned and paid for the poll, which was conducted by Irish Marketing Surveys (IMS). 'I was having some business difficulties at the time, but I wanted to get things moving so I paid for the poll myself. The results were very positive.'[8]

The findings were given to the media on 18 April and received extensive publicity the following day. They showed that 39 per cent of people surveyed were in favour of a new political party headed by O'Malley, while 35 per cent were against it. An interesting feature of the poll was that the most positive reaction to a party led by O'Malley came from the AB social category and the large farmers. The strongest support was located in Munster—not surprising in view of O'Malley's home base and the residual anger there at Haughey's treatment of Jack Lynch. The poll was released to the media by O'Malley, who made a public statement saying he had not commissioned the research nor been consulted on the questions. Nonetheless, he said that the results were personally gratifying and, taken in conjunction with all the messages of support he had received, seemed to reflect a growing and heartfelt dissatisfaction with the general political situation in the country. 'Consideration will have to be given to how the aspirations of so many for a fresh approach can find expression in Irish political structures,' he added.[9] 'The gestation of the party was a poll that Barra Ó Tuama carried out. Seamus Brennan organised it, but I never got the sense that he was going to get involved in a new party,' recalls Mary Harney.[10]

Ó Tuama recalls his surprise at Brennan's decision not to get involved after his initial burst of enthusiasm. 'I met Brennan on his own and with others, like Mary Harney and Des O'Malley, a number of times in the spring of 1985. He was all enthusiastic about a new party until the facts were produced showing that it could succeed.'[11]

Less than a week after the publication of the poll, O'Malley finally got around to responding to McDowell's letter of two months earlier: '*I apologise for the delay in replying to your letter of the 27th February but I have close on two thousand to answer and I have not necessarily answered the more important ones first, particularly as I was waiting to see how certain matters would develop.*'

O'Malley went on to thank McDowell and his wife for their good wishes and support and suggested that the barrister should ring him at his Dáil office and arrange to come in for a chat. McDowell duly made contact and invited the former minister to come to his house in Mount Pleasant Square for dinner on 9 May. McDowell, who also invited Michael O'Leary, was surprised at how cautious O'Malley was about the formation of a new party.[12]

O'Malley was in a quandary at this stage because most of his leading supporters in Fianna Fáil, with the notable exception of Harney, had gone cool on the idea of a new party after the publication of the poll. Seamus Brennan, in particular, decided to pursue his political career within Fianna Fáil. O'Malley's supporters in Limerick were also dubious about the notion of a new party, with most preferring their TD to stay on as a sort of Independent Fianna Fáil deputy who might one day be reconciled with the party.

McDowell, though, was galvanised into action and he produced a detailed memorandum on the formation of a new party. 'Time is of the essence,' he wrote in his introduction. 'If the Party is not established in the autumn there is the prospect that the impetus to get it going will flag all round. Likewise the chance of being forced into a by-election or a general election while unprepared is increased.' He went on to suggest a launch in early October, to coincide with the autumn Dáil session, followed by a national conference in the third week of November to get the party off the ground. 'I feel that there is a great deal of urgency in this enterprise. To maintain momentum, to avoid unforeseen problems and to keep the political initiative, this Party must be functioning in late 1985.'

McDowell was worried that the prospects for a new party would be scotched if there were any great delay. 'Everyone is taking a risk of sorts; those with established political links will be more exposed and less enthusiastic as each week goes by without any knowledge that the planning phase has commenced.' He then went on to outline the structure he envisaged, first for a foundation committee and then for the party itself, the need to acquire a national headquarters and the necessity of putting the party finances on a sound basis from the outset. He also dealt with the party name and image, the broad policy objectives and the nuts-and-bolts of the constituency organisation. McDowell suggested a number of names for the party, including New Democrats, New Republic, National Party, Radical Party; Progressive Democrats was not on his list. He maintained that it would be helpful if the name of the party could be translated easily into Irish, along the lines of 'Poblacht Nua'.

On the question of image he wrote in the memorandum: 'Distasteful though it may be, expert advice should be sought on image. While policy is not a matter for PR consultants, image is. Use of colour, symbols and suggestive associations are very important and will have to be decided on before the Party launch and the foundation conference. The help of professional visualisers and publicity men could be invaluable.' This injunction was directed at O'Malley, who had insisted at their meeting that he wanted nothing to do with handlers or political spinning.

On the broad thrust of party policy and rhetoric he said the party should be:

(a) pro-enterprise;
(b) in favour of economic participation by all;
(c) liberal and pluralist, but not aggressively secularist;
(d) hostile to institutional dependency;
(e) favourable to incentives;

(f) pro-self reliance;

(g) deregulating where possible;

(h) anti-monopoly and pro-competition, but not overly emphatic on 'privatising';

(i) low-key on nationalism;

(j) stressing real republican values rather than nationalistic myths.

He suggested that detailed policy should be worked out by a policy group established by O'Malley and other TDs who were supporting the initiative. At this stage McDowell envisaged six to eight members of the Oireachtas joining the party and felt that the presence of this number of high-profile politicians at the launch was essential. 'Above all any hint of amateurism must be avoided. That is the label that [Peter] Prendergast and [Frank] Wall will most want to hang about our necks. It is a line that the media will be easily fed.'13

At this stage McDowell believed that O'Malley was going to bring at least a handful, and possibly a significant number, of anti-Haughey Fianna Fáil TDs into the new party. For his part, he drew up a list of potential Fine Gael recruits. TDs such as John Kelly, Brendan McGahon, Paddy Harte, Liam Skelly, Ivan Yates, Hugh Coveney, John Bruton and Avril Doyle were on the list. Prominent figures like T.K. Whitaker, Paddy Lynch and Miriam Hederman were also mentioned.

McDowell was ready and anxious to get moving at this stage, but O'Malley was reluctant to commit himself. With local elections scheduled for June 1985, there was an argument for waiting to see what would happen. In the event, Fianna Fáil did well in those elections and Labour did badly, with Fine Gael performing reasonably well. When the elections were out of the way O'Malley continued to prevaricate, and it was not until early July that he wrote to Paul Mackay and asked him to get in touch.

Mackay telephoned O'Malley on 10 July and made an appointment to see him the next day in his Dáil office. 'He was sitting up there on his own with his secretary, Marie McLoughlin. He looked like a guy who was at a low ebb—just going nowhere—but said he had made up his own mind that he was going to set up a new party by September or October of that year.' O'Malley told Mackay that it was crucial to have a good general secretary and that he wanted to find a Seamus Brennan-type: 'He thought that was very important.'14

O'Malley suggested that Mackay should go to the Fianna Fáil senator and former party fundraiser, Des Hanafin, and ask him to help work out the cost of establishing and running a new party. 'I subsequently met Hanafin at his home. There weren't too many people hanging around at that stage. I submitted a document to O'Malley after my meeting with Hanafin, setting out some sort of budget. Forecasts of potential income and what costs would be on an ongoing basis in the first year.'[15]

That document was a detailed budget of revenue and expenditure for the first full year of what Mackay termed 'Product X'. It estimated that the new party would have to spend £130,000 in that period. Funding for that was to come from membership fees (£30,000), a national collection (£60,000) and fundraising (£40,000). Salaries for a general secretary, a policy advisor, an administrator and two part-time staff were factored into the budget, as were the costs of office accommodation and leasing charges for two cars. For the purposes of comparison a breakdown of Fianna Fáil's expenditure for 1983 was supplied, a figure of £504,000.[16]

Mackay didn't waste any time and was in a position to send a draft costings for 'Product X' to O'Malley on 23 July. In an accompanying letter he informed O'Malley that he was going to Kerry on holidays, but would be available on his return for 'any jobs you wish me to undertake on your behalf'. Mackay went on to say that during his break he would complete his notes on the economic situation and make discreet enquiries about a potential general secretary. 'I have already prepared a list of names and addresses of potential members/workers, together with a list of possible subscribers, many of whom were in sympathy with the late George Colley.'[17] (George Colley died in September 1983.)

O'Malley passed on Mackay's budget document for the new party to McDowell, who in turn telephoned Mackay on 12 August, to keep things moving. 'It was the first time I had heard of Michael McDowell,' recalls Mackay and he admits his immediate reaction was to think: Who the hell is this guy?

'I was very cautious. I was on the suspicious side so I immediately phoned Mary Harney and said McDowell wanted to see me for lunch. He had seen the document I had produced for O'Malley in relation to costs and income projections.' Harney reassured Mackay that McDowell was all right. 'He's okay. He has met O'Malley and we have talked. He's okay,' said Harney.

Mackay went ahead and met McDowell for the first time the following day, at lunch in the Hibernian United Services Club. Mackay's diary entry for Tuesday, 13 August is telling: 'Good meeting. Intelligent guy. He left me with his document which he has sent to O'Malley—Very impressive.'[18] It was an important date in the formation of the PDs.

A week later Mackay invited McDowell around to his home in Rathgar. The two men talked for about two hours, but came to the conclusion that continued planning was fruitless until they got firm riding instructions. Mackay recalls:

'Funnily, we thought we were in the outer circle. We thought there was a whole host of people in the middle there around O'Malley. We subsequently learned there were damn-all and that we, in fact, were in the centre and not in the outer rings. But at this particular stage we thought we were in the outer ring and were wondering what all these fellows close to O'Malley were doing. What was their plan of campaign? We wanted to get involved but thought we were being kept at arm's length. In fact, there were very few around as we found out later.'[19]

O'Malley, meanwhile, was taking soundings up and down the country to make his own assessment as to whether a new party would be a runner. He was determined to be very discreet: 'When it came to planning for a new party, I didn't want to do anything too publicly. As well as meetings in Dublin, I had some in Limerick and Cork. We had to be careful where we held meetings as we did not want to alienate potential allies.'

Barra Ó Tuama arranged for O'Malley to meet some leading Fianna Fáil figures in Cork. One of the people O'Malley met was Mairin Quill, who had been elected as an alderman to Cork City Council in June 1985. 'I met Des in the Metropole Hotel and he told me he was thinking of forming a new party. I encouraged him to go ahead and said that if he did, I would be happy to join.'[20]

Harney returned from a long visit to the United States in early September to find that O'Malley had gone cool on the idea of a new party. 'I was invited to the United States by the State Department and I was away for a couple of months. I was on my own, staying in hotels a lot of the time and I did an awful lot of thinking. I made up my mind that on the next big issue of conflict that arose in Fianna Fáil, I would leave the party. I was really unhappy.' However, on her return she found that O'Malley had become pessimistic about the idea of a party because of newspaper articles stating that a number of prominent anti-Haughey TDs, like David Andrews, would never leave Fianna Fáil. 'Des said, "We are not going to get anybody" and he was totally off the idea.'[21]

She didn't give up, though, and kept egging him on to take action. Mackay also kept the pressure on. He went to O'Malley's home on 18

September and the two men had a long talk. That galvanised O'Malley into action and planning finally began in earnest. A meeting at O'Malley's house was arranged for the following week, to bring together all the key planners. O'Malley wrote to McDowell to invite him to the meeting in his home at 9.00pm on 24 September, saying he had made arrangements with 'certain others to attend at that time also'. Harney, McDowell, Mackay, Labour senator Helena McAuliffe and a number of people from O'Malley's constituency organisation in Limerick attended and discussed in detail the formation of the party.[22]

Another meeting was arranged for McDowell's house on 29 September. Michael O'Leary was at that meeting and so too was the outspoken Fianna Fáil TD, Charlie McCreevy, who attended on the invitation of Mary Harney. McCreevy was enthusiastic about the new party and became very active in its planning over the next couple of months. A chartered accountant, McCreevy held firm views on the need for tight control of public spending and prided himself on speaking his mind regardless of the consequences. At this stage he also had the reputation of being a bit of a rake and attracted far more media attention than the average back-bencher.[23]

Two days later, at another meeting in O'Malley's house, a decision was taken to place a newspaper advertisement seeking a suitably qualified administrator. What they were looking for was the right kind of person to act as party general secretary. 'O'Malley was very anxious to have the right person as general secretary. He appreciated the role Seamus Brennan had played for Lynch in Fianna Fáil and he wanted somebody of a similar ilk to get involved. He is a terrible administrator himself so recognised the need for a good general secretary,' says Mackay.[24] There were a few replies to the ad, but nothing came of it. At that same meeting a launch date of mid-November was discussed. The names of a number of prominent Cork politicians were mentioned as likely members, including Fianna Fáil TDs Pearse Wyse and Joe Walsh, as well as two prominent city councillors, Mairin Quill of Fianna Fáil and Jim Corr of Fine Gael.

The key planners held meetings every couple of days, but they frequently disagreed and there were many rocky moments over the next couple of months before the party got off the ground. 'After a lot of persuasion and encouragement we got the thing moving again with O'Leary, with Charlie McCreevy and McDowell and Paul Mackay and we used to have regular meetings,' recalls Harney.[25] The participants remember some of these meetings as being very fraught. 'Disaster' is the descriptive entry in Mackay's diary after a meeting in his house on 3 October involving

O'Leary, Harney and McDowell. The main problem at this stage was indecisiveness, something that McCreevy and McDowell found infuriating. One of the reasons for this indecision was the way in which the three attempts to remove Haughey had been botched: that had generated a lack of trust among some of the plotters about the reliability of the others.

Des O'Malley's wife, Pat, for one, was very dubious about the whole project at that point. Pat O'Malley was a hugely popular figure across the political spectrum. Bright, amiable and with a flair for politics, she played a crucial role in her husband's political career. Her unfailing good humour and courtesy provided an ideal counterbalance to Des's reserve and impatience, and her involvement was a critical factor in his electoral success in Limerick. Des and Pat were a team in politics, as well as being a devoted couple, so her doubts about the project counted for a lot. Harney remembers the difficulties they faced at that time:

> 'Pat was sick of politics and all the hassle that Des and herself had gone through in the previous couple of years. She genuinely felt that Des was being used again after all the attempted *coups* and false dawns. Now Pat is a lovely person, as everybody knows, but when she heard that people like McCreevy, who she regarded as totally unreliable, were involved in the meetings, she kicked up murder and encouraged Des to call it all off.'[26]

Because of her opposition, meetings were no longer held in the O'Malley home. But the group did continue to meet, even though the mood swung wildly from pessimism to optimism. A week after the 'Disaster' in Mackay's house another meeting was held at McDowell's home, which lasted from 10.00pm to 12.30am. This time Paul Mackay recorded in his diary: 'A good meeting.' After that he made a number of appointments with auctioneers to look at premises for the new party. He went to view properties in South Frederick Street, Duke Street and Harcourt Street and recalls that O'Malley behaved in a furtive manner, which only served to attract attention to them as they examined the properties.

On 17 October they held a long meeting to discuss policy. Again Mackay records this as being a good meeting, particularly as McCreevy insisted that a clear policy position on economic issues was vital if the party were to succeed. 'McCreevy said that we should all put our thoughts down on paper, but he said that we should not put our names on the individual papers for security reasons. "O'Malley will be number one and I will be number two, because I am sitting beside him," said McCreevy. The result was we all got a number,' recalls Mackay. 'Only McCreevy and myself and one other did actually produce a piece of paper on the policy lines we should adopt as a new party.'[27]

The McCreevy document, entitled *Ideas by Number 2*, contained an introduction, a preamble and a set of ten principles on which the new party should be based. He suggested that the principles needed to be accompanied by the preamble to make it clear to people why the party was being established.

> 'What we are really hoping for is a realignment in Irish politics and to break the traditional Fianna Fáil/Fine Gael voting patterns. By having the preamble we are putting down on paper something that nearly every-one realises, i.e. that the Tweedledum/Tweedledee political approach of these parties has failed.'

He stressed that it was important to lay down basic principles not only to attract people who agreed with them but also to exclude those who would not feel happy with 'our objectives on liberal social legislation and/or the economic approach'.

In his preamble McCreevy maintained that, due to the absence of brave, visionary political leadership, the Irish people had lost their enterprise, initiative and hope in the future:

> 'We believe that barring some economic miracle, the viability of Ireland as an independent, economic unit is threatened . . . We believe that there is no difference between Fianna Fáil and Fine Gael and that any difference is superficial and stems from Civil War positions, and such considerations have no place in the political consciousness of modern Ireland . . . We believe that the populist, all things to all peo-ple approach of Fianna Fáil and Fine Gael has resulted in the Irish people having no real alternative at elections.'

He also maintained that real social change, attended by the appropriate legislative action, was being hindered by the absence of any clear philosophy to guide the major parties, which allowed them to be blocked by powerful interest groups, such as the Catholic Church.

McCreevy then set down ten principles for the new party, beginning with the aspiration to the unity of Ireland by consent. One of his principles stated: 'Our economic policies will be enterprise based and on the need to restore initiative.' Another was: 'To reduce the level of State involvement and interference in the economic life of the country'; while another stressed that the State should live within its means. On the other hand, McCreevy also proposed the principle that: 'Our social welfare policies will be biased in favour of the under-privileged sections of Irish society' and another was 'to eliminate discrimination in all areas'.[28]

McDowell came up with a detailed policy document, which stressed the need for tax reform as a fundamental prerequisite to turning the economy around. He proposed a substantial reduction in tax on work, but further proposed that there should be a tax on all other forms of income, as well as a tax on property, to fund local government. He highlighted what he regarded as the absurdity of the State taking money from taxpayers to distribute back to them in schemes like food subsidies and children's allowances. McDowell's document would later form the core of the party's economic policy.

Mackay's document adopted a similar approach to McDowell's on the issues of taxation and the economy, but he also dealt with the need for a thorough reform of the civil service, a more efficient system of revenue collection, a radical reform of the labour laws to improve business efficiency, the abolition of various State subsidies and a moderate approach to the North.[29]

The McDowell, McCreevy and Mackay documents were circulated at a meeting held in the home of Paul O'Malley, a relation of Des, at Highfield Road in Rathgar. By this stage planning was far advanced and there was even a formal agenda for the meeting. Item one was discussion on the first draft of a party policy document. The appointment of a general secretary was also discussed and McDowell asked Mackay if he would act as general secretary on a part-time basis. The response was, 'Thanks, but no thanks.' Mackay told the others about his search for a headquarters and gave the South Frederick Street location as his favoured option. The launch date was also an item on the agenda, but no decision was taken. One important decision that was taken was the name of the party, which it was agreed would be called the Progressive Democrats. McDowell didn't particularly like the word 'Progressive' in the title and continued to argue for other names, like the Radical party. However, Harney and the others wanted the term 'Progressive' in the title, so they settled on Progressive Democrats.

A week later, at a meeting in Mackay's house, Pat Cox—then a presenter with RTÉ's 'Today Tonight' programme—turned up. Paul Mackay says,

'O'Malley brought Cox along. He knew him from Limerick and I remember him saying at one stage: "Unless Cox comes on board there is no party. I have to have Cox as my general secretary." I had not met Cox before although I knew him from television. O'Malley wanted to introduce him to the others and see how they would all react to each other. It was a get-to-know-you meeting.'[30]

The following night, 31 October, the embryonic party was almost aborted at another meeting in Mackay's house: O'Malley suddenly got cold feet and wanted to call the whole thing off. 'He said to leave it for a month. We had a general debate on the whole thing,' recalls Mackay. McDowell was furious and he launched into a diatribe against O'Malley's lack of decisiveness. Mackay's diary entry says it all: 'Last Supper atmosphere.' After the meeting there was even talk of Harney going out on her own as the leader of the new party.[31]

O'Malley remained unhappy with the involvement of O'Leary and McCreevy, both of whom made him uneasy for different reasons. O'Leary had just done a solo run on the issue of divorce: with considerable help from McDowell, he had published a private member's Bill on the issue in the Dáil and, while only five TDs supported the measure, it added to the pressure on the Fine Gael–Labour coalition, which was theoretically committed to holding a referendum on divorce. O'Malley was impatient with what he regarded as a distraction at that stage, but, more importantly, he thought that O'Leary's record of having switched parties once before would be damaging for the new party. He feared that it would be regarded as a refuge for failed politicians.

O'Malley's attitude to McCreevy remained one of deep suspicion. While Harney held McCreevy in high esteem, as did most of the others, O'Malley was doubtful. In essence, he was not prepared to commit himself to such a big project until he was satisfied that everything was right, and he still had his doubts. After storming away from the meeting feeling furious at O'Malley's lack of decisiveness, McDowell calmed down and the following day wrote a letter to O'Malley apologising for the tone of his remarks. However, he repeated his view that the time had come to make a binding decision. 'I wrote O'Malley a note saying, it is time to make up your mind. Pee, or get off the pot.'[32]

Chapter 3 ∽

PROGRESSIVE DEMOCRATS

A few days later O'Malley came within an inch of his life in a road accident. The top half of his car was sheared off when he drove under a lorry on the Naas Road on 4 November. On impact he threw himself across onto the passenger seat; if he had not done so, he would almost certainly have died. It was a trauma that might have been expected to confirm O'Malley's doubts about the wisdom of embarking on a momentous political enterprise, and for a time his co-conspirators felt the whole project might be shelved. McDowell felt guilty about his scathing attack of a few days earlier, believing it may have upset O'Malley's concentration, while Mackay thought that was the end of it: 'Coming immediately after the Last Supper, it meant we really didn't know where we were going.'[1]

Mackay remembers calling in to O'Malley's Dáil secretary and being told not to go near him in hospital. He got the same response from Pat when he rang looking for him at home. 'The word was none of us was to go near Des. It was not that he was badly injured, just she didn't want any of us annoying him about politics or the new party. She would have wrung our necks at that stage and I can understand why.' Mackay, Harney and McDowell continued to meet and plan for the new party, but they were not sure if their leader was still interested in being involved.

Harney recalls how guilty everybody felt when news of the car crash was received: 'You know the way the media reports things. It sounded terrible: "Des O'Malley has been rushed to Naas hospital after a serious road accident." Of course everybody, having felt really angry with him for not going ahead, felt really upset. We thought at first he might die. He was in Naas hospital for a while and Charlie McCreevy went to see him.'[2]

Mackay sent a letter to O'Malley's Limerick address wishing him a speedy recovery. 'I telephoned you in Limerick last Tuesday but Pat advised me that you were under doctor's orders to rest and not to be disturbed. When you are feeling better and have an opportunity, I would appreciate a telephone call.'³ Mackay's letter conveys something of the sense of anxiety felt by the planners about O'Malley's intentions following the accident.

Finding it impossible to get in touch with O'Malley, Mackay came up with a novel way of sending a coded message to him. He sent a letter to RTÉ's three most popular radio shows—presented by Gay Byrne, Mike Murphy and Ronan Collins, respectively—asking them to wish O'Malley a speedy recovery. More importantly, he asked them to read out the following message: 'Perhaps you might advise him that he is particularly missed at this crucial time and that his many friends in Dublin are looking forward to his return.'⁴

O'Malley was badly shaken by the crash, which left him on crutches for a few months, but it did give him time to think and ultimately hardened his resolve to go ahead with the project. The catalyst for action was the signing of the Anglo-Irish Agreement by Garret FitzGerald and Margaret Thatcher on 15 November 1985. The Agreement represented a milestone in Anglo-Irish relations and was FitzGerald's crowning achievement. It led to the Downing Street Declaration and the Good Friday Agreement in the 1990s. The Anglo-Irish Agreement provided an institutional role for the Irish government in running the North's affairs, but was denounced in the strongest possible terms by Haughey as a betrayal of the constitutional claim to Irish unity. The Fianna Fáil leader even dispatched his deputy leader, Brian Lenihan, to the United States to lobby leading politicians against the proposed Agreement.

'When the Anglo-Irish Agreement was signed in November 1985, Haughey sent Lenihan out to the United States to try and get Tip O'Neill and the other leading Irish-Americans to oppose it. That was a treacherous and unpatriotic act by Haughey,' says O'Malley. 'The government of Ireland had signed an international Agreement and it was approved of in the Dáil, yet he tried to undermine it. It was the ultimate treachery.'⁵ This attempt to sabotage the Anglo-Irish Agreement backfired on Haughey in a number of ways. For a start, it infuriated Irish-American politicians, particularly the Speaker of the House of Representatives, Tip O'Neill, and did nothing to enhance Haughey's reputation when news of the intervention eventually leaked out. More significantly, the Agreement exposed the old fault line in Fianna Fáil once again.

The deal was publicly welcomed by O'Malley and by former Taoiseach, Jack Lynch. Harney issued a statement in favour of it and followed this by going through the government lobby along with O'Malley. The decision of O'Malley and Harney to vote with Fine Gael on the issue of the North marked the ultimate breach with Haughey and convinced O'Malley of the need to proceed with the formation of a new party, particularly when Harney was expelled from Fianna Fáil a week later. He was convinced that if Haughey won the following general election, the implications for the country's future would be very serious.

On 20 November Harney attempted to speak in the Dáil during the debate on the Anglo-Irish Agreement. The Fianna Fáil whip had refused to allocate speaking time to her and an attempt by Fine Gael Junior Minister, George Birmingham, to give her some of his speaking time failed. Harney then issued a statement saying that she intended to vote for the Agreement. 'Important day. Harney breaking with party,' recorded Mackay in his diary. The following day Harney and O'Malley went through the division lobby with Fine Gael and Labour. Now there was no going back to Fianna Fáil for either of them.

On 27 November, Harney was expelled from the Fianna Fáil parliamentary party and that night there was a meeting in O'Leary's house on Wellington Road that has gone down in the annals of the PDs. After her expulsion, Harney was feeling bruised and needed reassurance. McCreevy, by contrast, was becoming increasingly impatient with what he regarded as a scheme that was going nowhere. He felt he had taken a big political risk by producing his document of basic principles for the party and was really fed-up at a renewed bout of indecision on O'Malley's part.

The meeting became argumentative and emotional and the mood was not helped by the consumption of a fair amount of alcohol by some of the participants. 'Harney was in tears. McCreevy kept needling her and it suddenly became like a boxing ring at the National Stadium when Paul Davis, a friend of Harney's, took a cut at McCreevy. Davis was defending Mary, being the gallant,' recalls Mackay.[6]

McCreevy, impatient with the delay and indecision that had impeded them for months, threw down the gauntlet to the others. He proclaimed that if the new party did not go ahead that night, he was out and would have nothing more to do with it. They did not take the threat seriously, but it was in fact the last meeting attended by McCreevy. 'It was very bitter and very rough,' recalls Harney. 'I remember McCreevy saying, "That's it. I don't care. I'm gone. There's not going to be a new party." He told Des he didn't have the bottle for it; actually the word he used was "balls". These were the days when Charlie was drinking and the only thing Michael O'Leary had in the house was whiskey and thanks be to God I don't like whiskey. So Charlie was very pissed and sticking it to Des. It was all a very morbid scene and it ended in complete debauchery in Wellington Road.'[7]

O'Malley was not too perturbed by McCreevy's departure and, if anything, was relieved that someone he regarded as an unpredictable maverick was now out of the picture. 'Harney used to bring McCreevy to the meetings and he was there in the background during the planning. But I was still furious at his behaviour in October 1982, and didn't trust his judgment at all,' he says.[8]

Harney's expulsion from Fianna Fáil accelerated the move towards the launch of the Progressive Democrats. She joined O'Malley as an Independent in the Dáil and applied strong pressure on him to launch the party. Fianna Fáil's utterly negative attitude towards the Anglo-Irish Agreement convinced him that the national interest now required the formation of a new party and he committed himself fully to the project. Perhaps unsurprisingly, given the divisions that dated back to the arms crisis, it was therefore his strong feelings about the North, rather than his disillusionment with economic policies, that provided the real incentive for O'Malley to throw caution to the winds and go ahead with founding the Progressive Democrats. A detailed analysis of all the letters and messages received by O'Malley since his expulsion showed that his perceived integrity and honesty would be the strongest cards held by any party led by him.

By the end of November the momentum for the formation of the PDs was unstoppable. Harney telephoned Mackay in ebullient mood to say she had received a letter of support from Jack Lynch following her expulsion from Fianna Fáil. She also received a letter from Church of Ireland bishop, Walton Empey.[9] Then, on 4 December, a crucial meeting was held in Mackay's house at which the project was carried beyond the point of no return. 'Good meeting. The word was go,' recorded Mackay in his diary. He says that a lot of people later claimed they were at that meeting, at which the launch of the new party was at last irrevocably decided. 'It was in one of the smallest rooms in the house and I think there were about four or five people there.' Mackay's diary records that the people present, apart from himself, were O'Malley, Harney, McDowell and Michael Kerins, a Fianna Fáil councillor from Carlow who had become involved during November. 'We decided to go with the party being launched in January 1986. We planned two levels of activity. Political activity through O'Malley and organisation through McDowell and myself. A decision was taken to go ahead with the premises in South Frederick Street. December 4 [1985] was the date on which we agreed to launch.'[10] (One of the reasons why so much of the planning took place in Mackay's house was that Pat O'Malley remained doubtful about the enterprise, particularly after the car crash that nearly killed her husband.)

On 17 December, Mackay collected the keys of 25 South Frederick Street. Harney went to see it for the first time and then there was a meeting with O'Malley and others in his house and a decision was taken to go ahead with the launch before Christmas 1985, rather than wait for the New Year. They judged, rightly as it turned out, that there would be very little news in the days before Christmas so a new political party was sure to grab the headlines. A launch date of Saturday, 21 December 1985 was agreed. Mackay then went to a friend of his, Ig Lyons, who was manager of the St Stephen's Green branch of the Bank of Ireland, and he agreed to provide an overdraft facility of £5,000 to cover the initial expenses. 'Nobody put their hands in their pocket at all. We kept ourselves out of the financial end and didn't look for money. We decided we would borrow five grand and be responsible for it.' O'Malley and McDowell signed the bank documents.

Then, at this very late stage, another problem arose. Key people in O'Malley's organisation in Limerick began to get cold feet. 'They didn't know us. This was a new crowd up in Dublin who had got involved with their man and they were wondering if we were leading him astray,' recalls Mackay. At the very least the Limerick organisation wanted to hold off on the launch until after Christmas. I got a call from O'Malley saying we had to go down and see these fellows in Limerick and reassure them that everything was okay. So I said I'd get hold of McDowell and we would go down and show ourselves the next day and explain what was going on.'[11]

The next day Mackay and O'Malley went down to the Four Courts to collect McDowell, but he was embroiled in a complicated landlord and tenant case. Mackay went into the court, pulled at McDowell's sleeve and said: 'Michael, we have to go down to Limerick and explain ourselves.'

'"I can't," he says. "I am in a case on here." He had excused himself with the judge and was talking to me as if I was a witness, or a solicitor giving instructions. He said, "I just can't come down."'

So O'Malley and Mackay headed off without McDowell and arrived in Limerick at 6.00pm. McDowell travelled down later that evening.

Pat O'Malley insisted on meeting Mackay before he met with the Limerick organisation to discuss the planned launch. 'I had never met her, but she insisted she had to speak to me,' he recalls. "Do you know this man at all? Do you know what type of man he is; how difficult he is?" she asked. She was laying it on the line to me. "If you get involved with this man it is going to be a rough, rough ride. It is like becoming involved with Jesus Christ. Once you declare yourself for him you have to forget everything else and be with him. He is difficult," said Pat. I said I thought I knew what to expect. Of course I didn't, but I was well warned at any rate,' says Mackay.[12]

After that Mackay went to O'Malley's house and met the Limerick group. He recorded the mood in his diary: 'Who are you? Dublin versus country. Is this a rent-a-crowd? Will there be any Limerick representation.'

Mackay explained the organisation that had gone into the planning stage and after some time a consensus was reached. The Limerick group gave the go-ahead on the basis that there would not be a big crowd at the launch, that it would simply be a declaration of intent by O'Malley. They wanted to keep the focus on O'Malley rather than on the new party. 'It was agreed he would make a speech with the press there. No hullabaloo or razzmatazz, no food.' Mackay agreed to this, but when he telephoned Harney to tell her, he found that she had already arranged for certain people to be there and had arranged for food to be provided. 'We stayed overnight in Limerick and arrived back in Dublin by 12 noon.'

The following night, the eve of the launch, there was a final meeting in O'Malley's house. 'We had a question-and-answer session for the next day. At this stage now, Pat was acting up. She was very apprehensive; she was not happy at all about the whole thing and she was giving O'Malley a hard time and this was all being done in front of us all. It was embarrassing. So I left his house and was home at 10.30pm,' says Mackay.

Harney waited until that night before formally resigning from the Fianna Fáil organisation. In a letter to the party general secretary, Frank Wall, she told of her growing frustration and disillusionment with the authoritarian trend in Fianna Fáil under Haughey's leadership. 'Until relatively recently I remained firm in my hope and expectation that the party would again find that progressive republican spirit which I endorsed when I joined in 1973,' she added. Her emphasis on the words 'progressive' and 'republican' was no accident. They were the core values of the new party.[13]

The Progressive Democrats party was launched on Saturday, 21 December 1985 in a blaze of publicity that exceeded all the expectations of the planners. There were last-minute jitters. Despite the assurances given in Limerick, a crowd of supporters and well-wishers did turn up— including many of the Limerick people who had insisted that it be a quiet affair. Mackay recalls how 'The nerves were at us that morning. I told a doctor from Limerick to bring Pat O'Malley out of the building and to drive her around until it was time for the launch. I pulled O'Malley himself down into a small room and said, "Just sit down there and wait until the off".'[14] Harney also recalls the tension: 'Pat was very apprehensive, but a guy called Michael Cleary, who is a doctor from Hospital in County Limerick, took her out of the building. I met him only recently and he said to me, "I keep reading about you and Des O'Malley and Michael McDowell, and all ye have done over the past twenty years, but only for me that morning, there'd be no party." He took Pat out to lunch. She was threatening to go in and disrupt the launch. Now she would never have done that, but Michael kept her away in any case and everybody calmed down.'[15]

Media speculation about the new party had been building for days and the launch attracted a great deal of publicity. 'The Sunday papers went bananas,' says Mackay. 'One of the reasons we picked Christmas was that we had decided among ourselves that this was the silly season. They needed news and we gave it to them. It was a good talking point over the whole Christmas holidays. That was why I pushed the Limerick crowd. We got great publicity, much more than we thought we'd get. It was beyond our wildest dreams.'[16] 'We were extremely lucky there was less news than normal,' says McDowell. 'We caught the political establishment by surprise, which was another big plus.'[17] The newspapers, radio and television programmes were full of the story for days. The seriousness of the business impressed journalists. 'There were no marching bands nor high-kicking cheerleaders about; no paper hats nor streamers,' wrote Miriam Lord in the *Irish Independent*.[18]

There may not have been any marching bands, but an enthusiastic crowd assembled in South Frederick Street that winter's day to cheer on O'Malley and his associates. McDowell and Mackay joined the party's two founding deputies, O'Malley and Harney, on the platform, while Brigid Teefy represented the Limerick organisation. In acknowledgment of his work in establishing the party, McDowell was appointed chairman. This also served to emphasise that the PDs was not merely a Fianna Fáil dissident rump. A group of O'Malley supporters from Limerick joined well-wishers from Dublin at party headquarters to applaud the launch and give the television cameras something to film.

O'Malley delivered a typically crisp speech that outlined the PD message with clarity and precision. He made the case that the formation of a new party was essential for the health of Irish democracy:

'The high hopes we held in the past and our belief in ourselves as a strong and independent nation have been replaced by a crisis of confidence, evidenced by rising unemployment and emigration and the fact that national morale is now at an all-time low. Two generations have passed since the present shape of Irish politics emerged. In those sixty years such democracy has borne the marks of division, hostility and suspicion based less on our vision of the future than our view of the past. Whatever logic there was in those divisions, there is none today.'

The speech, drafted with the aid of McDowell, spelled out the core philosophy of the party. It focused on the need for a peaceful approach to the problems in Northern Ireland, the need for fundamental tax reform to favour enterprise and employment and the requirement for a clear distinction between Church and State.

'It is clear that in the eyes of ordinary people much of what passes for politics is a futile confrontation between power *blocs* which differ little on many major issues. Where there is a difference the choice posed sometimes seems unfair. There is no choice on the real issues that face our society, such as taxation, unemployment, public spending, rebuilding of local government and difficult social and personal problems. These issues call for a different political response. Parties aligned on issues of history offer no such response. There is a danger for democracy itself in the failure of the party political system.'

Declaring his confidence in the support available for a new initiative in Irish politics, O'Malley said he was prepared to be a vehicle for facilitating change.

'I do not feel that I have the right to deny my services, limited as they are, to that growing segment of the public requiring such change. Accordingly, I am today giving notice of my intention to seek support for a new initiative in Irish politics . . . I am addressing all democrats of goodwill who share my beliefs and my confidence that the face of Irish politics can be transformed. I am asking for their support in building a new progressive democratic force in Irish politics. I am confident of its success. I believe that the people will give such support to our venture that it will command a substantial voice in the next Dáil.'

O'Malley added that he was not launching a new and complete political party, but rather looking for support to build one from the ground up.

'I am not at this stage putting forward definitive and detailed policies. These must await the full establishment of the party and be drawn up as its organisation is built up. My general views are well-known, however. I particularly seek the active involvement of young people who have so much more to lose if drastic improvements are not brought about in the economy and in Irish society generally. Together we can build up such a party in the next few months and in that way give a voice to the new politics which this country so badly needs.'[19]

It was a stirring call to arms, but at the time neither O'Malley nor his leading supporters had any real idea of how things would develop. 'Forming the party was a leap in the dark. We didn't know what was going to hit us; whether we were going to crash to the ground or have a soft landing,' says O'Malley, looking back almost twenty years on. He is still surprised that his political 'leap in the dark' engendered such a durable political force. 'I wasn't sure how long the party would survive and I certainly wasn't sure the party would ever be in government, never mind be in government three times in less than two decades.'[20]

Mackay remembers asking O'Malley, in the very early stages, how many seats he thought the PDs would win in the next election. 'If we had two or three, I'd be happy. I'd be very happy,' responded O'Malley. 'The plan was to get five seats and have the balance of power,' recalls McDowell. 'We had to develop a party within a year in circumstances where it was clear the people were going to get rid of the existing government.'[21]

O'Malley sounded much more confident than he felt as he went on radio making a plea to the electorate for donations of £150,000 a year to make the PDs a viable proposition as a political party. Michael O'Leary, whom O'Malley continued to keep at arm's length, issued a statement welcoming the formation of the new party and saying: 'It is possible it may be seen as the most significant political event of 1985.'[22]

Others in Fine Gael had a more jaundiced reaction. Education Minister Gemma Hussey recorded in her diary how McDowell's involvement came as a blow to Fine Gael: 'Dessie O'Malley's new party, the Progressive Democrats, was announced today. Michael McDowell is the chairman. Will it hurt Fianna Fáil more than us? It is depressing that Michael did this; it must be hurtful to Garret.'[23]

Fianna Fáil feigned indifference, but the hostility of Haughey and his supporters was palpable. A spokesman for the Fianna Fáil leader insisted that the party would suffer 'not at all' from the advent of the PDs and dismissed suggestions that other party TDs might defect and join up. The Haughey reaction was unsurprising, but there was some disappointment among the PDs when Senator Eoin Ryan, a respected figure and an arch opponent of Haughey who had spoken in favour of the Anglo-Irish Agreement, made it clear he was not going to leave the party his father had helped to found. 'I have no intention of leaving Fianna Fáil,' he declared unequivocally. Sean O'Rourke, the political correspondent of the *Irish Press*, speculated that the primary purpose of the new party was to prevent Charles Haughey becoming Taoiseach after the next election, and he reported speculation that the PDs would vote for any other Fianna Fáil nominee for Taoiseach, as long as it wasn't Haughey.

Chapter 4 ~

THE FIRST YEAR

In the early days of 1986 things just got better and better for the PDs. Mackay placed front-page advertisements for the party in the New Year issues of all the national newspapers. The ad contained a message from O'Malley, seeking members and subscriptions for the new party:

> 'Our country faces grave economic and social problems. Unemployment, high taxation, violence and emigration are the outward signs of a crisis of confidence and a faltering belief in ourselves and our future. To tackle these problems we need a new kind of politics. That is why I am asking you to help me build the Progressive Democrats. We need members, skills and finance. Join us in changing the face of Irish politics and let us work together for a better future.'

The ad proclaimed that telephone lines would be open twelve hours a day to enrol new members and an application form was also carried in the newspapers.[1]

The response was astonishing. On 2 January, the day the ad appeared, over 700 people telephoned or visited party headquarters. Sufficient pledges of money rolled in on that first day to cover the initial outlay of £15,000, which was being spent on renting the offices and paying for the newspaper ads. O'Malley, Harney and McDowell joined a group of volunteer workers answering the telephones on the first day of the appeal. By 6 January over 4,000 people had enrolled as members and £25,000 had been contributed by public subscriptions. While all the planners were delighted by the response, they had no idea whether their plans would work in the longer term.

The party's first public meeting was planned for the Marine Hotel in Sutton on 8 January and a reasonable crowd was expected on foot of the success of the initial appeal. Mackay recalls the events of that night:

'I got a phone call over the Christmas from a fellow called Noel Peers who was a Fianna Fáil activist from the Howth/Sutton area. He said he'd love to arrange a meeting in the area and asked if O'Malley would come out. So he made a booking for the Marine Hotel and organised a room for about ten or twelve people.

Then, when we came back from our holidays and the momentum had started and the whole thing snowballed, I said you had better arrange a room for about sixty people because this is getting a bit out of hand. So he said grand and all of a sudden all hell broke loose. On the night it was just sheer bedlam. I drove O'Malley out to the meeting in his own car and we actually got stuck in the traffic jams going into Sutton. The place was unsuitable for that sort of a meeting. It was just sheer bedlam, but it was beautiful bedlam. Here was a Messiah. People felt so downtrodden and they were looking for anybody who would help them out of the morass. So the meeting that was planned for twelve people became 1,200 or 2,000. I was chairman of the meeting. It didn't last too long. People were shaking hands and wanting to know when the next meeting would be. It was great to be there. It was just amazing.'[2]

O'Malley recalls his own astonishment at the turnout for that first public meeting. 'The response amazed me. The meeting was held without much notice, but something like 2,000 people turned up. We had to rig up loud-speakers in the car park to cater for the crowd. After that we became more ambitious.'[3]

If the PDs were surprised by the reaction, the other political parties were stunned. Haughey went on radio a few days later and expressed the view that the PDs were 'not in the national interest'. Seán MacBride, leader of Clann na Poblachta, which had briefly threatened to break political moulds in the late 1940s, was equally dismissive: 'I don't think the PDs can become a major voice in Irish politics. It is basically a replica party, a mixture of Fianna Fáil and Fine Gael.'[4]

Nonetheless, the crowds continued to flock to the public meetings. At these early meetings O'Malley hammered home the party's core message: the State is strangling the economy through an involvement matched only by the communist countries of Eastern Europe. He committed the PDs to cutting taxes as the essential first step in putting the economy to rights. To an electorate disillusioned with a stagnant economy, rising unemployment and renewed emigration and crippled by high rates of personal taxation, which touched 70 per cent at the marginal rate, the new party's message sounded attractive, particularly as Fianna Fáil had failed to come up with any coherent response to the economic crisis. O'Malley's imposing presence and Mary Harney's abilities as a speaker contributed to the air of excitement generated at those early meetings. 'That was the period when Des and Mary were in hot gospelling mode and it was something to behold,' recalls one early convert.

John Dardis, a Kildare farmer and well-known agricultural journalist, remembers going along to the first party meeting in Newbridge, just to see what it had to offer.

'I remember Des O'Malley being asked two questions and being won over by the way he responded,' says Dardis. 'The first question was from a man who demanded to know why the PDs wanted to abandon the claim to the North. Des told him firmly that he saw peace as the first priority rather than the old talk about a united Ireland. He was then asked by a teacher if the PDs would support their case for a pay increase and his response was, "You have something that a lot of other people in this country would like to have—a job, and a safe and secure one at that. That comes at a price." I was really impressed by him and joined up that night.'[5]

It was a very unsettling time for Fianna Fáil. A significant number of their activists in constituencies like Dún Laoghaire, Dublin South and the two Cork City constituencies deserted to the PDs. The question was whether the deputies for those areas, particularly those who had been close to O'Malley, would follow suit. Charlie McCreevy, Seamus Brennan and David Andrews were the most frequently mentioned candidates for defection. Brennan, however, had long before made up his mind to stay with Fianna Fáil, after a brief flirtation with the concept of a new party almost a year earlier. In fact, he had spent a lot of time in the early weeks of 1986 trying to persuade wavering Fianna Fáil deputies to stay with the party. In mid-January, when rumours abounded that Cork TD, Pearse Wyse, was on the verge of leaving to join the PDs, Brennan and Bobby Molloy were dispatched by Haughey to talk to him and try to get him to stay on. Despite the persuasion, Wyse turned up at the first major PD rally in Cork, on 20 January, and announced that he was joining the new party. The Cork meeting overflowed the Metropole Hotel into the street outside and consolidated the revivalist mood that now permeated PD rallies.

If the Cork meeting was emotional, the first rally in Galway, three days later, was sensational. Bobby Molloy—who just a week earlier had assisted Seamus Brennan in trying to persuade Pearse Wyse not to leave Fianna Fáil—jumped ship on the day of the PD rally in the Leisureland complex in Salthill. The move stunned Fianna Fáil; Molloy had given no inkling of his departure to anybody in the party leadership. On the day of the PD rally in Galway, 23 January, he set off from Dublin in the early afternoon, later ringing his secretary from a phone booth along the road. He told her to open his filing cabinet, take out a letter he had left there and bring it to Haughey. The letter was his resignation from the Fianna Fáil party, which he had served as a TD for twenty years.[6] 'I was a very true-blue Fianna Fáil loyalist right from my youth and I held the party's aims and ambitions in the highest esteem, as I did its founder,' says Molloy. 'I became totally disillusioned, but I didn't rush out. The process happened over the years I was on the front bench of Haughey's shadow Cabinet. Despite my position, I felt a complete alienation from what was going on. It was a totally different party from the one I joined.'[7]

The Dáil was sitting that day and the shock among Fianna Fáil TDs was palpable. 'That was the biggest shock,' says Charlie McCreevy. 'If you ever got Charlie Haughey up close to ask him, he'd say that was the biggest shock as well. Molloy was party, through and through and through, and he left. I had great admiration for Molloy for doing that, strange as it may seem. He had the courage to get up and do it, I'm afraid I didn't have myself.'[8] Mairin Quill recalls that Molloy's decision to join the PDs came as a pleasant surprise for her, but it stunned Fianna Fáil. 'Bobby represented the true, decent, traditional side of Fianna Fáil and he was also a politician of enormous ability and experience. His decision to join the PDs was hugely important for us,' she says.[9]

Over the following days Fianna Fáil TDs speculated feverishly as to who would be the next to go. The PDs expected that Andrews would be next. 'Andrews was going to be the big one. He was coming. He was definitely coming,' says Mackay. 'And then there was the rugby match. Ireland against France in Paris. Andrews headed off for that weekend in Paris and we were assured that when he came back he was going to declare on the Monday. Something happened, though, because when he came back he said no way and we never saw or heard from him again. He was obviously got at. Who got at him I don't know, but he was got at.'[10] Harney also remembers how close Andrews came to joining. 'He confirmed to Des, I think it was on a Thursday night, because Des confirmed to me in the morning. Then David went off to a rugby match the next day and whoever he was with said, "You must be mad," and that was the last we heard of it.'[11]

When Andrews did not jump, the mood in the Fianna Fáil camp stabilised. Joe Walsh, a friend of O'Malley's, was, like Andrews, also regarded as a possible defector, but in the end he too stayed put. Rumour persisted about McCreevy and a small number of others, like Noel Davern from Tipperary, but when, after another few weeks of uncertainty, none of them had left, confidence gradually surged again within the party. Mairin Quill recalls that she and other early members were surprised that McCreevy did not join. McCreevy—whose involvement in the planning stages of the party remained a well-kept secret—decided to wait for a few weeks to see how things would develop, but he received no encouragement from O'Malley to join.

In early February McCreevy gave an interview to the *Sunday Press* in which he firmly nailed his colours to the Fianna Fáil mast: 'What is at stake now is the survival of our great party [Fianna Fáil]. I welcome recent converts to what I term the Charlie McCreevy/John Kelly school of responsible Government leadership, especially from politicians who were leading lights in foisting a lot of these problems on the Irish people.'[12] This was a dig at O'Malley, who had been a powerful member of the Fianna Fáil leadership that had produced the disastrous 1977 Fianna Fáil election manifesto. Harney and McDowell regretted then, and later, that O'Malley had not encouraged McCreevy to join the PDs, but in the longer run his continued involvement in Fianna Fáil was to prove a vital link between the two parties at critical stages over the next two decades.

Looking back nearly twenty years later, McCreevy confirmed that he had considered joining the party:

'In the lead-up to the formation of the Progressive Democrats, it is only true to say that a lot of talking had been done by people who thought of like mind, some people who are now in the PDs, some who are not and who never left their political parties, and some who have never been in the public domain. I certainly would have considered it, but when they were formed in Christmas week in 1985 I didn't hesitate at all. I made a clear-cut statement that I wasn't joining them and wished them the best of luck.'

In fact, McCreevy didn't make his announcement until February and for over a month there was intense speculation that he would jump ship.

'I suppose when it came to the crunch I felt that all my people that preceded me, like my mother and her brothers, would have got up out of their graves and haunted me for the rest of my life. Fianna Fáil, whatever people say about us, and lots of critical things, and some justifiably critical things are written about us over the years, we are an extraordinary tribe.'[13]

The decisions of McCreevy and Andrews to stay put calmed nerves in Fianna Fáil, and it soon became clear that the departure of Molloy marked the end, rather than the beginning, of the drift from the party to the PDs. The cautious attitude of the PDs was a factor in discouraging some potential recruits from joining. At the very first meeting of the interim National Executive of the PDs the acting chairman, Michael McDowell, was mandated to 'discourage high-profile aspirants whom the executive feel might not be of benefit to the party'.[14]

The impact of the PDs on the public imagination was something no one had bargained for and it was soon reflected in the opinion polls. The first national poll to measure the impact of the party was carried out by IMS for the *Irish Independent* and published on 17 January. It showed the PDs making an immediate impression, winning the support of 19 per cent of the electorate—Fianna Fáil was on 41 per cent, Fine Gael on 29 per cent, Labour, 6 per cent and Others, 5 per cent. However, the media coverage did not reflect the significance of the poll, with commentators forecasting that the party might get five or six seats on the basis of the findings, if things went well. The PDs commissioned economic consultants Davy Kelleher McCarthy (DKM) to do an analysis of the poll. That analysis came up with some startling conclusions. It suggested that if the poll findings were reflected in votes at the next election, the PDs would win 31 seats, Fianna Fáil would get 74, Fine Gael, 53, Labour, 5 and Others, 3. 'The IMS poll implies that the Progressive Democrats would get 30 seats at minimum. The poll could of course be wrong as a predictor of the election outcome, for all sorts of reasons. But if it is at all accurate, the political arithmetic of the Republic of Ireland has been rewritten,' said DKM.[15]

This carefully drawn assessment showed that the media and the other political parties were completely underestimating the electoral prospects of the PDs. The problem was that the PDs themselves did not quite believe it either, and their electoral strategy never reflected the belief that the party could actually win twenty seats or more on the basis of the latent public support that was so evidently present in the first year. An

Irish Times poll conducted by MRBI in February held even better omens for the PDs, giving the party a 25 per cent share of the vote, ahead of Fine Gael on 23 per cent, with Fianna Fáil taking 42 per cent and Labour just 4 per cent.

Fianna Fáil deputy leader Brian Lenihan claimed that the PDs' showing in the polls was merely 'a temporary response' to the electorate's worries about jobs and taxation, but its transitory nature didn't stop him denouncing the new party, describing it in pejorative terms as a party of the right: 'It's a negative rather than a positive response. The only end product of right-wing radicalism is destabilisation of the political system, leading to class antagonism, which we have never had here. It's based on extreme *laissez-faire*, selfish materialism, which takes no cognisance of the weak, deprived and less well-off in our society.'[16]

Fianna Fáil regarded the PDs with deep-seated suspicion and hostility; Fine Gael could not make up its mind. The party leader, Garret FitzGerald, gave a more objective analysis of the new party than Lenihan, describing it as a classic party of European liberalism, which rejected State intervention on both economic and social issues. The PDs' subsequent decision to join the liberal group in the European Parliament vindicated FitzGerald's analysis. The stumbling block for Fine Gael was that the party was unsure if the PDs should be regarded as a threat to be feared, or an opportunity to prevent Fianna Fáil gaining an overall majority at the next election. Some Fine Gael strategists saw the PDs as a possible coalition partner in place of Labour, but ordinary Fine Gael TDs regarded the party as a potential rival that threatened their seats. A number of Fine Gael TDs, like Maurice Manning, Monica Barnes, Hugh Coveney, Ivan Yates, Michael O'Leary and Michael Keating, were rumoured to be considering moving to the PDs, but nothing immediate happened.

The PDs were desperate to get a recruit from Fine Gael, as the minutes of the National Executive from 23 January reveal: 'It was agreed following a discussion that it was imperative that if further deputies were to join the party, strenuous efforts should be made to ensure that some members of Fine Gael should be among them. Des O'Malley agreed to speak to a number of named deputies.'[17] It took some time for efforts to lure a Fine Gael recruit to pay dividends, and even then it proved to be a mixed blessing. While a number of leading Fine Gael politicians toyed with the idea, only one TD, Michael Keating, eventually jumped.

If Fine Gael TDs were reluctant to join, the new party did have two surprising Labour recruits, senators Helena McAuliffe and Timmy

Conway, who were very much on the moderate wing of that party. McAuliffe was close to Harney and had attended some of the party planning meetings in the autumn of 1985. While neither McAuliffe or Conway was regarded as a senior Labour figure, the fact that two Labour members of the Oireachtas joined the PDs helped to counter the image that the party had no social conscience and the sole aim of helping the better-off. If the other parties had been more objective in their analysis, they might have seen in the Labour recruits a reflection of the frustration felt by so many ordinary, working-class taxpayers at the iniquitous burden of taxation.

Adrian Hardiman, a close friend of McDowell, put in a lot of work in the early stages of the PDs' development. He chaired a policy group on the economy charged with devising outline policies for the party's first conference. Another young barrister, Gerard Hogan, was also a power-house of ideas, policy documents and ongoing advice. Early on he expressed the valid concern that 'the party's image will be tarnished if we are perceived as a refuge for the "Club of 22" or a flag of convenience for other politicians worried about their seats.'[18]

There was a delay in appointing key headquarters staff because Pat Cox wanted to finish a television programme he was making about alleged links between the Workers' party and the Official IRA. Therefore it was not until the end of March that he took over the vital role of general secretary, with responsibility for setting up a professional political organisation. His experience in Ógra Fianna Fáil was a vital asset in the development of the party. Cox was joined in the PD backroom by another prominent journalist, Stephen O'Byrnes, news analysis editor with the *Irish Independent*, who had previously worked on the political staff of the *Irish Press*. Ironically, O'Byrnes had just completed a book, not yet published, on the development of Fine Gael under Garret FitzGerald. Unlike Cox, O'Byrnes had no involvement in the foundation of the party and did not know Des O'Malley particularly well, but the fact that both were from Limerick gave rise to comments about a 'Limerick mafia' running the new party.

It was at this early stage in its development that the PDs came up against the harsh political reality that spending cuts, while all very well in theory, are difficult to implement. The coalition was involved in an ongoing and extremely bitter row with the teachers' unions over a pay award, which involved a huge drain on scarce Exchequer resources. Naturally Fianna Fáil did everything possible to encourage the teachers and put the coalition under pressure by tabling a Dáil motion calling on the government to agree to the pay increase recommended by an independent arbitrator. The PDs initially backed the government's attempt to resist the award in order to control public pay and were roundly abused by the teachers' unions for their trouble. A teacher from Clonmel wrote to Michael McDowell on 7 March saying: 'It is with regret that I inform you of my decision to withdraw my support from the Progressive Democrats. I am a teacher and I bitterly resent the decision by the PD TDs to vote against our independent arbitrator's pay award in Dáil Éireann.'[19]

In the face of such a hostile reaction the PDs backtracked and sought a compromise solution. The government eventually conceded to the teachers, but the episode showed that PD rhetoric on spending cuts might not apply in practice. Although this gave the party some inkling of the difficulties being faced by the FitzGerald government, the PDs didn't evince much sympathy for FitzGerald and his government as they wrestled with the problems involved in implementing public-spending cuts.

Despite the immediate impact on the general public, in the spring of 1986 the PDs was still a party of four former Fianna Fáil TDs. Despite discussions with a number of Fine Gael TDs they had failed to get a positive commitment from any of them to join and the party was wide open to the jibe that it was merely an anti-Haughey splinter group. Finally, on 9 April, the Fine Gael TD for Dublin Central, Michael Keating, announced that he was joining the new party. He spoiled the move somewhat by issuing denials to the media on the morning of his defection. The PDs, however, were very glad to have a Fine Gael TD on board and in recognition of the significance of the move he was appointed deputy leader, a position many felt should have gone to the co-founder of the party, Mary Harney.

Although he was a former front-bench spokesman and a junior Minister for Sport in FitzGerald's first government, Keating was widely regarded within Fine Gael as a maverick. He had not been reappointed as a junior minister by FitzGerald when he formed his second government, mainly because of bizarre and undisciplined behaviour during his term as a Minister for State. His senior minister, John Boland, had complained to the Taoiseach about the way he spent Departmental funds in unorthodox ways, such as buying sets of football jerseys for youth teams in his constituency and, more damaging, attempting to get the Department to pay some of his bills for election literature. There had also been a row in 1981 when he had sought to buy Adare Manor for the State without government authorisation. When the government was informed of his intentions, a Garda car was sent to intercept him on his way to Limerick before he could place a bid on the property. Consequently, FitzGerald developed a distrust of Keating and did not appoint him to any position in his second administration.[20]

Reports of these misdemeanours were leaked to the *Irish Press* after Keating joined the PDs and served to spoil the impact of his accession.[21] O'Malley never really trusted him and his role as deputy leader was a hollow one. In the eyes of most PDs, Harney was the rightful number two and as she retained the absolute confidence of O'Malley, that was effectively what she was, in all but name. The PDs suffered in another way from Keating's move in that there was criticism from women's groups about the party's failure to appoint Harney as deputy leader when she was clearly entitled to that role.

'The Keating thing was a bad experience and it never worked out,' says Harney. 'I remember Des saying, "Do you mind if he is deputy leader?" and I didn't give a damn because we were only a few people. But he never really gelled with the other members of the party.'[22] Stephen O'Byrnes, who, with Cox, had been instrumental in landing Keating, recalls ruefully the day Keating joined. 'I met Maurice Manning outside the Shelbourne Hotel and he said, "You will regret the day you signed him up. He is completely unreliable." Of course, Maurice was right.'[23]

In the days after the Keating move there was once again widespread speculation about the intentions of other Fine Gael TDs, but ultimately no one else defected. Michael O'Leary had already been turned down by the party and the attentions of maverick Fine Gael TD, Liam Skelly, were also spurned, as were those of Lord Henry Mountcharles. O'Malley strongly held the view that the PDs should not be seen as a safe haven for disgruntled politicians who were out of favour with their own parties, as that would undoubtedly cause enormous damage to party credibility.

However, the party did attract a number of big political names. Anne Colley, daughter of George, joined in Dublin South and was quickly selected as a prospective candidate. Some of the children of Kilkennyman Jim Gibbons, who had been one of Haughey's staunchest opponents in Fianna Fáil, also joined up and Martin Gibbons emerged as the likely Dáil contender. The prominent names in the PDs—O'Malley, Molloy, Colley, Gibbons and Wyse—read like a litany of the defeated faction in Fianna Fáil. Among this group a strong motivating force was deep antipathy towards Haughey, rather than a burning commitment to a new form of liberal politics. After their initial, high-flying performance in the polls the PDs settled back to very respectable ratings of around 15 per cent, although there was still widespread scepticism about the ability of the party to achieve anything like that figure in a general election.

In advance of the party's first national conference in May, O'Malley agreed to appear on RTÉ's 'Late Late Show' with his wife, Pat. He was led to expect a relaxed chat about his life and times and was even asked to select a poem to recite. What transpired, though, was anything but a relaxed chat. The show's legendary host, Gay Byrne, could barely disguise his hostility towards O'Malley and dragged him into a bitter and fruitless discussion about his distrust of Charles Haughey. In particular, Byrne honed in on why O'Malley had met Haughey two weeks before the 1970 arms trial commenced. The net effect was to make O'Malley appear like a politician with a grudge, embarking on a personal mission to stop Haughey at all costs.[24]

Vincent Browne, in a *Sunday Tribune* editorial, led the chorus of disapproval. 'At the heart of Mr O'Malley's break from Fianna Fáil has been the accusation that Mr Haughey is unfit for public office. Mr O'Malley's remarks on this issue are reminiscent of the disgraceful speech which Garret FitzGerald made in the Dáil on the nomination of Mr Haughey as Taoiseach in December 1979.' Calling on the PD leader to produce the evidence against Haughey, Browne added: 'Mr O'Malley should either put up or shut up: either he should state what evidence he has for claiming that Mr Haughey is unfit for public office or he should withdraw the allegation.'[25]

The controversy over Haughey did not blight the party's first conference on 24–25 May, which proved to be a resounding success. The venue was the then slightly down-at-heel National Stadium in Dublin, which has since been refurbished. Pat Cox recalls going to inspect the venue a few days before the conference and finding that many of the toilets were not in working order: 'We had to get our own plumber in to make sure the toilets flushed.'[26] The attendance was large and, more importantly, interested and enthusiastic. RTÉ's inimitable presenter, Brian Farrell, recalled how he was shushed by members of the audience when he attempted to have a conversation with a colleague during one of the routine debates. The delegates were enthused by the fact that they were participating in the formation of party policy. They were presented with position papers on a range of issues, but the final shape of each policy was left open to allow all members to participate in the process.

They enjoyed the novelty of making policy; the first motion carried at the conference called for the abolition of the Seanad.

The economic policy discussion document suggested that the party commit itself to bringing down the standard rate of tax to 25 per cent, introducing a 15 per cent VAT rate on all goods and services, completely abolishing employee PRSI, making sizeable cuts in public spending, creating a property tax and a programme of privatisation. In relation to the North, the discussion document supported the Anglo-Irish Agreement, called for changes in Articles 2 and 3 of the Constitution and suggested closer security operations with the British authorities to combat the IRA. These aspirations were to form the unchanging basis of the PD policy in the years ahead. In October 1986 that policy was being fleshed out in detail, with discussion papers giving way to actual policies. The central feature remained the commitment to lower personal taxation.

In her speech to open the conference, Harney made the point that there was no picture of the party leader on display. 'It's not Des O'Malley's party and it's not Des O'Malley's country. It's *your* party and *your* country.'[27] The point Harney was really making was the contrast with Fianna Fáil *árd fheiseanna* under Haughey, at which a giant picture of the leader served as a backdrop to the platform and dominated the entire proceedings. O'Malley was keenly aware that the future of his party depended on the success of its first conference. He was wracked by nerves before going on stage to address his followers; he actually had to go to the bathroom to throw up before delivering his keynote address. Unlike the routine for other party leaders at their conferences that speech was not carried live on television because RTÉ argued that the PDs did not meet the requirement of having won 5 per cent of the vote at the previous general election. Nonetheless, the speech featured prominently on the main evening news bulletins televised by RTÉ.

In that speech O'Malley again identified lower taxation as the central plank of party policy, and committed the PDs to fighting its first election on a policy platform of reducing the lower rate of tax from 35 per cent to 25 per cent. He maintained that lower taxation was the key component of policy aimed at rolling back the control exercised by the State over people's lives. 'Government is inert and the community has been so alienated and disaffected by the crippling tax system that its attitude is one of acceptance and toleration of the tax-fiddler and dole-abuser. What we are witnessing is the death of legitimate business.' O'Malley said that although scarcely 5 per cent of Irish voters would support extreme socialist ideas, in practice there was even greater State involvement in Ireland than in any other democratic European country. 'Big Brother is bigger here than anywhere else west of the Berlin Wall,' he declared to great applause.[28]

Conor Cruise O'Brien, a former foe of O'Malley's, was deeply impressed by the conference and particularly by the PD leader's speech.

'The magic was not in the words themselves but in the manner of their delivery. Mr O'Malley has a peculiar personal style which I myself don't find particularly congenial, but which at the present stage of his career exudes masterful determination and carefully controlled aggression. There is a peculiar rasping crackle that comes out with a subliminal effect of menace, from under the softness natural to the Limerick speech. You can't listen to him these days without feeling that this might be a difficult man to stop, that airy dismissal of this phenomenon as a flash in the pan may not be serviceable for much longer.'

O'Brien noted that, having attended the conference all day, he wondered whether the 'nice people' there were hungry enough in a political sense to take on Fianna Fáil. 'After listening to Mr O'Malley I felt reassured on that point at least. This is as hungry a leader as any around at present and his party too will feel the pangs.' While O'Brien was mainly attracted by the capacity of the new party to stop Haughey winning an overall majority, he had no difficulty identifying the PDs as a typical European liberal party.

'The policies on which they put most emphasis, drastic reductions in income tax and public spending, are those of economic liberalism. Other policies, pro-divorce, anti-capital punishment, reduced emphasis on nationalism (in relation to the North) are characteristic of liberalism in a more general way. And the general tone of almost all the interventions was liberal.'[29]

'That conference was very successful and there was a great buzz about it. It captured the momentum that was there and distilled it down to policies and a political platform,' recalls Cox.[30]

One talking point right through the first few months of the PDs' existence was what the party would do if it held the balance of power in the Dáil. It was assumed that the PDs would never vote for Charles

Haughey as Taoiseach, but on the weekend of the first conference O'Malley was careful to rule out nothing. He poured scorn on Fianna Fáil's claim that it was the only party capable of forming an alternative to the existing government and claimed that Ireland was on the verge of having coalition governments of various hues, as was common on the Continent. 'I can foresee a time when Irish politics will be like those of Holland or Denmark with governments made up of different coalition partners. This has not happened in the past because of the strength of civil war politics but that is now dying. The rise of the PDs is evidence that people are prepared to look at things in a different way.'[31] At the time, this vision of the future of the development of Irish party politics and coalition government was widely regarded as belonging to the same cloud-cuckoo-land as a standard tax rate of 25 per cent or less.

Chapter 5

PREPARING FOR BATTLE

I n June 1986 the PDs were pitched into their first electoral contest, on the issue of divorce, just six months after their foundation. This was only appropriate as the party had played an important role in nudging Garret FitzGerald's government into holding a referendum. The issue had been propelled to the centre of the political stage by Michael O'Leary and Michael McDowell at the same time as they were trying to organise the launch of a new party in 1985. A private member's Divorce Bill was introduced in the Dáil in the autumn of 1985 by O'Leary, but its provisions were actually drafted by McDowell. In the Dáil the Bill was supported by only five TDs and did not get a second reading.[1] While the government was committed to the introduction of divorce, it did not want to be pushed into an untimely referendum, therefore the whips encouraged Fine Gael and Labour TDs to give the O'Leary initiative a wide berth.

However, once the PDs were established as a party the government feared that it would be outflanked by a second Divorce Bill, which might attract enough support to get a full debate on the floor of the Dáil, with a possibility of it being passed.

Fine Gael had supported the removal of the constitutional ban on divorce since 1978 when a motion calling for an end to the ban was passed at FitzGerald's first *árd fheis* as party leader. Although a vocal minority in the party was opposed to change, FitzGerald moved the issue on by establishing a Joint Oireachtas Committee on Marital Breakdown in 1983. Two years later the committee produced a report that came down in favour of removing the ban. It was unclear for some time whether the government would act on this report, but ultimately the coalition parties decided to hold a referendum.

Fear of a PD move on the issue helped the coalition partners to make up their minds, although FitzGerald was adamant that he had always intended to confront the issue during the lifetime of his government. The prospects for success appeared to be good, with opinion polls showing a consistent lead for the pro-divorce lobby, but the government was woefully unprepared for the kind of campaign that was to develop. Even within the government the decision to proceed was not unanimous. The Minister for Education, Patrick Cooney, was opposed to the move, so the decision to hold a referendum was taken by the two parties in government rather than by the government as a collective unit: it was a bad omen.

FitzGerald and Spring held a press conference to announce the decision to hold a referendum and the PDs rowed in quickly to express support. The first opinion poll of the campaign, in early May, encouraged optimism as it showed 57 per cent in favour of a Yes vote, 36 per cent against, with 7 per cent having no opinion. This was the signal for those who wanted to defeat the government—whether from sincere or cynical motives—to launch a massive counteroffensive.[2]

On 29 April the PDs' National Executive decided that the party would support the Divorce Referendum Bill in the Dáil and the Seanad. A rider to the decision stated that 'any member of the parliamentary party who had reservations about publicly committing himself to the principle of divorce would be under no pressure or obligation to take any public stance on the issue thereafter.'[3] It was also decided not to spend a large sum of money on the referendum campaign. Pearse Wyse proposed that no party money should be spent on the campaign, but eventually £7,000 was allocated. O'Malley and Harney had no difficulty supporting the call for a Yes vote and at the party's first annual conference in May the members overwhelmingly endorsed their stand. It was not as easy for Molloy and Wyse, who both had sympathy with more traditional attitudes on the subject.

In the event, the liberal position on social issues did not alienate supporters in counties like Limerick, Cork and Galway, which constituted the bedrock of the organisation, while the decision to support the Yes campaign was vital for the PD image in middle-class, urban areas. One of the reasons ordinary PD members had no difficulty with the party position, regardless of their own private views on the matter, was their contempt for the cynicism of Haughey and some other leading members of Fianna Fáil who opposed divorce tooth-and-nail. While many in Fianna Fáil were sincerely opposed to divorce, no one in politics doubted that the position taken by the party leadership was heavily influenced by the calculation that it had the potential to embarrass the FitzGerald government and cause further splits in Fine Gael. In theory, Fianna Fáil was neutral on the issue, but Haughey and most leading members of the front bench attacked the proposal vociferously.

Haughey expressed his views in the following terms:

> 'For my own part, I approach this issue from the point of view of the family. I have an unshakeable belief in the importance of having the family as the basic unit of our society. My experience of life tells me that this is the best way in which to organise a society . . . I want to make the valid point that there is a price to be paid for the intro-duction of divorce and that people must decide on whether they wish to pay that price. It is not reasonable to suggest that there is some form of divorce that could be introduced which would not have many definite consequences for society, for the stability of the family and for the rights of existing family members.'[4]

What really galled the supporters of divorce was that Haughey was carry-ing on a celebrated extra-marital affair with the *Sunday Press* fashion correspondent, Terry Keane, whose husband, Ronan, was a High Court judge. The general public may have been unaware of this, but it was well-known among politicians, officials and journalists—the so-called 'chattering classes'. Despite Haughey's cynical double standards the media refrained from raising the issue, although at one stage *Sunday Tribune* editor, Vincent Browne, threatened to name hypocritical politicians whose lifestyles were in clear conflict with their position on divorce. Browne drew the line at naming names, however, and the wider public was left in the dark. But in political circles, knowledge of the contra-diction between Haughey's private behaviour and his public stance caused anger and cynicism.

To make matters worse, Haughey absented himself from the Dáil debate on divorce and there were persistent rumours around Leinster House that he had gone to Paris for a romantic tryst with Keane. The ostensible reason for his absence was that he was visiting the European Parliament in Strasbourg, but the rumour about the other reason for his trip to France spread around Leinster House like wildfire.

Speaking in the divorce debate, the late David Molony, Fine Gael TD for Tipperary North, referred to Haughey's absence from the country when such a serious issue was being debated. This provoked an immediate reaction from Pádraig Flynn, and the following exchange took place:

'MR FLYNN: That is miserable and the Deputy knows it.

MR MOLONY: It is a fact.

MINISTER FOR HEALTH (MR B. DESMOND): He is in the cathedrals in Strasbourg.

MR FLYNN: I will—

MR MOLONY: It is a fact.

MR B. DESMOND: He is locked in contemplation in Strasbourg.

MR FLYNN: That is mischievous and the Minister knows it.

AN LEAS-CHEANN COMHAIRLE: Deputy, please.

MR MOLONY: Deputy Haughey should be noted as being meticulous in his attentions to this House.

MR FLYNN: He is.

MR MOLONY: Of all times in the history of this Dáil when we are discussing a most important amendment to the Constitution he finds himself absent from the House. I find that extraordinary. If there is a reason, I will be glad to hear it.

MR FLYNN: The Deputy will swallow his words before the year is out.

MR MOLONY: I am merely citing as a fact that Deputy Haughey is not here this week. If Deputy Flynn can explain it, so be it, but I am very surprised that the Fianna Fáil spokesman or somebody from Fianna Fáil did not find it necessary or even desirable to explain to the nation and to this House at the beginning of the debate why Deputy Haughey was absent. On Tuesday he was visiting his MEPs in Strasbourg, something he can do at any time. Deputy Flynn has the explanation for this. It was described in one newspaper as a strategic absence.

MR FLYNN: I wonder who inspired that little gem.

MR MOLONY: I do not know just how strategic it was or was not intended to be, but I submit to this House that it is a slight on the House and on the importance of this historic debate that Deputy Haughey should absent himself for it.'⁵

Of course the public had no idea of the background to this exchange, but it explains the bitterness felt by those politicians who supported divorce and were forced to listen to Haughey's pro-family platitudes. Even more galling was the fact that he had the full support of leading members of the Catholic hierarchy.

In the Dáil debate Mary Harney expressed her unequivocal support for the measure: 'I am very pleased that this matter has now come before the House in this form and that, for the first time, the people are likely to be given an opportunity, in a matter of weeks, to vote on the important matter and to allow us, the legislators, to bring into law legislation in relation to divorce.'

Harney went on to express her disapproval of some of the language being used by Fianna Fáil speakers: 'We heard words like "sledge hammer" from Deputy Woods, and "Frankenstein is going to stalk the land". This morning we heard words like "the monster" from Deputy Treacy.' At the end of her contribution she summed up the reason why the PDs backed the Yes campaign:

> 'It is not just because of the hard cases or because I believe we must face up to the issue in a realistic way, but because I want to see our Constitution and our legislation reflect the ethos of a republic and not the ethos of a State dominated by one particular Church.'

One of those speakers who articulated the hardline position adopted by most Fianna Fáil TDs was Pádraig Flynn:

> 'I believe divorce based on failure as now proposed in the Bill will have a very serious impact on society. It will have serious moral and social consequences. It will change the character of society for the worse in this country. It will introduce a radical change into society and change the complete legal understanding of marriage as we now see it. It will weaken family structure here and will make the upbringing of children much more difficult. It will put them at risk in certain circumstances.'[6]

The PDs supported the pro-divorce campaign around the country. They did not, however, commit much money or resources to the campaign, preferring to concentrate their efforts on the general election, whenever it would be held. By the time the referendum came around opinion had turned decisively against the government's proposal. The well-organised anti-divorce campaign had focused on the economic hardships divorce would impose on women and children, the effect on property and pension rights and the long-term consequences of marriage breakdown for society. The government simply did not have answers for all these questions. The negative attitude of most Fianna Fáil TDs proved decisive in transforming a clear pro-campaign Yes majority into a decisive majority against the proposal, which was lost by 63 per cent to 37 per cent. The defeat of the divorce proposal further demoralised the coalition government and made it a virtual certainty that it would lose office at the next election.

One thing the PDs feared in the first half of 1986 was that FitzGerald might opt for an early election before they had time to organise properly. Michael McDowell recalls that their strategy was 'to develop the party as quickly as possible because at the back of our minds was the fear that FitzGerald might call a snap election to nip our progress in the bud, as de Valera did with Clann na Poblachta in 1948.'[7] In April, Mackay went to the bank and obtained an overdraft facility of £250,000, to be drawn down in the event of a snap election.

It was the responsibility of Pat Cox to build the party organisation and to work with Stephen O'Byrnes to prepare for the forthcoming election campaign. Cox was convinced that the FitzGerald coalition would break on the 1987 Budget—the only question was the timing of that break. In September 1986, Mackay and the PD finance committee agreed on an election Budget. The PDs were reasonably well-off, but contrary to much media commentary they did not receive much funding from big business. Instead, the bulk of the money raised in that first year came in the form of relatively small contributions sent in the post by ordinary people in response to the newspaper appeal that followed the party launch, and from party fundraising activities. By August the party had raised £200,000, but only £20,000 of that came from corporate donations.

Cox had enough money to commission market research to measure the party's standing and to establish what values the public associated with the new party. The research, carried out by IMS in the early autumn of 1986, showed the PDs on 18 per cent of the vote, with Fianna Fáil on 49 per cent, Fine Gael on 23 per cent and Labour polling just 5 per cent. The focus-group findings were just as interesting. The strongest association with the party in the public mind was with its leader, Des O'Malley. Another great strength was the newness of the party, which appealed to people who were in despair at the state of the country. It was clear that the two greatest assets the PDs would have going into an election were the public perception of its leader and its dramatic policies on issues like taxation. After discussing the findings, the party's National Executive noted the need to devise a strategy to pull Fianna Fáil back from its 49 per cent standing if the PDs were to have any chance of holding the balance of power. It was also noted that the most significant deficiency for the party was the absence of good candidates to convert the obvious potential support into votes.[8]

As the party organisation developed, one of the things that surprised Cox was the fact that the vast majority of the members had no previous political experience. While the IMS research showed that potential PD voters came in a ratio of two-thirds Fine Gael and one-third Fianna Fáil, the membership of the party was quite different. Cox made a point of asking those attending PD meetings what their previous political experience had been and he calculated that up to 90 per cent had never before been involved in party politics. In the second half of 1986 he organised seminars for constituency officers and, with O'Byrnes, produced an election hand-book, modelled on Fianna Fáil's legendary blueprint *Coras Bua*, which was distributed to the members.[9]

In tandem with the building of the organisation work was proceeding on the preparation of a detailed economic policy document. O'Malley and Harney knew that the success or failure of the party would depend on the credibility of its economic policies more than anything else. A number of policy teams were established in the early months of 1986 with a taxation committee—under Dan Hickey, a banker with the State-owned ICC—having responsibility for the key area of party policy. Adrian Hardiman and Michael McDowell, who was in charge of the party's constitution and rules committee, also had significant input into the formation of economic policy.

In June Hickey gave an interview to Geraldine Kennedy, then political correspondent of the *Sunday Press*, in which he said that the introduction of the 25 per cent tax rate had not been fully worked out and would depend on the scale of government spending cuts but, he said, the current Budget deficit would not be increased to pay for the tax cuts. He accepted that the PDs wanted to introduce a standard rate of VAT on all goods, which meant that the price of food would rise by 15 per cent. He also suggested that £1 billion could be raised through the sale of State assets, like forests, or State-owned companies, like Telecom Éireann or An Post. The public airing of the party's economic policy before it had been fully worked out provided an opportunity for the Minister for Finance, John Bruton, to question its credibility. Bruton maintained that PD tax-cutting policy was based on the mirage of 'self-financing tax cuts', an old and discredited catchphrase of Haughey's from the dark days of 1982.[10]

As a result of the controversy, which Fianna Fáil finance spokesman, Michael O'Kennedy, also joined with gusto, the PDs decided to keep a tight rein on future interviews. The party policy group worked away in private for months and the fruits of their labour emerged in October 1986, in the shape of a document entitled 'A Nation that Works: A Blueprint for jobs, fair taxation and social justice'. It put flesh on the bones of the broad policy objectives announced at the party's annual conference six months earlier and set out a number of steps designed to change Ireland from a heavily taxed economy, with high government spending, into a low tax regime that would revitalise the economy. The document proposed that the three existing income tax rates of 35 per cent, 48 per cent and 58 per cent should be reduced over the next five years to two rates: one at 25 per cent and the other at 40 per cent. It also proposed that employee PRSI, which added another 7.5 per cent to the basic tax rate, should be abolished completely.

The document, which attracted massive publicity, did not just set out aspirations, it gave details of what would happen in each year of a five-year programme of spending cuts and tax reductions. The party produced its own Budget for 1987 in which it proposed to cut the 58 per cent top rate of tax by 3 per cent, the middle 48 per cent rate to 43 per cent and the 35 per cent bottom rate to 31 per cent.

'The Progressive Democrats offer a different way of looking at the economic world. A fair taxation system is the cornerstone of our economic strategy. Achieve that objective and we believe that economic activity will gather momentum, arising from people's willingness to work, to employ and to invest,' said the document. It spelled out how tax would be reduced in incremental steps over a five-year period in order to reward individual effort, restore the incentive to work and encourage people to build their future in Ireland rather than emigrating.

Hand-in-hand with the promise of low tax rates was a commitment to crack down on tax evasion through new enforcement measures, the seizure of bank accounts and the attachment of earnings. A corresponding crackdown on welfare fraud was also proposed, involving a national identity card for everyone in the country over the age of sixteen, increased referral of disability benefit claimants and the redeployment of staff into a special investigations unit.[11]

The big question, though, was how the PDs intended to finance dramatic tax cuts and the abolition of PRSI at a time when the government was being forced to borrow massive amounts to keep public services going. The programme suggested that current public spending could be slashed and the capital programme pruned by a clampdown on public spending.

A total of £370 million in itemised public-spending cuts was listed in the programme. Among the measures proposed were a policy of non-replacement of vacancies in the civil service, the abolition of the Office of Public Works, the abolition of bread and dairy subsidies for those on welfare, the integration and abolition of a number of State agencies and cuts in capital and training grants to industry. The sale of State assets, including the State forests, was proposed as a means of raising revenue in tandem with the cuts. Some eye-catching cuts were also proposed in the document, including the abolition of ministerial pensions, a reduction in the number of junior ministers from fifteen to seven and the abolition of the Seanad.

The party's opponents pounced on the document, saying that it simply could not be done. The Tánaiste and Labour leader, Dick Spring, indicted the document as 'absurd', 'totally unrealistic' and 'immoral' because it would benefit those at work at the expense of the unemployed. Referring to the spending cuts he said: 'Such changes could not be made without substantial negotiations with the parties concerned and it was nonsense and totally unrealistic to think otherwise.'[12] Stephen O'Byrnes remembers how the PDs were attacked and treated as pariahs by the other political parties and by much of the media. 'The PDs were viciously denounced in the early days as being right-wing, Thatcherite, yuppie, uncaring, and all the rest of it. Of course the left liked to have a polar opposite to attack, but the tone of the criticism was often very nasty.'[13]

The government responded to the PD policy document by asking the Minister for Finance, John Bruton, to have his Department carry out a detailed analysis of it. This analysis, completed by the end of October 1986, focused on the public-spending cuts proposed by the PDs and concluded that the figures simply did not add up. 'My assessment is that the expenditure savings proposed by the Progressive Democrats would save far less than the amounts they claim. Further the cost of their income tax/PRSI proposals is understated by at least £70 million to £80 million,' said Bruton in a confidential memo to Cabinet colleagues dated 3 November 1986. 'Overall, I am satisfied that the policies advocated by the Progressive Democrats, far from improving our public finances, would result in a significant worsening of the current Budget deficit in 1987.'

A major flaw Bruton identified in the PD proposals was that they did not take into account the £551 million increase in public spending that would arise in 1987 simply from underlying increases in public service pay, social welfare and debt-servicing costs. In his memo, Bruton freely conceded that an Opposition party could not be expected to make any detailed assessment of the 'no policy change' expenditure base for the following year, but he was critical of the PDs for not factoring in a substantial figure for the pay, welfare and debt-servicing increases that should have been obvious to everybody.[14]

Bruton's critique of the PD policy on public expenditure may well have been correct in its detail, but his memo did not confront the underlying policy issues at the heart of the PDs' analysis. The question of whether it was feasible to tackle the country's economic crisis through a fundamental shift in budgetary policy towards cuts in public spending and an easing of the tax burden was not addressed. At this stage Bruton was locked in a struggle with his Labour colleagues in government to get them to accept the need for spending cuts, while he was being criticised by the PDs for not cutting enough on the basis of figures his officials told him did not add up.

In fact, there was a growing realisation in Fine Gael that something dramatic would have to be done to cope with the economic crisis and that a continuation of existing policy was not a viable option. Bruton was already preparing a Budget for 1987 based on the notion that severe cuts in public spending would simply have to be implemented, whether or not Labour ministers agreed. He was naturally dismissive of the apparent ease with which the PDs proclaimed public spending could be cut substantially, although he did accept that side of the PD policy in theory. What neither he or anybody else in government or Opposition was prepared to accept at this stage was that tax cuts were feasible in the circumstances. The notion that tax cuts would actually be self-financing through the boost they would provide to economic activity was widely regarded as pie in the sky: it was suspiciously reminiscent of Charlie Haughey's phoney Budgets of the early 1980s.

The PD policy of cutting taxes and spending was dismissed as both unachievable and undesirable by the government parties, Fianna Fáil, the trade unions and an array of voluntary organisations. Nonetheless, it struck a chord with a significant number of ordinary voters. Brendan Keenan, the astute business editor of the *Irish Independent*, was critical of the document for its lack of detail on spending cuts and its casual attitude to borrowing, but he still maintained that the PDs deserved all the positive publicity they had achieved. He identified the reason for the massive publicity as 'the yearning of the PAYE struggling masses to be free of the present crushing burden of tax. Any party which seems to have an answer to that conundrum is guaranteed an attentive ear, at the very least.' Keenan remarked that the thrust of the PD approach to cuts in public spending would find favour among most economists, business leaders and professional commentators on the economy. 'These people may be in a minority, but their voices do get heard.'[15] The people listening most attentively were not the business élite or even the self-employed, as the left fondly imagined. Many of those who finally heard a message they had been longing to hear from a political party were highly taxed PAYE workers, particularly those in the private sector who did not have the clout of the public service unions to win them compensatory special pay awards. The PDs struck a chord with the grassroots electorate; whether or not their sums added up did not really matter to a lot of voters. The party had flown the flag of low taxation and that in itself was enough to shape the future of Irish politics.

Chapter 6 ∿

ELECTION TRIUMPH

As the country slid inexorably towards a general election at the end of 1986, the PDs were ready, with draft policies and an organisation in place. The new dynamic in Irish politics represented by the party had a definite influence on the timing, tactics and atmosphere of that general election. For a start, the arrival of the PDs served to stiffen the resolve of those in Fine Gael, like John Bruton, who wanted to take decisive action to deal with the economic crisis, regardless of the attitude of the Labour party. Fine Gael TDs could sense the disillusionment among their supporters and were all too aware of just how devastating that might be in a general election campaign.

The sense of foreboding in the Fine Gael camp was summed up in an anecdote told by Fine Gael TD John Kelly, who had refused office in FitzGerald's second government because he felt the party was disappointing its own supporters by accepting dictation from Labour. In late 1986 Kelly was showing a visiting group of German politicians around Leinster House and he brought them into the Distinguished Visitors' Gallery.

'The door opened and Des O'Malley came in. As I was pointing out the more notable people, I explained that this man had just started a new party. "Indeed," said the leading German, "and what gap in the market has he identified?" I had to tell him that it was the gap which Fine Gael had left yawning open. The PDs reflected exactly what we had left undone: that part of the spectrum which we used to stand for and had ceased to represent.'[1]

The other side of the coin was that Fine Gael perceived the PDs as an alternative coalition partner to Labour. The two parties were at one on the North and the liberal agenda and were in broad agreement on the need to cut public spending. While Taoiseach Garret FitzGerald was less enamoured with the PDs than some of his colleagues and always preferred the Labour option, he was persuaded to take a tougher attitude towards Labour in the final months of 1986. Bruton was encouraged to draft a Budget that would meet Fine Gael requirements and if that meant losing Labour, so be it.

One of the reasons Fine Gael ministers saw a possible opening for the PDs was the behaviour of Fianna Fáil under Haughey. It was not just on the divorce referendum that he had displayed a cynical attitude that took no account of the national interest. Fianna Fáil attacked every aspect of the coalition's record, particularly the tough economic policies aimed at controlling the debt. Government spending cuts were singled out for derision and the main slogan of the Fianna Fáil pre-campaign was: 'Health cuts hurt the old, the poor and the handicapped.' Months before the election campaign even started this message was plastered up on billboards all over the country. Haughey's record of fighting the government tooth-and-nail on every single public-spending cut over the previous four years suggested that he would adopt a much more relaxed attitude towards public spending. He had maintained again and again that spending cuts were unnecessary and he lambasted the government for its policies in this area. 'We had a profligate government being criticised by the Opposition for not being profligate enough. Where in God's name is the country going? There was even talk of the IMF coming in,' says O'Malley.[2]

Policies and organisation were all very fine, but the PDs also needed viable candidates who could win elections. Throughout 1986 the party attracted a number of well-known individuals who looked as if they had the potential to be good candidates. Some of them came from the old aristocracy of Fianna Fáil families and had been elbowed out of the way by Haughey: Anne Colley, daughter of the former Tánaiste, George Colley, became the PD standard-bearer in Dublin South; in Kilkenny, Martin Gibbons, son of Jim, stepped forward to run for the party; while in Louth, Frank Aiken, son and namesake of the famous founder of Fianna Fáil, joined the ranks of the PDs; in Limerick, former Fianna Fáil TD, Peadar Clohessy, switched to PD; while in Cork, Mairin Quill, a close friend of Jack Lynch, took on the challenge of running in the difficult territory of Cork North Central. Others who had never been heard of in national political circles joined the party around the country and were not shy about their ambitions: Martin Cullen in Waterford; John McCoy in Limerick West; and Pat O'Malley, a cousin of Des, in Dublin West were just some of the new, ambitious, potential PD politicians.

By November 1986 it had become obvious that the Fine Gael–Labour coalition could not last much longer. The two parties had been negotiating the contents of the following year's Budget throughout the autumn and by mid-December it was clear they would not be able to agree. The haggling continued through the first weeks of 1987, but the inevitable break came on 20 January when the four Labour ministers left the government, refusing to accept Bruton's Budget strategy. FitzGerald asked President Hillery to dissolve the Dáil and opted for a long, four-week campaign in the hope that he could bring the electorate around to accepting Fine Gael's tough Budget proposals.

The PDs had prepared for the election by setting up two committees in the summer of 1986: a strategy committee, under Cox; and a communications committee, under O'Byrnes. They merged in November into an election committee and the data produced by the IMS poll regarding the potential support base proved invaluable to their work. About 100,000 posters, 5.2 million canvassing cards and 2.2 million election addresses were printed by PD head office, with a similar output by individual constituencies. The party also produced 40,000 paper hats, 800,000 lapel-stickers, 50,000 car-stickers and 5,000 rosettes. Campaign expenditure by headquarters came to £450,000, with another £330,000 being spent by the constituencies.[3] 'By late 1986 we were ready to roll whenever the election came. There was nothing left to do in the field with ten days to go,' says Cox.[4]

There were still some last-minute loose ends to be tied up, however. Cox recalls the director of elections in Sligo–Leitrim ringing him the day after the election was called and saying, 'Pat, we have an office, a telephone and a fax machine, but we have no candidate.' It did not take long to find one. In Dún Laoghaire—a prime target for the party—there was a different problem: too many candidates. Just before the election was called the *Sunday Press* political correspondent, Geraldine Kennedy, announced that she was resigning her job and seeking a nomination in the constituency. Kennedy had been approached in 1986 about running for the PDs. She had been reluctant to make a decision until she knew the outcome of a High Court action she was taking with Bruce Arnold, of the *Irish Independent*, against the State for the illegal tapping of their home telephones by the Haughey government in 1982.

'The result of the case was not announced until January 1987. It represented an independent judgment on my treatment by the Haughey government that I felt was necessary,' says Kennedy. 'Once it was announced I felt free to run for the Dáil, so I told O'Malley I would stand for the PDs. I was prepared to stand anywhere and had no problem about looking for a nomination. He told me Dún Laoghaire would be the best constituency for me, but said not to seek a nomination as it was too late. The party would select one candidate and he would add me to the ticket.'[5]

Rumours of Kennedy's arrival in Dún Laoghaire generated enormous publicity, but caused deep resentment in the fledgling PD constituency organisation. At the selection convention the delegates attempted to block Kennedy's candidature by flouting the direction from the party leadership to select just one candidate. They selected Helen Keogh, a leading light in the Women's Political Association and an active PD member, along with another hopeful, Larry Lohan. Despite the rebuff, the party National Executive went ahead and added Kennedy to the ticket, so that the PDs fielded three competing candidates in Dún Laoghaire.[6] In the campaign the PDs spent more money in Dún Laoghaire than in any other constituency, in any election, then or since.[7]

Dún Laoghaire was not the only constituency in which there was conflict over electoral strategy. In Longford–Westmeath, Senator Helena McAuliffe, who had taken a huge political risk and endured a lot of aggravation for leaving Labour to join the PDs, was annoyed to find that she was not to be the party's sole candidate. Dan O'Sullivan, a lecturer in Business Studies at Athlone Regional College, was added to the ticket in what was a very difficult constituency for the party. In Wicklow, former Fianna Fáil TD Ciaran Murphy, who had joined the PDs and had been selected as a candidate, resigned in protest when a second candidate was added to the ticket.

While the candidates were being sorted out, the PDs prepared in great detail for other aspects of the campaign. The first two days after the election was called, on 20 January, were spent in Dublin finalising the manifesto and mapping out candidate and constituency strategies. O'Malley was sent off to spruce up his image: he bought a few new suits and got his hair cut.[8] Suitably attired, it was off on the campaign trail for the party leader and his wife, Pat. Travelling by train, car and helicopter he criss-crossed the country in the early days of the campaign. Cox decided that a whirlwind helicopter tour at the beginning and the end of the campaign would have maximum impact. The cost of hiring a helicopter was steep, but he was quite happy to spend money on it because in publicity terms it delivered far better value for money than newspaper advertising.[9] For instance, on Monday, 26 January the party leader departed from Dublin by helicopter at 9.15am and managed to take in Arklow, Wexford, Waterford, Clonmel and Thurles before lunchtime. After a light meal it was on to Ennis, Clifden and Galway for a big public meeting. After staying overnight in Galway he departed by helicopter the next morning to Loughrea, Athlone, Tullamore, Navan, Dundalk, Tallaght, Newbridge, Carlow and finally Kilkenny, where he had time for a meal before an evening public meeting.[10]

The PD policy, which was hammered home again and again up and down the country, was a commitment to cut taxes and to give the people more of their own money to spend. The slogan on the posters, 'Dessie Can Do It', made the most of O'Malley's credibility. The party's IMS poll had shown the importance of O'Malley's image to the party's fortunes, but the strategy committee had had a heated debate as to whether the slogan should be 'O'Malley Can Do It', or to use the leader's first name to convey a more human image. O'Malley himself was very dubious about the slogan, feeling that it smacked of the politics of personality that he had found so distasteful in Fianna Fáil under Haughey's rule. After a fraught meeting, during which the PD leader launched a scathing attack on an advertising executive who sought to explain the rationale behind the personalised slogan, O'Malley's objections were overruled by the election committee and the posters were printed.[11]

During the campaign Cox made no bones about the fact that the election was make-or-break for the new party.

'We need a significant take-off. We need double-digit figures on the Dáil benches. We want to show that we are a force to be reckoned with and that we did it all with our own hands. It has been a fantastic piece of risk-taking, made real by a group of people who believed hard enough in the thing to make it happen.'[12]

The party's newspaper advertisements promised a new deal for the taxpayer: 'This time the Progressive Democrats will make all the difference. The country needs real change. A government courageous enough to confront the crisis. With the integrity and strength to work for lasting jobs, tax reform and social justice. Give us the balance of power. We're ready. TOGETHER WE CAN DO IT. Vote Progressive Democrats.'[13]

The PD manifesto, which was launched on 2 February, focused on the themes that had by now become the mantra of the PDs. 'The Progressive Democrats have identified reform of the tax system as the central issue in this election and as the fundamental component of their plan for economic recovery,' reported the *Irish Press*. Their policy document, 'A Nation that Works', advocated a progressive reduction in the basic rate of tax to 25 per cent by 1991, with the process being launched by a 2 per cent reduction in 1987. The tax cuts were to be paid for by a reduction in public spending, receipts from privatisation and the postponement of public sector pay increases.

'The PD's insistence on the importance of the tax issue and the link between taxation, a reduction in public spending and employment, introduced a very specific focus into the campaign. Drawing explicitly on a supply side argument the PDs argued that low taxation would stimulate employment,' wrote one political scientist in an analysis of the campaign. He added that the PD policy document's emphasis on the need to ensure the independence of State institutions from political interference was important. 'This gives the party a certain distinctiveness in the Irish context, since it advocates a minimal, but not a weak, State. The State should not be hindered by unnecessary involvement in the economy or social affairs but when it does become involved, its power should be used decisively.'[14]

Speaking at the launch of the manifesto, O'Malley forecast that Fianna Fáil would not win an overall majority and he predicted his party would hold the balance of power. As to what would happen in that scenario, the PD leader made it clear that his preference would be for Haughey and FitzGerald to stand aside and allow a government to be formed. 'If the PDs had anything to do with it, neither Garret nor Charlie would be Taoiseach, but someone untarnished with the fiascos of the last five years,' noted Fergus Pyle of *The Irish Times* in his report on the manifesto launch. 'His [O'Malley's] strongest aversion was, predictably, to the Fianna Fáil leader, an aversion shared, he said, by most of his party, who would prefer someone else as Taoiseach in the national interest. As for Garret he said, "I would find it difficult to offer support to the man who has presided over the affairs of the nation for the past four years." It took a bit of prying to get that order of preferences out of him.'[15]

The presence of the PDs radically changed the political landscape. Instead of Fianna Fáil and the Fine Gael–Labour axis the voters were now presented with a range of options. The PDs offered a combination of spending cuts and tax cuts; Fine Gael offered spending cuts as the way back to economic health; Labour was opposed to cuts and made a priority of protecting welfare and health spending; while Fianna Fáil just condemned the government, made hardly any commitments, but implied strongly that spending cuts were unnecessary and would be reversed.

At the launch of the Fianna Fáil manifesto, Haughey carefully avoided making promises or any specific commitments regarding the public finances. He maintained that a Fianna Fáil government would stimulate growth to navigate the country out of the economic doldrums. O'Malley responded by accusing Haughey of insulting the electorate and looking for a blank cheque. 'Imagine such a statement [of no commitments] after he has spent the past four years promising everything to any sectoral group that pressed claims, no matter how extravagant and costly.'[16]

O'Malley, like almost everybody else, assumed the clear implication of Fianna Fáil strategy was that spending cuts would be reversed. When Fine Gael followed the PDs in announcing that they were in favour of selling off some State companies, Haughey immediately sent a letter of reassurance to the Irish Congress of Trade Unions (ICTU) pledging that a Fianna Fáil government would never countenance the privatisation of State enterprises. Nothing was said by Fianna Fáil during the campaign that would alienate any interest group in the country, but no firm commitments were made either.

The first opinion poll of the campaign confirmed the widespread belief that Fianna Fáil was on course for a resounding victory. The MRBI poll in *The Irish Times* gave the party 52 per cent, with Fine Gael way back on 23 per cent, Labour on just 5 per cent and the PDs with a very impressive 15 per cent. As the long campaign wore on, however, Fianna Fáil's commanding lead in the opinion polls began to slip. Although polls showed the PDs running at between 12 per cent and 15 per cent, few gave the new party much chance of getting more than ten seats. Leading figures in the party were later to bemoan the fact that they did not run enough candidates to take advantage of the considerable groundswell of support.[17]

As well as being at one with the PDs on the need for spending cuts, Fine Gael also found common ground on the issue of the North. Haughey had denounced the Anglo-Irish Agreement on a number of occasions since it was signed in November 1985 and had pledged to renegotiate it, if elected. At the start of the campaign he changed tack and pledged to continue working the Agreement, though he maintained he still could not accept the constitutional implications of recognising partition. The PDs, by contrast, were wholehearted supporters of the Agreement.

The strength of the PD campaign remained a double-edged sword for Fine Gael. The new party was mainly staffed by former Fianna Fáil activists, but appealed mainly to disillusioned Fine Gael voters. On the other hand, the Fine Gael leadership knew that the PDs represented the only chance of preventing Fianna Fáil from getting an overall majority, and there was even hope that between them the two parties might have the capacity to form a government.

As the campaign wore on Fianna Fáil became increasingly worried about the potential impact of the PDs. On the eve of the election the party bolstered its defences by publishing an advertisement that gave a stark warning to the voters: 'Tomorrow you have two choices: The wrong choice—A vote for the PDs, FG, Labour or others is a vote for another disastrous coalition. It risks a hung Dáil. It leaves Ireland open to wrangling minority rule by small parties and a worsening of unemployment, emigration, taxation, the health services and the national debt.'[18]

In the latter stages of the campaign there was a botched attempt to organise a pre-election pact between the PDs and Fine Gael. Cox held detailed discussions with the Fine Gael director of elections, David Molony, about the possibility of a transfer pact. Both men were acting on the instructions of their respective party leaders and by the last weekend of the campaign, Fine Gael believed that a pact was on. Despite an initial acceptance of it by Des O'Malley, senior ex-Fianna Fáil figures in the party, particularly Bobby Molloy, were adamant that such a move would lead to an electoral disaster.

As a result, the PDs pulled back, but FitzGerald went ahead anyway and made a speech calling on Fine Gael voters to give their second preferences to the PDs. O'Malley spurned the offer and studiously avoided any reciprocal gesture, leading to a great deal of bitterness and lack of trust between the two parties.[19] McDowell believes that the talks were an attempt by Fine Gael to neuter the PDs: 'It was an effort by Garret to suffocate us and kill us by offering us a coalition deal in the lead-up to that election.'[20]

When the votes were counted on 18 February, the result was a triumph for the PDs. The party won 14 seats and almost 12 per cent of the vote, the only regret, with hindsight, was that it did not run more candidates to take advantage of the wind in its favour. A number of the party candidates romped home at the top of the poll. In Limerick Des O'Malley had his best election ever, polling over 12,000 votes and helping to bring in his running-mate, Peadar Clohessy. Mary Harney, who had struggled to get elected while in Fianna Fáil, topped the poll in Dublin South West. Bobby Molloy, always a poll-topper in Galway West, delivered as usual, while in Cork South Central, Pearse Wyse found himself at the head of the poll. Former Fine Gael TD Michael Keating was the only sitting PD deputy not to top the poll, but he was still comfortably elected in Dublin Central. Newcomer Anne Colley topped the poll in Dublin South, while Michael McDowell was comfortably elected in Dublin South East. Geraldine Kennedy made it in Dún Laoghaire, edging out Helen Keogh, while Mairin Quill was elected in Cork North Central and Martin Gibbons made it in Carlow–Kilkenny.

Then there were the PD victors that nobody in national politics had ever heard of before. Martin Cullen was elected in Waterford and Pat O'Malley came from nowhere to win in Dublin West. But probably the biggest surprise of all was the victory of John McCoy in Limerick West.

Despite a flawed electoral strategy that led too many candidates in Longford–Westmeath and Wicklow and too few in places like Dublin South, Cork South Central and Galway there was euphoria on the night of the count. The PDs had made the kind of breakthrough few had dared to hope for, indeed, even in their own ranks. 'There was little doubt about which was the happiest political headquarters last night. An atmosphere of calm triumph pervaded the PDs' in South Frederick Street,' wrote Ann Marie Hourihane in the *Irish Press*.[21]

In Limerick East O'Malley announced joyfully that the PDs had achieved their objective of ending Civil War politics: 'We have now smashed these politics into smithereens and broken the mould.' Harney announced that she was not in favour of the PDs going into coalition with anyone, and that was the prevailing mood within the party. 'I think if we perform well in the next Dáil, we will do extremely well in the next election.'[22]

In Fianna Fáil, by contrast, the outcome was a bitter disappointment as the party won just 81 seats, three short of an overall majority. For Fine Gael it was a disaster, with almost 20 seats being swept away to leave the party with 51. Labour held on to 12 seats in the face of great odds and, even though it polled just over half the votes won by the PDs, managed to cling on against the tide to fight another day.

Fianna Fáil supporters couldn't come to terms with the result. The party had confidently expected to sweep into power with an overall majority; from grassroots members up, they were gutted by their failure to achieve that objective. It was the fourth time in a row that Haughey had failed to deliver an overall majority and some senior figures now began to despair of him ever being able to do so. What made it all the more galling was that the PDs had done so well. By preventing Charles Haughey winning an overall majority, they had achieved one of their major objectives. There was deep disappointment, however, that the party had narrowly failed in the second strategic objective of holding the balance of power. The ostensible reason for this was the ambition to force the party's tax-cutting programme onto the political agenda, but it was an ill-disguised secret that many in the party harboured the ambition of holding the balance of power so that they could force Fianna Fáil to ditch Haughey as the price of their support.

Keenly aware that this was still a possibility, Haughey hid his deep disappointment at the election result and conducted himself as if there were no question but that he would succeed FitzGerald as Taoiseach. As three of the four Independent TDs elected to the Twenty-Fifth Dáil had voted for his nomination as Taoiseach back in 1982, he had some grounds for optimism on that score, but with a minority government his prospects of keeping office for any substantial period didn't look good. Haughey brazened it out and announced that he was not going to do deals with anyone. In response, the PDs held their nerve and made it clear they would not be voting for Haughey, even if that meant another general election.

The arithmetic was simple: Haughey needed 83 votes out of the 166 members of the Dáil to be elected as Taoiseach, so the first priority was not to lose one vote by filling the Ceann Comhairle's chair. A deal with former Labour TD Sean Treacy, who had been Ceann Comhairle during the 1973–1977 period, solved that problem and left all of Fianna Fáil's TDs free to vote for Haughey. There was still no certainty that Haughey would win it, however, as Fine Gael, the PDs, Labour, the Workers' party and Jim Kemmy were all committed to voting against him. That meant there were 82 certain votes against Haughey, as opposed to 81 Fianna Fáil votes for him. His fate, therefore, lay in the hands of two Independents: Neil Blaney and Tony Gregory.

In this uncertain atmosphere the PDs waited anxiously to see if anybody in Fianna Fáil would take the obvious course of suggesting that in the national interest Haughey should step aside and allow another Fianna Fáil nominee for the Taoiseach's Office. There were some murmurings about Haughey's position as Fianna Fáil leader because it was an open secret that any other Fianna Fáil nominee for the Taoiseach's post could be elected with PD support. Haughey moved quickly to remove any threat to his leadership. Just two days before the Dáil vote

Ray Burke was dispatched to put the position clearly:

'Let nobody outside Fianna Fáil have any feelings that since they've left the party they can influence our leadership. They tried that when they were on the inside and they're not going to do it from the outside. He will remain leader, and let there be no misunderstanding for any member of the Dáil, the only alternative to Mr Haughey being leader and being Taoiseach is a general election.'[23]

On the day of the crucial Dáil vote, Haughey repeated the same message to his front bench. Convinced that Tony Gregory would vote against him, the Fianna Fáil leader called his front bench together and told them to prepare for an immediate election. He did so to get the word out around Leinster House in order to terrify all and sundry. In actual fact, if the worst had happened, Haughey would not have been in a position to call an election. That would have been the prerogative of FitzGerald, who would have continued as Acting Taoiseach and who certainly had no intention of asking President Hillery for an immediate dissolution. In the circumstances, the President would also have had the right to refuse a request for dissolution from FitzGerald because he no longer commanded a majority in the House. The country was facing the prospect of a constitutional crisis, but Haughey was determined, whatever the outcome, not to relinquish his leadership of Fianna Fáil and the chance of once again being Taoiseach.

In the event, when the critical moment came Sean Treacy was elected Ceann Comhairle unopposed and Haughey scraped into office. Blaney voted for him and Gregory abstained, leaving the vote tied at 82–82. Treacy then gave his casting vote in favour of Haughey, and he was Taoiseach once again. The PDs were left to grind their teeth at having come within a whisker of their second strategic objective. 'If things had tumbled slightly differently, we would have had the balance of power and a very, very difficult first outing,' says McDowell.[24] Stephen O'Byrnes takes the opposite view and regrets that the party didn't do a bit better in the election. 'Pat Cox and myself were green in 1987. We could have pulled a few more seats with the vote we got and that might even have got us into government at that stage. Things would have been very different if that had happened.'[25]

Chapter 7 ~

THE MORNING AFTER

With Haughey installed in office the PDs waited anxiously to see what would happen next. There was a widespread view that he would return to the old habits of financial profligacy that had characterised his earlier periods in office. Instead, he moved quickly to signal that he intended to get to grips with public spending, and his appointment of Ray MacSharry as Minister for Finance suggested that he was serious. The PDs claimed that Haughey's conversion to the path of righteousness was due to their arrival on the scene.

'Our performance convinced Haughey that he could afford to take the risk of doing the right thing. The fact that he put MacSharry into Finance showed he was convinced of the necessity to do it and he stuck to it. I attribute the Fianna Fáil change of mind, the 180-degree turn, to the success of the PDs in the election. The policies we had put before the people caused him to change his mind,' says O'Malley.[1]

When MacSharry introduced his first Budget, in March 1987, it contained even bigger cuts than the Bruton version, which Fianna Fáil had repeatedly denounced throughout the election campaign. The PD Finance spokesman, Michael McDowell, had no hesitation in supporting the Budget cuts and claiming part-ownership for his party.

'The Progressive Democrats were founded as a new and separate political party in order to make the Irish political process not more divisive but more decisive. I venture to suggest that the tone of the debate today and what was done by the Fianna Fáil party in bringing forward this Budget would not have happened had the Progressive Democrats not come into being.'[2]

That assertion was disputed by Fine Gael, who instead pointed to an offer by Garret FitzGerald, on the night of the election, to support Haughey if he did the right thing on the economy. The fact that there was an overwhelming Dáil majority in favour of tackling the crisis in the public finances certainly pushed Haughey in the direction of rectitude.

FitzGerald stepped down as Fine Gael leader and was replaced by Alan Dukes, who announced on the day of his election as party leader that one of his priorities was to take on the PDs. 'Dukes declares war on the PD,' was the headline in the *Irish Press*, whose political correspondent, Sean O'Rourke, went on to quote the new Fine Gael leader as saying: 'I would take the view that the PDs are a factor of instability in Irish politics and therefore cannot last.'[3] In a radio interview he expanded on the theme, saying the PD economic policies did not hang together. 'They would be financially impossible to carry out and on that basis I find that the PDs have been built on a certain illusion as to what can be done in economic policy.'

O'Malley responded by accusing Dukes of using exactly the same language about his party as that employed by Haughey a year earlier; it was not a good omen for future cooperation between the two Opposition parties. In fact, they embarked on a fruitless game of one-upmanship, which benefited neither of them. 'I should like to comment briefly on our colleagues on my extreme right,' remarked Fine Gael Finance spokesman Michael Noonan in relation to the PDs during the Dáil debate on the Budget. 'First of all they adopted the Anglo-Irish Agreement; then it was Fine Gael's social policy and Fine Gael's economic policy. The PDs, with all the zeal of the convert, advocated those policies in a frenetic manner which caused one revered Deputy in this House to refer to them as the military wing of the Fine Gael party. I prefer to think of them as the provisional wing of Fianna Fáil.'[4]

The PDs and Fine Gael both struggled to find a coherent strategy that would allow them to retain their identity and push their own political agendas, while keeping Fianna Fáil in office. Both parties ultimately suffered for the very different strategies they adopted as they each sought to keep Haughey on the right track. They faced the difficult task of ensuring that Haughey was not given an opportunity to call a general election, which might have given him an overall majority.

On the Fine Gael side, the strategy outlined by FitzGerald on the night of the Budget was soon followed by intense criticism of the Fianna Fáil U-turn and a crisis on the issue of health cuts that almost precipitated a general election in the summer of 1987. Dukes backed down at the last minute and in September, deciding that he did not want to be placed in the same position again, announced what became known as the Tallaght Strategy. In a speech delivered in the Tallaght chamber of commerce, Dukes offered to support Haughey's minority government as long as it adhered to strict control of the public finances. The strategy effectively ended adversarial politics between the two biggest parties in the country for the remainder of the Twenty-Fifth Dáil and saw Fine Gael supporting more and more aspects of government policy as time went on.

The PDs, meanwhile, went in the opposite direction. The supportive strategy initially outlined by McDowell in the Budget debate gave way to a more selective approach. This sometimes involved blatantly opportunistic denunciation of the government, especially when it came to Dáil votes on unpopular spending cuts. At times it seemed as if the PDs believed in spending cuts in theory, but not those that involved any degree of public opposition. Fine Gael's decision to underwrite the government let the PDs off the hook on major issues and the party subsequently began to succumb to the temptation of playing populist politics.

The problem facing both the PDs and Fine Gael was that Haughey surprised everybody by the way he went about his third term as Taoiseach. Having begun by cutting public spending, he appeared determined to continue the process and in May circulated a letter to all government Departments spelling out in clear language the kind of cutbacks he wanted for 1988. The letter was aimed not just at the ministers, who already knew what he wanted, but at the senior civil servants in each Department who traditionally sought to squeeze extra money out of the Exchequer each year, regardless of the overall financial position of the State.

To be fair to Haughey, there was one major aspect of the economic recovery that was very much his own policy. After making various cuts in public spending, he opened talks with ICTU, employers' and the farmers' bodies on a new national agreement to cover the following three years. The trade unions were the key to the deal as control of public service pay was a vital requirement for the government if it wished to keep inflation down and get borrowing under control. Haughey's overriding concern was to get a national pay deal. In this he started off with the great advantage that the trade union leaders liked him.

Apart from Haughey, the other minister who did most to bring the process to a successful conclusion was Bertie Ahern, then Minister for Labour. Newly promoted to the Cabinet, having served Haughey well as chief whip during the three leadership heaves, his low-key, conciliatory approach was well-suited to the delicate task. Haughey pursued the two prongs of his policy in tandem and had no compunction about reassuring the unions from time to time by uttering public denials that huge cutbacks in public spending were planned. His ministers devised plans for swingeing cutbacks while a deal with the unions was hammered out. The Programme for National Recovery, as the deal was called, was the first of a series that guaranteed industrial peace for almost two decades. The nub of the Programme was an agreement with the unions on a public service pay deal that pinned back wage increases to just 2.5 per cent per year for three years and deferred a range of special pay awards. Taken together with the public-spending cuts, it was just the medicine the ailing economy needed.

It was not only on the economy that Haughey performed a complete U-turn. On the question of Northern Ireland he did precisely the same and implemented the policy developed by the Fine Gael–Labour government and supported by the PDs. In many ways this was even more extraordinary than the turnaround on the economy. Haughey's denunciation of the Anglo-Irish Agreement was all of a piece with his record as an irredentist nationalist since the 1970s arms crisis. He had pledged to tear up the Agreement, but in fact did nothing of the kind. 'When Fianna Fáil got into government fifteen months later they worked the Agreement without a whimper,' recalls O'Malley.[5]

Even when it came to the thorny issue of extradition, Haughey stunned many in his own party by his decision to work the system agreed by Fitz-Gerald, with a few minor modifications. There was considerable opposition to this in Fianna Fáil, but the party swung in behind him after one of the most appalling IRA atrocities of the Troubles: the Remembrance Day bomb in Enniskillen in November 1987, which killed eleven people and wounded sixty-three.

With the Tallaght Strategy in place from the autumn of 1987 the minority government was regularly able to command majorities of more than 100 in Dáil divisions. TDs on all sides of the House were puzzled by what was happening. Fianna Fáil back-benchers had not expected to be implementing public-spending cuts even more severe than those of the Fine Gael–Labour coalition, and the last thing Fine Gael TDs had ever expected was to be supporting a government led by Charles Haughey. Garret FitzGerald, now a back-bencher, summed it up well:

'There seemed to be two Fianna Fáil parties. Fianna Fáil in Opposition and Fianna Fáil in Government and any resemblance between them has become totally coincidental; in fact not only coincidental but almost unfindable at this stage.'[6]

The emergence of the PDs as a serious political force and the introduction of the Tallaght Strategy transformed the nature of Irish politics. In the Dáil, Fine Gael was prepared to troop through the lobbies with Fianna Fáil on division after division, or at the very least to abstain. The PDs sometimes voted with the government, or more often abstained, but they were much more critical of government policy than the main Opposition party.

O'Malley needled Haughey regularly in the Dáil and stuck much more closely to old-style adversarial politics than Dukes, even if the PDs often ended up on the same side in the division lobbies. As a result, tension in the relationship between Fine Gael and the PDs developed in the early months of the Twenty-Fifth Dáil. Just after his accession to the leadership, Dukes had declared his intention of targeting the PDs and the smaller party responded by trying to embarrass Fine Gael at every opportunity. In the Dáil this meant that O'Malley regularly tried to, and succeeded in, upstaging Dukes. His much greater experience gave the PD leader the edge in Dáil exchanges and he found it easy to score points both against the government and against Fine Gael. The old animosity between Haughey and O'Malley added spice to the exchanges. The Taoiseach did not try to conceal his contempt for the PDs, to whom he generally referred as 'that party'.

Haughey developed a particular animosity towards McDowell, who rivalled O'Malley as his pet hate figure in the PDs. 'I have seen fairly nasty pieces of work come into this House in my long career here and you are aiming well towards becoming one of the best,' he told McDowell during one Dáil exchange. 'Wagging a threatening finger at me, Deputy McDowell, cuts no ice. I was about to say that I do not particularly blame you for your irresponsibilities but I do blame your colleague, Deputy Des O'Malley, because he has Government experience.'[7]

O'Malley's political skill and experience in the Dáil was a crucial asset for the PDs. 'Des had very high expectations of us and made us work extremely hard,' says Mairin Quill. 'We had fourteen people in the Dáil, most of them brilliant in different ways, but they had to be brought together into a cohesive team and Des did that brilliantly. It was a stimulating and challenging experience.' Quill remembers one occasion when she missed a crucial Dáil vote. 'I was given a severe dressing-down by Des. As a teacher myself, I felt what it was like to be treated as the boldest girl in the class and I had nightmares for months afterwards about missing a vote. In fairness, though, while Des expected a lot he more than gave it back in terms of loyalty and commitment to his TDs.'[8] John Dardis echoes the point: 'O'Malley is the kind of man you would have followed over the top on the Somme. I have had enormous rows with him over the years, but he never took a difference of opinion personally. Half-an-hour after a row you could have a pint with him in the bar and it would never be mentioned again.'[9]

The newly elected TDs took some time to adjust to parliamentary life. Bobby Molloy was a great help to them, providing advice and assistance until they got to know the ropes. 'Bobby was a truly decent man,' says Geraldine Kennedy. 'He always made himself available to help us frame Dáil questions or explain parliamentary procedure. He was a father figure in the party because he knew how politics worked and he took the trouble to talk to the new bunch.' She also remembers his emphasis on high standards in political life. 'He said to us early on: "Always remember you are Dáil deputies now and you have to live up to the highest standards. Only claim the expenses you are strictly entitled to and don't let others lead you into using your position for personal gain." I'll always remember that.'[10]

Despite O'Malley's confident Dáil performance the PDs found the going difficult at times as they tried to act as a critical Opposition party while generally supporting the government. Some senior party members came to the conclusion that they had made a big mistake by not adopting a formula like the Tallaght Strategy. 'The Fianna Fáil government was doing what we had advocated. I believe that if we had actually advocated the Tallaght Strategy we would have done an awful lot better out of it than Fine Gael did,' says Harney. 'So many of our members came from the Fianna Fáil stable, and they were not long out of it, they automatically assumed that when in Opposition you must oppose.'[11] Stephen O'Byrnes agrees: 'Dukes and the Tallaght Strategy took the economic high ground from the PDs. The depth of bitterness post-1987 was so deep that the instinct of Dessie and Bobby was not to back Haughey. Fine Gael's adoption of the Tallaght Strategy smothered the PDs.'[12] The same view is shared by Geraldine Kennedy. 'The PDs should have done something like the Tallaght Strategy. I believe that had it been done properly, without giving Fianna Fáil a blank cheque, as Dukes did, it would have worked to the advantage of the party. Voters in constituencies like Dún Laoghaire and Dublin South expected something like that from us.'[13]

In many ways the Tallaght Strategy would have made more sense for the PDs than it did for Fine Gael, but O'Malley was rightly reluctant to give Haughey the blank cheque that Dukes had written, even if Fianna Fáil appeared to be on the right track. With the operation of the Dáil tied up by a cosy deal between the Fianna Fáil and Fine Gael whips, the PDs often found themselves in the same camp as Labour and the other left-wing groups, attacking the government on specific issues while rarely voting against it.

The credibility of the PDs took a bad knock over the party's attitude to the closure of Barrington's Hospital in Limerick. The closure of the out-dated hospital was one of the cuts proposed by Minister for Health, Rory O'Hanlon. There was a furious reaction in Limerick and O'Malley sided firmly with the popular cause and even took part in a protest march. In the Dáil the PDs put down a private member's motion against the closure and forced Fine Gael to back the government line. It was an opportunistic and populist policy to adopt and in the longer term did considerable damage to the credibility of the party. Of course, it was a very difficult issue for O'Malley in his home base, but in choosing the soft option the party lost a vital element of its electoral appeal.

'I was totally against what we did on Barrington's Hospital. We have never recovered from it,' says Harney. 'Here was an issue in Des O'Malley's backyard and the party adopted a position that did not fit with its overall policy. Des' position was that a hospital in Limerick should close, but it should be St John's, not Barrington's. That message was impossible to get across and the issue was a huge disaster for us.'[14]

'It was very difficult for us in that Dáil and the PDs did wobble on the subject of Barrington's Hospital,' recalls McDowell. 'To some extent what MacSharry was doing was what we said we would have done—cutting back public spending to get the public finances in order. So it was a trying period.' He says the enmity expressed towards the PDs from everybody else in the Dáil made things difficult for the party. 'The degree of hostility to us in the Dáil was huge. Alan Dukes in his first speech said his policy was to eliminate us. Labour had a dreadful election and were bitterly hostile to us. We were as isolated in the Dáil as the Workers' party chose to be.'[15]

O'Byrnes, too, regards this as a low point in PD history: 'Barrington's Hospital did enormous damage. Here we were, the party of fiscal rectitude, not being prepared to follow the prescription in the leader's own constituency. In my view it was fundamental as it represented a failure of the party to live up to one of its fundamental principles.'[16]

Still, the party continued to insist that the government was implementing PD policies. 'The battle now being successfully waged by the present Government against excessive public spending draws its inspiration from the new realism which this party pioneered in October 1986, when we published our economic document 'A Nation That Works'. There, for the first time in Irish politics, a party in Opposition, in the run-up to a certain election had the courage not only to advocate cutting public spending but also to spell out in detail a programme of over £350 million in such cuts. Our electoral success caused Fianna Fáil, happily for the country, to dishonour their promises,' maintained O'Malley at the PD annual conference in Cork in May 1988.[17]

At the same conference another issue emerged that caused severe and unexpected damage. It arose from a decision by the party to press for a new Irish Constitution. In January 1988 the party published a remarkable document entitled 'Constitution for a New Republic'. It was a complete reworking of Éamon de Valera's 1937 Constitution, Bunreacht na hÉireann, and was designed to bring the original document into the modern age while retaining most of the fundamental liberal values contained in it and in the first, 1922 Constitution. The ban on divorce was dropped completely and the territorial claim in Articles 2 and 3 abandoned in favour of a new clause expressing the desire for Irish unity by consent. Among the other key proposals were a reduction in the size of the Dáil, the abolition of the Seanad and the appointment of two extern ministers from outside the Dáil.

The public reaction was broadly positive despite the not unexpected controversy over the decision to drop the territorial claim and remove the ban on divorce. The draft document was brought before the party conference on 29 May for a full day of debate before being formally approved. In his keynote speech the night before the debate, O'Malley expressed his pride in the draft constitution produced by his party:

'It is the most comprehensive review published by any political party in the Republic of Ireland in the last fifty years. We have elevated the debate to a new plane. We have moved from the rhetoric of the need for change into the substance of how that change can be accomplished and what it should embrace.'

He went on to tell the delegates that by endorsing the draft constitution they would have an opportunity to underwrite the party's commitment to personal rights and freedoms for the citizen, to clarify Church–State relations, to radically reform the institutions of government and to seek Irish unity by consent only.[18]

All those lofty aspirations foundered on an issue that barely anyone had noticed since the publication of the draft five months earlier: there was no reference to God in the preamble to the PDs' draft constitution. Even at the conference debate on Sunday morning the matter was remarked on by only a few speakers, most of whom favoured the change. It was not until the following day's *Irish Press* hit the streets that the issue suddenly jumped up to bite the party. 'God will be banished from the constitution if the PDs have their way. At the closing session of the conference in Cork yesterday they voted for a 'Godless' preamble to any new constitution,' wrote the *Press*' Cork correspondent, T.P. O'Mahony. The story was highlighted by RTÉ's 'It Says in the Papers', whose presenter, P.P. O'Reilly, pointed out the irony that the PDs had taken the decision to drop God on Trinity Sunday.[19]

Fianna Fáil immediately pounced on the issue as a stick with which to beat the PDs. 'The party that wants to take God out of the Constitution' was how the PDs were suddenly labelled and all the good work in the document was forgotten in what quickly became a public relations nightmare. After a few days of damaging controversy the PDs announced a retreat back to God, which only compounded the initial damage. In August, at a special party conference held solely to debate the new Constitution, delegates voted by a large majority to insert a reference to God in the preamble. Even that did not dispose of the issue and it rumbled on for years, providing an ideal whispering campaign against the party on the doorsteps. It also helped to bury the PDs' proposed new constitution as an issue for debate in the months and years to follow. In time, major aspects of the PD draft constitution—an end to the ban on divorce and the removal of the territorial claim to the Six Counties— were actually implemented, but the party got little credit on either score. What should have been a strong positive for the party was turned into a negative because of a silly controversy.

In November 1988 the PDs produced a new, comprehensive economic policy document entitled 'Employment, Enterprise and Tax Reform'. The document restated the party's objective of radically reforming the income tax code with the introduction of just two rates, 25 per cent and

40 per cent, over a five-year period and a switch to tax credits rather than tax allowances. Finance spokesman, Michael McDowell, also proposed changing the tax treatment of married couples so that each would be taxed individually. These were ideas that would be implemented a decade later by Charlie McCreevy, but in 1988 they were still regarded as PD fantasies. As well as tackling personal taxation, the plan proposed a major change in the corporate tax structure, including the abolition of a range of allowances, and it proposed the concept of a minimum level of tax, regardless of the allowances available. Detailed measures to tackle the black economy and the sale of some State assets were also proposed in the document, which proclaimed the objective of creating a pro-employment economy. It was a radical document, but it provoked a disappointing level of debate.[20]

By early 1989, as a result of tough economic policies underpinned by the Tallaght Strategy, Haughey had never been in a stronger position. The PDs, Labour and the Workers' party deeply resented the neat arrangement between Fianna Fáil and Fine Gael, but there was little they could do about it. In fact, the PDs began to suffer an erosion of credibility because of their hostility towards the government. The electorate expected left-wing parties to attack Fianna Fáil for spending cuts, but they expected something different from the party of fiscal rectitude. Haughey, who had recovered from a serious illness that affected his breathing, appeared to be in a powerful position. According to the opinion polls support for the PDs had begun to wane, while Fine Gael was making little headway and neither was the left. Opinion poll ratings of 50 per cent and more painted a rosy picture for Fianna Fáil and indicated that the electorate was happy with Haughey's minority government.

Nonetheless, Haughey's old enemies in the PDs were sure the leopard had not changed his spots. There were a few indicators that not everything was as it seemed. The visit of a Saudi royal prince raised all the old doubts about Haughey's character. A political storm blew up when it emerged that the Saudi visitor had presented Haughey with a jewel-encrusted dagger and that Mrs Haughey had received a valuable necklace. The gifts, which were worth a substantial amount of money, were simply pocketed by the Haugheys and the Taoiseach refused to give any explanation to the Dáil about them.

Haughey's behaviour in accepting the valuable gifts was not only unethical, it was in flagrant contravention of the Government Procedure Instructions, which were binding on every member of the government.

The Instructions stated that while there were no formal guidelines on the subject of gifts, 'the practice has been for Ministers and Ministers of State to accept relatively inexpensive gifts to mark occasions such as official openings etc and not to accept expensive gifts or when presented return them. Any gift of national significance would be regarded as the property of the State and dealt with accordingly.' The Instructions added that in any case of doubt, the Taoiseach should be consulted.[21]

Another development that drew the fire of the Opposition was the decision to establish an Independent Radio and Television Commission (IRTC) to oversee the establishment of commercial radio and television channels. The initiative was taken by the Minister for Energy and Communications, Ray Burke. A strange feature of politics during this period, and one that was widely commented upon, was that Burke retained the Communications portfolio as he moved on through three different Departments—Energy, Industry and Commerce and Justice. Some of the Opposition's concern stemmed simply from left-wing opposition to ending the State monopoly on broadcasting, but there were other, deeper worries about the way the licences were being awarded. The most controversial decision taken by the IRTC was the allocation of the national commercial radio licence to the Century consortium, headed by a well-known Fianna Fáil supporter and concert promoter, Oliver Barry. It emerged over a decade later that Barry had paid a donation of £30,000 to Ray Burke during the 1989 election campaign, which followed shortly after Century went on air. Rumours about that donation circulated for years before finally being confirmed by the Flood Tribunal in January 2000.[22] Ironically, the granting of the licence to Century resulted in a financial disaster for Barry, who lost a lot of money on the ill-fated national station before it eventually closed down. On the positive side, many local stations were quickly established and over the next few years became an integral part of Irish broadcasting.

Haughey's credibility, which was always a tenuous thing, took a bad knock when the PDs dragged into the light his relationship with Larry Goodman, the beef baron whose rags-to-riches story was as remarkable as Haughey's rise to the top in Fianna Fáil. On 18 June 1987, within months of achieving power, Haughey had given a major press conference to promote a massive development in the beef industry, to be undertaken by Goodman Companies. A grandiose scheme for the industry was unveiled, which entailed a planned investment of £260 million in Goodman's operations. It was the biggest investment programme ever devised for the food industry. Funding was to consist of: £60 million in assistance from the Industrial Development Authority and the European Community; a £30 million investment by Goodman himself; and a package of loans under Section 84 of the Finance Act, which involved a benefit of £170 million to Goodman Companies.[23] The ambitious plan never got off the ground, however, despite the continuous prodding of Goodman by the State agencies involved. While no government agency made any direct investment in the plan, Goodman Companies did draw down a considerable portion of the Section 84 loan finance.

One result of the massive publicity surrounding the project was that it inextricably linked Haughey and Goodman in the public mind. This association became a hot political issue in the early months of 1989. First, the Oireachtas Committee on State Sponsored Bodies became embroiled in controversy when it emerged that Goodman was interested in buying the State-owned Sugar Company through a company he controlled called Food Industries. Haughey's appointee as chairman of that Oireachtas committee, Liam Lawlor, was also a director of Food Industries and the potential conflict of interests was raised by the PD committee member, Pat O'Malley. Lawlor was put under severe pressure and was eventually forced to resign as chairman, but only after putting up a dogged fight to retain the role. Agriculture Minister Michael O'Kennedy also came under attack in the Dáil and faced a series of questions on the issue.

It was not long before a second controversy arose concerning Goodman. This time it involved the operation of the State export credit insurance scheme and the way in which Goodman's meat exports to Iraq were being underwritten. Cover for all exports to Iraq had been withdrawn in 1986 by the Fine Gael Minister for Industry and Commerce, Michael Noonan, because of the risks involved in trading with that country. A series of Dáil questions from Pat O'Malley in April 1989 established that on Fianna Fáil's accession to office in 1987, that cover had been restored. The vast bulk of the cover went to Goodman Companies: in 1987 export credit for beef exports to Iraq was £41.2 million; in 1988 it had risen to £78.5 million. In fact, almost one-third of all the available export credit insurance for all Irish exports was absorbed by Goodman's trade with Iraq. The figures further showed that the export credit insurance cover provided for the trade with Iraq in 1987 and 1988 actually exceeded the total value of beef exports to that country by £57 million.

The Opposition demanded to know why the Fianna Fáil government had provided this level of cover for Goodman. 'Members of this present

Government, from the Taoiseach down, are extremely close personally to the leading figure in the group concerned,' Des O'Malley told the Dáil. The Minister for Industry and Commerce, Ray Burke, who had cancelled the export credit for Iraq on taking over the Department from Albert Reynolds in January 1989, responded by attacking O'Malley and accusing him of leading a witch-hunt against the Goodman group. 'Throughout it has been my impression—and it has been confirmed tonight—that many of the questions raised on this matter have been characterised by insinuation, innuendo and hints of abuse regarding the operation of the scheme.'[24]

The rows over the Saudi jewels and the allocation of the radio licence took some of the gloss off Haughey, but it was the Goodman controversy that caused genuine public disquiet. The PDs and Labour latched onto the issue and pursued Haughey relentlessly over it. He fought back with equal vehemence and the political atmosphere during the spring of 1989 became poisonous.

Chapter 8 ~

ELECTION DISASTER

The PDs were as stunned as everybody else when Haughey, in a fit of temper, decided to call a general election in June 1989. The vast majority of TDs had reckoned on the Fianna Fáil minority government remaining in office for another two years and the parties had planned for the future on that basis. But when Haughey returned from an official visit to Japan at the end of April he threw a tantrum when he discovered his government was about to be defeated in a Dáil private member's motion that called for the allocation of £400,000 to counter the problems of haemophiliacs who had been infected with the AIDS virus through bloods supplied by the Blood Transfusion Service.

Following the Dáil vote Haughey's closest associates in Cabinet, Ray Burke and Pádraig Flynn, encouraged him to use the defeat as an excuse to call an election. Urging Haughey to appeal to the nation, both men pointed to a succession of opinion polls that showed Fianna Fáil's support level at well over 50 per cent. They were convinced that the party would win an overall majority in a snap election. Another argument in favour of an election was the decline in the PDs' standing in the polls. It seemed that the time was right to wipe out O'Malley and his party. Even though Haughey had calmed down in the days after the Dáil defeat, the temptation to go for the overall majority and eliminate the PDs in the process proved irresistible in the end.

A decade later it emerged that Haughey, Burke and Flynn had all used the 1989 election campaign to raise enormous amounts of cash for their own personal use from a variety of wealthy Fianna Fáil supporters. Whether the fundraising potential of an election campaign influenced the decision it is impossible to say, but the calling of the election certainly took most politicians by surprise.

Having made up his mind to go to the country, Haughey waited for a few weeks so that he could run a general election in tandem with the

European elections, already scheduled for 15 June. He dissolved the Dáil on 25 May, but weeks of media speculation after his return from Japan had given the Opposition plenty of time to prepare. Drafts of party policies, advertising strategy and the preparation of election literature and posters had all been completed by the Opposition parties before Haughey dissolved the Dáil and printing houses all over the country were on stand-by, geared up and ready to go once the formal announcement was made. In fact, the Opposition parties seemed far better prepared than Fianna Fáil. It was not just a matter of nuts-and-bolts, the Opposition had a strategy whereas the government appeared confused and was content to rely on its record.

By the time the Dáil was dissolved the PDs were ready in terms of policies and campaign structures, but the party was in deep trouble. For a start, its credibility had taken a knock because of the way it had flip-flopped on some of the high-profile spending cuts introduced by Fianna Fáil. At the beginning of the campaign the party TDs knew they had a fight on their hands, but they had no idea just how tough the campaign was going to be. Some were lulled into a false sense of security because they were so well prepared in policy terms. The economic policy published the previous autumn provided a handy basis for an election manifesto, but its credibility, too, had been damaged by the party's voting record in the Dáil. In later years the PDs managed to pull off an impressive *coup* by implementing the core aims of that manifesto, but the difficulty facing the party in the summer of 1989 was that its patchy record in Opposition for the previous two years had undermined its authority.

The party's confidence was rattled at the very beginning of the campaign when its deputy leader and TD for Dublin Central, Michael Keating, announced that he was not going to run again. In truth, Keating had proven to be a huge disappointment to the PDs. The sole Fine Gael TD to join had proved to be a loner who remained an isolated figure in the party. He was totally eclipsed in the Dáil by PD stars like McDowell, Harney and Kennedy, and had no rapport with his colleagues. In practical party terms he was therefore no great loss, but in terms of image and credibility the departure of the deputy leader at the start of the campaign was a huge blow. The Limerick West TD John McCoy, who had been one of the completely unexpected victors in 1987, also decided not to run. A novice in politics, McCoy had not found the Dáil a very agreeable place and decided to quit while he was ahead. The loss of two TDs before the campaign had even begun was ominous.

Another problem was that in March Pat Cox had been selected as the PD candidate for Munster in the European elections. The party had nominated Cox in Munster, Harney in Dublin, John Dardis in Leinster and Bobby Molloy in Connacht–Ulster. At that stage, of course, nobody had any idea there was going to be a general election and, in fact, Cox had decided to run only when a high-profile candidate could not be found.[1] His selection meant that the key figure in the organisation was missing when the general election campaign was called. Stephen O'Byrnes tried to fill that gap as best he could, but he also had to fulfil his responsibilities in terms of policy and media relations. The campaign was a radically slimmed-down version of the 1987 one due to, on the one hand, lack of resources and, on the other hand, the fact that the climate was not right for the razzmatazz that had characterised the party's first campaign. In any case the PDs didn't have the money for that kind of election; after the initial surge of financial contributions in 1986, funding began to dry up. The PDs received very little support from corporate Ireland, so the membership was squeezed to contribute money and to raise funds through raffles and race nights. 'After 1987 we had to live in the real world and spend a lot of time whipping the organisation into raising a few bob,' says Cox.[2]

Paul Mackay was appointed director of elections. He divided the constituencies into three categories. There was an A list of seats regarded as Bankers, which included seven constituencies and eight TDs. There was a B list of six constituencies regarded as Probables. And a C list of eight constituencies regarded as Possibles. The remaining thirteen constituencies where the party was fielding candidates were dubbed Also-Rans.[3]

Launching the PD campaign, O'Malley set down five principles that defined his party. The first was that 'the Progressive Democrats stand for honest, open government, which will not fudge the issues and which will tell it as it is.' The second principle was that the party stood for radical change while ensuring there was real social justice. 'The PDs stand for consensus, not conflict, in our society,' said O'Malley, adding that the party wanted to restore a sense of community while promoting individual effort and responsibility. The emphasis on social justice was a response to the campaigns of Labour and the Workers' party, both of which focused on the effect of the health cuts and got huge media coverage for their plans.[4]

O'Malley's emphasis on the need for honest, open Government didn't capture the imagination of the media, nor of the electorate, which depended on the media for information. It was not just that the PD leader had a profound distrust of Haughey's integrity that dated all the way back to the arms crisis of the 1970s, there were persistent rumours around Leinster House in May and June of 1989 which raised serious questions about the integrity of the Taoiseach and his cronies. In the rarefied atmosphere of Leinster House there were well-founded whisperings that suggested Haughey had gone to the country simply as an excuse to raise money for himself, under the guise of legitimate electioneering. As far as most media commentators and politicians were concerned, this was a bridge too far, even for Haughey, but O'Malley believed there were no depths to which his opponent would not stoop.

Almost a decade later the information obtained by the tribunals about the fundraising activities of Haughey and some of his chief lieutenants substantiated the rumours that had abounded in 1989. It emerged that two days before the election, on 13 June, Haughey had drawn down a £150,000 contribution from Ben Dunne of Dunnes Stores, part of the £1.3 million he received from the supermarket tycoon between 1987 and 1992. Also, in early June the Minister for Justice and Communications, Ray Burke, received £30,000 in cash from James Gogarty at his home. During the course of the campaign Burke received a further £30,000 from Rennicks, a subsidiary of the Fitzwilton Group, and later in the year he again received a sum of £30,000, this time from Century Radio boss Oliver Barry. Meanwhile the Minister for the Environment, Pádraig Flynn, was also fundraising. During the campaign he met property developer Tom Gilmartin, who gave him a cheque for £50,000 and left it up to the minister to fill in the name of the payee. Gilmartin says the donation was meant for Fianna Fáil, but the party never got it and it ended up in foreign bank accounts in the names of Flynn and his wife, Dorothy.[5]

. Two days after the election was called the PDs pulled a rabbit out of the hat and announced that they had done a deal with Fine Gael to offer the country an alternative government. Haughey's month-long delay in calling the election had given the two parties time to negotiate a pact, which they presented as an agreed agenda for action. Despite the time available to lay the groundwork, the pact had almost collapsed on the eve of the announcement. Dukes, who had attacked the PDs so bitterly on his election two years earlier, was very dubious about it and had to be pushed and prodded by his deputy leader, John Bruton, who believed strongly in it. Fine Gael's director of elections, Sean O'Leary, and the party press officer, Peter White, were not enthusiastic either. It would never have got off the ground if Bruton had not pushed relentlessly for it.[6]

At this stage positions were the reverse of those pertaining in the 1987 election when Fine Gael had badly wanted a pact but were spurned by the PDs. This time around the polls were reasonably good for Fine Gael, giving the party a solid 28 per cent, while the PDs had slumped to 5 per cent at the start and increased only marginally during the campaign. The polls, as usual, had grossly overestimated the Fianna Fáil vote at the start of the campaign, but that served to focus minds in both Fine Gael and the PDs on the fact that unless the voters were offered an alternative government, Haughey was likely to win an overall majority. In a joint statement launched on 27 May, O'Malley and Dukes attacked Haughey for turning his back on the consensus politics that had enabled the country to get to grips with the problems facing the public finances.[7]

The first item in the joint programme committed the PDs and Fine Gael to a budgetary strategy that would reduce the Exchequer borrowing requirement to 3 per cent, or less, of GNP by 1993. The second objective was the reduction of income tax rates to 25 per cent and 40 per cent in the lifetime of the next government. The former aim reflected Fine Gael's overriding concern with the national finances, while the latter reflected the PDs' belief that tax cuts were vital in order to create a healthy economy. Privatisation of State companies was also included as an objective of the government.[8] The parties did focus some attention on Health as an important issue, but during the campaign it was the left-wing parties that made most of the running on that subject. The emphasis of the media, particularly RTÉ, on the Health issue to the virtual exclusion of everything else hurt Fianna Fáil, but it also damaged the PDs and their Fine Gael allies because the deeper economic fundamentals did not raise a great deal of attention.

The PD–Fine Gael pact failed to capture the public imagination, but it did unsettle Fianna Fáil and it stopped the two Opposition parties attacking each other during the campaign. Instead they joined with the left-wing parties in a systematic assault on the government. This multi-faceted assault began to erode the government's lead in the opinion polls. As had happened in almost every election since polling began in 1977, Fianna Fáil lost support as the campaign progressed.

The PDs, though, were too weak to capitalise on this decline in public support. The party's own support had dipped suddenly a year earlier and the slide continued right up to the election. According to the polls conducted by MRBI, support for the PDs was a very solid 14 per cent for the year after the 1987 election. It then dropped to 10 per cent in the summer of 1988, was down to 7 per cent by October of that year and dropped again, to just 5 per cent, at the start of the general election campaign.[9] O'Malley and his colleagues did not believe party support could have simply evaporated like this, but they were to get a rude shock in the election results.

Geraldine Kennedy, who had established herself as a politician with a national profile, had no idea, until it was far too late, that she was going to lose her seat. 'I did not foresee this swing before or during the election campaign. The cool reception I received outside the polling stations on 15 June—particularly at the Progressive Democrat strongholds of Foxrock and Dalkey, where people whom I recognised as being positive when I canvassed them did their utmost to avoid eye contact—was the first inkling I had that something could have gone terribly wrong.'[10]

What puzzled her in the aftermath was that she had gone into the 1989 election campaign far better prepared than two years earlier when she had been successfully elected. With hindsight, she believes a number of factors combined to cause the loss of her seat, but one of those factors was the campaign strategy devised by PD headquarters: 'It was not sufficiently responsive to the climate emerging from the opinion polls and the canvass. In my view the negative, anti-government issues were over-emphasised to the detriment of the positive contribution of the PDs to the creation of consensus politics. The national campaign was affected by the fact that the newer party deputies were not included or involved in fronting the campaign.'[11]

The voters went to the polls on 15 June and turnout was a respectable 68.5 per cent. When the results came in the following day, it proved a bitter blow for the PDs. The fact that Fianna Fáil had also suffered a setback, dropping four seats from 81 to 77, seemed little consolation at first. Fine Gael and Labour improved marginally, while the Workers' party made a big breakthrough, winning almost as many votes as the PDs and securing one more seat.

The scale of the setback for the PDs was stunning. The party dropped from 14 seats to 6, with its share of the vote down to 5 per cent. In the process the PDs lost many of its brightest stars. Michael McDowell, Geraldine Kennedy, Anne Colley, Pat O'Malley and Martin Cullen all bit the dust, despite having performed very well in the Dáil over the previous two years. On the night of the election count it seemed the party was heading for oblivion. Ray Burke, smarting from his own party's failure to win a majority, remarked bitterly: 'It couldn't happen to a nicer bunch of people.'[12]

The result was a shattering blow for the PDs. McDowell concluded glumly that Ireland had 'reverted to a failed formula of closing the windows on opportunities for change'. Anne Colley suffered the indignity of going from topping the poll in Dublin South in 1987 to losing her seat just two years later, while in neighbouring Dún Laoghaire Geraldine Kennedy suffered the same fate, despite a fine performance in the Dáil. 'Politicians from all other parties, including Fine Gaelers in private, will take pleasure at their demise, but the average intelligence of Dáil deputies will fall with their departure. Almost without exception the party's fourteen deputies in the last Dáil were very capable performers, working very hard in their designated areas of policy and making intelligent contributions to Dáil debates and at committee level,' wrote Mark Brannock in *The Irish Times*.[13]

'It was a disaster,' says Harney. 'It was an amazing result in many ways. We held our two seats in Limerick, but we lost Anne Colley, Geraldine Kennedy, Michael McDowell, Pat O'Malley, Martin Cullen. The only seats we held were the six former Fianna Fáilers.'[14] Stephen O'Byrnes also mourned the loss of so much talent in the election. 'The result was a tragedy for us because we lost so many good people.'[15] Mairin Quill held her seat in Cork North Central against all the odds, but only just. 'I conceded defeat midway through the count, but I got an amazing transfer from the Workers' party to bring me over the line. I was the only newly elected TD from 1987 to survive,' recalls Quill.[16]

The pre-election pact with Fine Gael had clearly not worked to the advantage of the PDs and was of doubtful value to Fine Gael. O'Malley, though, was happy that it had been worthwhile, saying that without it the outcome of the election would have been a foregone conclusion. He said it was his duty to offer the electorate a non-socialist alternative to Fianna Fáil, but he accepted that the voters had refused that option this time. On the night of the count O'Malley seemed to be whistling in the wind when he maintained, in the teeth of disappointment, that the PDs would rise again: 'I think we have performed a great service and I think that the opportunity to perform that service will arrive again. I am determined to see that we rise from the relative ashes in which we find ourselves tonight.' Few took this long-term prophecy seriously, but they did pay attention to a more immediate forecast. He maintained that whatever happened when the Dáil met, the surviving PD deputies would not be voting for Charles Haughey as Taoiseach.

Looking back with hindsight, in the autumn of 2004, O'Malley still expresses surprise at the 1989 election disaster. 'I find it hard to explain what happened. In the previous two years the PDs, with fourteen deputies, was the best parliamentary party I have ever been in. More than half of them lost their seats. Some thought the Dáil chamber was all that mattered and didn't work their constituencies. Then there was the fact that some of the people who had supported us as the only salvation thought that Fianna Fáil had been converted to the right path and it was not as necessary to vote for us. The third factor was that we entered a pre-election alliance with Fine Gael. It didn't do us any good at all. It didn't do Fine Gael much good either.'[17]

The PDs barely had time to come to terms with the result when they had to confront the issue of what to do next. The unanswered question of the election was how a government could be put together. Fianna Fáil had 77 seats, Fine Gael 55, Labour 16, the Workers' party 7, the PDs 6, the Greens 1 and Others 4. Labour's Barry Desmond argued that the answer was obvious: Fianna Fáil and the PDs had the numbers between them, so Des O'Malley should go back to Fianna Fáil, from whence he had come, and they could form a government.[18]

Once the outcome became clear Haughey stated his willingness to form a government and said he was prepared to consult with the other political parties before the Dáil resumed on 29 June. He was confident he could form another minority administration and that Fianna Fáil could simply take up where it had left off under the Tallaght Strategy. The prospects for that looked good the following day when one of the surviving PDs, Mary Harney, took a different line from that articulated by O'Malley the night before and went on radio to say her party should support Haughey, if that were necessary to provide the country with a government. Many PD members reacted with fury to Harney's suggestion that the party should put Haughey back into power. Party headquarters was inundated by angry phone calls from members and Harney received a steady stream of outraged calls on her home telephone.[19]

'What happened was that the basic arithmetic of 77 and 6 generated a lot of media comment and I gave an interview giving some support to the idea of a deal with Fianna Fáil. And Haughey rang McCreevy and said "Is she serious?" McCreevy came to see me to find out.'[20] McCreevy immediately drove to Harney's home in Rathcoole to discuss the situation.

Since his involvement in the planning phase of the PDs four years earlier, McCreevy had been a solid member of the Fianna Fáil parliamentary party. He was delighted at Haughey's conversion to the economic straight-and-narrow and was back on good terms with 'the Boss'. While McCreevy had not been given any office by Haughey, he had established himself as one of the 'characters' of Fianna Fáil and was even consulted from time to time by the Taoiseach. This had not prevented McCreevy from keeping up his strong friendship with Harney, so he was ideally placed to act not just as a go-between but as an advisor to both sides. As the election results continued to trickle in that Sunday afternoon he tried to convince Harney to go with him to visit Haughey at his home in Kinsealy, but she was not impressed by the idea—particularly when the stream of hostile phone calls from PD supporters began.

When McCreevy returned home after talking to Harney, he discovered that government press secretary, P.J. Mara, had been ringing, looking for him. 'I've already been about my father's business,' McCreevy told Mara. The following morning he went to see Haughey and told the Taoiseach that in his view Harney was the key to resolving the political impasse. McCreevy explained to Haughey just how vital a role Harney had played in founding the PDs, that she was a tough fighter and had the ability to bring her party around to the notion of supporting Fianna Fáil.[21]

Immediately after briefing Haughey, McCreevy headed off to talk to Harney again, this time at her weekday flat in Dublin. The two of them listened to RTÉ's 'News at One' and an interview with Cork PD deputy Pearse Wyse, in which he said he could never bring himself to vote for Haughey as Taoiseach. McCreevy told Harney that he was interested to hear what Michael McDowell had to say about the situation, so contact was made with the party chairman and he arrived to talk to them. Despite the bitter disappointment of losing his Dáil seat, McDowell was keyed up about the possibilities of the new political situation. He immediately changed the nature of the discussion by arguing for full-blown coalition between the PDs and Fianna Fáil. Up to that point, Harney and McCreevy had been discussing the option of the PDs supporting a minority Fianna Fáil government on an agreed programme. McCreevy relayed Haughey's view that various problems the PDs had arising from the loss of so many seats could be fixed. The reduction in seats from 14 to 6 meant that the party faced the loss of its Dáil status and its party leader's allowance—more than half the party's secretarial staff would have to be let go and some of its former deputies were now out of work. 'Don't worry about those secretaries or anything else. They'll all be looked after, but you can't have ministers,' McCreevy told them.[22]

McDowell, however, was strongly opposed to PD involvement in some new version of the Tallaght Strategy and argued cogently that, bad and all as the election result was, it provided an opportunity for the PDs to get into government to implement their policies. 'The election result was a major catastrophe for the party and Haughey then tried to bully the PDs into external support. As soon as I saw that coming I became a very strong supporter of coalition. It was a question of political survival. If we didn't support him and he called another election, we would have been annihilated. The thing was to stay focused on policy as he was desperate to stay in office.'[23] Harney, McCreevy and McDowell, who had been at the core of the plan to form a new party four years earlier, recognised a fresh opportunity to break the mould of Irish politics. However, at that point the odds seemed heavily weighted against them.

Chapter 9 ∿

INTO OFFICE

O nce he had absorbed the immediate disappointment of the election result, O'Malley recognised that the arithmetic had created the possibility of a coalition between the PDs and Fianna Fáil. However, he could also see a whole host of obstacles blocking such a move. The first was that most of his own surviving TDs were adamantly opposed to voting Charles Haughey into the Taoiseach's Office. Secondly, he knew there would be fierce resistance within Fianna Fáil to any notion of coalition. The party had never shared office and had adopted the principle that coalitions were bad in themselves. That 'core value' was a hurdle that seemed insuperable to most people in the days after the election.

Haughey didn't waste any time contacting the other party leaders to discuss the election result, but coalition was far from his mind at this stage. Significantly, though, despite all that had passed between them over the years, the first party leader Haughey called was O'Malley. The two men met the day after McCreevy had discussed, with Haughey's approval, the prospect of government formation with Harney and McDowell. In that first short and formal meeting of the Fianna Fáil and PD leaders there was no reference to the possibility of coalition.

The first post-election meeting of the PD parliamentary party was a strange event because the former TDs, who had just lost their seats, were invited to take part. The hostility to the idea of coalition with Fianna Fáil among the six survivors was tempered by the views of the election casualties. A clear majority of the former TDs felt that coalition was the only way out of the election disaster; in contrast, a majority of the survivors were opposed to doing a deal with Fianna Fáil. In particular, the two Cork TDs, Pearse Wyse and Mairin Quill, had huge problems with the notion of voting for Haughey as Taoiseach—in any circumstances.[1]

'Our first instinct was to run a mile from a coalition with Haughey, but we had to sit down and reflect on it,' says O'Malley. 'If we walked

away, we would have been into another election and the PDs would
have been portrayed as the cause of it. We would not have been
thanked by the electorate for that. The media would have said that we
wouldn't form a government just because O'Malley didn't like
Haughey. We had very valid reasons for that deep dislike and distrust,
but it would have been trivialised into a personality clash.'[2]

It took time for the party TDs to come to terms with the political
reality being forced upon them by the result of the election. 'The six of us
sat down for three days and considered the matter very carefully. The
principal advocate of trying to do business was Harney. She saw there
was no future in opposition and gradually others came around to the
same view. We were stunned at having lost more than half our seats and
were fearful we would be wiped out altogether.'[3]

While the talking softened the mood, the six surviving PDs and their
new MEP, Pat Cox, were still torn asunder over the notion of voting for
Haughey: O'Malley, Harney and Cox were in favour of some kind of deal
with Fianna Fáil, preferably a coalition; Quill, Wyse, Molloy and Peadar
Clohessy were opposed. On the Fianna Fáil side, while Haughey was
attempting to devise a strategy that would hook the PDs he initially had
no thought of coalition. Strangely—in view of their differences over the
previous few years—McCreevy became a regular visitor to Kinsealy at
this stage and he relayed the mood within the PDs to Haughey. The
Taoiseach's only real confidant in Cabinet, Bertie Ahern, the Minister for
Labour, was the other regular visitor to the Taoiseach's home during the
post-election political crisis.[4]

Gradually the PDs edged towards a consensus on how to cope with the
political reality. After he had a week to reflect on their position, Molloy
accepted that coalition represented the best way forward for his party
and he conveyed this view to his colleagues. Intense discussions took
place at length in an attempt to bridge the impasse and reach consensus
—one meeting of the small parliamentary party lasted for a staggering
eight hours. Eventually, however, everybody came around to the view
that an offer of coalition should be made, although most consoled
themselves with the belief that it was all academic as it would not be
acceptable to Fianna Fáil anyway. O'Malley insisted that before anything
else happened, the PDs had to agree to honour their pledge to vote for
Alan Dukes for Taoiseach when the Dáil met on 29 June.

On the evening before that first meeting of the Twenty-Sixth Dáil,
Haughey sent word to O'Malley that he would like to meet him.

O'Malley asked Cox to accompany him and the two of them walked across the tunnel from Leinster House to the Taoiseach's Office. 'Des was wound up like a spring and sat on the edge of his chair, but Charlie relaxed back into his own comfortable leather armchair and surveyed the wreckage of the election result with equanimity,' recalls Cox. 'Charlie made the point that it was important for the country that a government should be formed and said it would be feasible to harmonise the policies of Fianna Fáil and the PDs.'[5] Haughey even got down to specifics and offered to provide revamped Dáil committees with expanded powers and to give the PDs the Chair of the important ones. He offered to provide the PDs with back-up staff and the important privilege of group status in the Dáil, even though the party was one TD short of the number required to qualify. In addition, he offered the post of Leas-Cheann Comhairle and three positions in the Seanad. O'Malley responded by saying he was not there to negotiate at that stage, but instead wondered if he might pose a hypothetical question about how Haughey would regard the prospect of PD participation in government.

'Des, even *I* couldn't sell that to the party,' replied Haughey.

'Charlie, from my experience I wouldn't be inclined to underestimate your selling ability within Fianna Fáil,' responded O'Malley.[6]

As they stood up to leave, Haughey enquired if O'Malley would be attending the Mass at the Pro-Cathedral the following morning to mark the opening of the Twenty-Sixth Dáil. 'We all need to pray to God from time to time,' retorted O'Malley. Both men laughed at the oblique reference to the embarrassing episode when the PDs had attempted to remove references to God from the Constitution.

When the Dáil met on 29 June, Haughey was beaten in the vote for Taoiseach, but Dukes and Spring were defeated by even bigger margins. It was the first time in the history of the State that the Dáil failed to select a Taoiseach after a general election. As if that wasn't sensational enough, Haughey added to the drama of the day by initially refusing to tender his resignation to the President, as the Opposition parties claimed was required by the Constitution. The Dáil was adjourned for two hours to give the Fianna Fáil leader time to meet his Cabinet and consider his position. As the TDs left the Dáil chamber O'Malley bumped into junior Agriculture Minister, Joe Walsh, who had acted as an intermediary between the two parties in the previous ten days. 'This won't make it any easier,' the PD leader remarked ominously. At a stormy Cabinet meeting Haughey at first insisted that he would not resign, but eventually he was persuaded by colleagues that, regardless of the legal rights and wrongs of the issue, it made political sense to resign formally.[7]

Haughey went back into the Dáil to announce his decision and then drove to Áras an Uachtaráin where he handed a written note of resignation to President Hillery. As the Constitution stipulates that an outgoing Taoiseach should remain in place until a successor has been appointed by the Dáil, Haughey and his ministers stayed in office, although there was considerable debate about the powers of an 'Acting Taoiseach' and whether these included the authority to obtain a dissolution of the Dáil in order to hold another election. Haughey was still in power for now, but it had been brought home to him and his party that they could remain in that position only if they really got down to business and made some genuine compromises with other parties. The one unmentionable compromise, then and later, was the possibility of Haughey stepping down as leader of Fianna Fáil to let somebody else take over and try to put a government together. Members of the Cabinet and most Fianna Fáil TDs knew that almost any leader other than Haughey would have taken the necessary steps to enable them to retain office as a minority government. However, nobody in the party dared to broach the subject and the PDs, too, carefully avoided raising it for fear of frightening Fianna Fáil away from the notion of coalition.

With the Dáil once again adjourned, until 3 July, Cox devised a bold strategy for the PDs. He drew up a nine-point Framework for Dialogue with Fianna Fáil, which was endorsed enthusiastically by his parliamentary party. The basic thrust of the Framework was that each party should appoint a negotiating team to discuss a programme for government and that nothing should be ruled in or out in advance. O'Malley asked Molloy and Cox to carry out the detailed negotiations, referring any issues that could not be resolved to himself and Haughey. The Framework document was given to Joe Walsh, who charged around to Government Buildings and interrupted a Cabinet meeting to deliver it to Haughey. After a quick consultation with his Cabinet colleagues, Haughey dictated a letter of reply that accepted the Framework for talks, handed the letter to Walsh and told him to deliver it personally to O'Malley.

A meeting between the negotiating teams was immediately arranged for that same evening, in the Mansion House. When Molloy and Cox arrived at the venue they found that Haughey had appointed Albert Reynolds and Bertie Ahern as his negotiating team. After an exchange of courtesies the four men sat down at a small table with three pints of Guinness in front of them and a soft drink for Reynolds, courtesy of the Lord Mayor.

'Bobby looked at me and the message was *start talking*,' recalls Cox. Never short of a word, Cox duly set about an analysis of the election result and its clear message that Fianna Fáil had not earned the right to form a government on its own. Molloy then intervened to suggest that they should discuss the possibility of coalition. 'Oh no. We have no mandate for that,' said Reynolds. Molloy insisted that participation in government was fundamental for the PDs and there was no point discussing anything else until that was accepted. The meeting broke up after less than half-an-hour without agreement on the fundamental issue. The negotiators met again the following morning, but it was as much for the benefit of the media as anything else and there was still no movement on the core issue. 'We got hot tea, warm toast and the cold shoulder,' recalls Cox. When the PD team went back to party headquarters and described the proceedings to O'Malley, they received another cool reception; the leader wondered if they had over-egged the coalition demand.[8]

Haughey and O'Malley gave press conferences later that day to put pressure on each other, but the issue had boiled down to the question of whether or not Fianna Fáil would countenance coalition. The two men met formally at the Mansion House before the day was out to see if they could find a way to breach the obstacle. They had no success and both subsequently spoke to the media, suggesting that agreement would be extremely difficult to reach. 'Coalition is completely ruled out,' Haughey told journalists as he left the Mansion House.

By that stage, however, Haughey was mulling over the issue of coalition. Two days earlier Ahern had drawn up a list of options open to Fianna Fáil: the first was a second election; the second was that Fianna Fáil stand down from government and allow Dukes to form a minority Fine Gael government; the third was for Haughey to step down as party leader; and the fourth was for a coalition with the PDs. At a meeting in Kinsealy, attended by McCreevy and P.J. Mara, Ahern outlined these options to Haughey, who replied that he didn't like any of them. Nonetheless, coalition was clearly the least painful option for Haughey and McCreevy was not shy about pointing that out to him.[9]

That meeting in Kinsealy took place on Sunday, 2 July, and while it did not impact on the deliberations of the Dáil the following day, Haughey made the decisive move the following Tuesday as media speculation about a fresh election reached a frenzy. On the morning of 4 July he

contacted O'Malley to arrange a meeting in the Berkeley Court Hotel for
5.00pm. Ahern spoke on a radio programme at lunchtime and hinted
that coalition might just be on. When asked if coalition was out in all
circumstances, Ahern replied: 'It's a matter for discussion to work
around. Nobody should ever say never in discussions because ultimately
people have to find solutions and in crises people always have to find a
way out of them.'[10] It was a clear signal to those on the inside track that
Fianna Fáil opposition to coalition was crumbling, but many senior
people in the party were the last to get the message.

That afternoon Haughey called a Cabinet meeting at which he directly
raised the subject of coalition with his ministers for the first time. Most
of them were stunned by the realisation that the Taoiseach was considering such a move. A clear majority of ministers, led by Albert
Reynolds, was strongly opposed to any coalition arrangement: Pádraig
Flynn, Michael O'Kennedy, Rory O'Hanlon, John Wilson, Michael
Noonan and Brendan Daly all spoke against a deal with the PDs. Flynn
was the most vehement and shocked everybody by accusing Haughey of
dubious motives—raising the coalition option out of a personal pursuit
of power. Two key ministers, Gerry Collins and Ray Burke, took the
opposite view and in coded language spoke in favour of a deal with
O'Malley, even if the price was coalition. As ever, Brian Lenihan supported Haughey and asserted that if that were the ultimate decision they
would be able to sell it to the organisation. By that stage Ahern was
already working to deliver a coalition deal, but he kept his views largely
to himself at Cabinet. No formal decision on policy change was taken by
the Cabinet and in a radio interview that evening Flynn said that refusal
to enter coalitions was a core value for Fianna Fáil.

At about the same time as that interview was being broadcast,
Haughey was meeting O'Malley in the Berkeley Court Hotel. He made it
clear to the PD leader that he was prepared to concede on coalition as
long as he could bring his party with him. Another meeting was arranged
for the following day to formalise the decision. Meanwhile Harney,
worried by the level of anti-coalition sentiment being expressed by
Fianna Fáil ministers, went to see McCreevy, but he was able to reassure
her that everything was now on track for a coalition deal. When she got
home, O'Malley rang to tell her the latest news and to explain the
arrangements for the follow-up meeting the next day.

Cox and Molloy accompanied their leader to this meeting, but
Haughey didn't invite either of his two negotiators. At the meeting

Molloy challenged Haughey about Flynn's widely publicised remarks of the evening before, to the effect that coalition wasn't on the cards, and also about anti-coalition views expressed by Reynolds that morning.

'It's all right. I just haven't told them yet,' was Haughey's cryptic response.

The audacity of the Taoiseach's reply didn't surprise the PD team, who knew his form only too well and, if anything, were impressed by the utter confidence and self-belief with which he conducted himself. Having agreed to coalition in principle, Haughey then went back to brief his Cabinet, but he didn't give them the full picture and he certainly didn't ask for their permission.[11] He hinted that a coalition deal might be on, but omitted to spell out the concession he had made to the PDs. Some of his ministers were appalled at the news and Reynolds, in particular, was deeply indignant at Haughey's effrontery in making the fundamental concession without informing his negotiators. It was salt on wounds when Reynolds and Ahern subsequently learned that the two PD negotiators had met Haughey along with their leader, while they had not even been aware that a meeting was taking place. Despite the misgivings of some ministers, there was no clear objection to an announcement that the negotiations with the PDs would resume.[12] The announcement was to be made that very evening.

Astonishingly, McCreevy was much closer to the action than any other Fianna Fáil minister, with the exception of Ahern. When there was an inexplicable delay in a reciprocal statement being issued by O'Malley to confirm that talks would resume, McCreevy rang Harney and in blunt language demanded to know what her leader was up to. McCreevy told her that Haughey was 'climbing the walls' in frustration at the delay. Harney personally delivered a copy of the PD statement to Haughey's office, where McCreevy and Mara were ensconced with the Boss.[13]

The negotiating teams got back to work the following day. Haughey instructed his ministers to discuss a policy programme, but to leave the actual make-up of the government, and hence the question of coalition, to him. There was little doubt in anybody's mind what that meant in practice, but some ministers still tried to avoid facing up to the reality. When the public announcement regarding the talks was made around 5.00pm, the media was in no doubt about what had transpired and that a Fianna Fáil–PD coalition was now on. Some ministers still clung to the belief that any deal would have to come back to the Cabinet for final approval, comforting themselves that they would ultimately have the final say. This didn't happen, of course, but Haughey read his Cabinet correctly in assuming that while they might huff and puff behind his back, none of them would do anything about it. His attitude to his ministerial colleagues was summed up in an encounter with one back-bench TD, who asked him if his Cabinet would agree to coalition. 'They are only a crowd of gobshites,' he responded brusquely.[14]

When the Dáil met the following day, 6 July, another adjournment was agreed to allow Fianna Fáil and the PDs time to negotiate their programme for government. Haughey, who had unequivocally ruled out coalition in any circumstances a few days earlier, told the Dáil that the 'higher national interest' required an arrangement to put a government in place. With the Dáil adjourned for six days to allow the two parties to conclude an agreement, there was intense pressure on both sides. Having conceded the principle of coalition, Fianna Fáil tried to limit the PD representation at the Cabinet table to just one minister, but again the PDs, and particularly Molloy, adopted an uncompromising negotiating stance and demanded that Haughey concede two Cabinet posts. The Fianna Fáil parliamentary party met twice to debate the issues involved, but on both occasions they gave Haughey a free hand without being told how many Cabinet places the PDs would get. Some deputies were strongly opposed to coalition at any price, among them junior Minister, Máire Geoghegan Quinn, Dick Roche of Wicklow and newly elected Meath TD, Noel Dempsey. While the majority didn't like it, they were very anxious to avoid another election and therefore were prepared to allow Haughey make whatever decisions he thought necessary to avoid that outcome. In the Fianna Fáil organisation the mood was very different, however, and there was total and utter astonishment that Haughey had given way to O'Malley, of all people.

At the negotiating table the question of Cabinet seats remained the hot issue. 'Bobby and myself were firmly of the opinion that it had to be two seats at Cabinet. One PD minister would have been totally isolated and in effect would have been merely a token at Cabinet. We had to have two ministers to have a proper coalition,' says Cox. 'We couldn't have pursued our tax agenda without a real coalition.' Haughey furiously resisted giving way on the question of the second minister.[15]

The issue was still outstanding on the morning of 12 July. Bertie Ahern went on radio to say that the PDs should not get more than one Cabinet seat and it seemed that Haughey had drawn a firm line under this. A nervous O'Malley went to see Haughey in his office at 10.30am, but the

Taoiseach refused to budge. Returning to an anteroom where Cox and Molloy waited for him, O'Malley reported anxiously: 'He says "no, no, no".' Molloy advised O'Malley to hold his nerve and just sit down and relax. An hour later Haughey asked him back to his office. A few minutes later a beaming PD leader emerged and returned to his negotiating team to report that Haughey had conceded two Cabinet posts. O'Malley was to be Minister for Industry and Commerce and Molloy the Minister for Energy. The PD team was ecstatic, but then realised that in the excitement O'Malley had omitted to pin down a number of other commitments on their political shopping list. That list included a junior ministry for Harney, the appointment of three PD senators, government press officer and places on the Council of Europe. O'Malley, Cox and Molloy went back to the Taoiseach's office to sort out these matters. Haughey, who was obviously as thrilled as the PDs, remarked that he couldn't concede everything. After a pause he added that Council of Europe places—the least important item on the list—were out. There were handshakes all round and just before the PD team left Haughey's office, the Taoiseach grinned at them and remarked, 'You know, nobody but myself could have done it.'[16]

While most political and media attention was focused on the coalition issue and the number of Cabinet seats for the PDs, negotiations on the Agreed Programme for Government 1989–1993 had been proceeding apace. The PDs worked feverishly to distil their policies on taxation, the economy, Northern Ireland, the environment and a range of social issues into a coherent framework document. They brought in a number of expert advisors to help them achieve this, including former Fianna Fáil minister, Martin O'Donoghue. By contrast, Fianna Fáil relied on briefing documents produced by the Department of Finance and other government Departments and capitulated on a range of policy issues. The PDs were effectively allowed to write the joint programme for government and all the party's pet policies, particularly its tax-cutting agenda, were included. The penny dropped with O'Malley that as long as he was prepared to vote Fianna Fáil into office, he could virtually dictate the programme for government. For their part, the PDs agreed to continue Haughey's successful programme of social partnership. It was a policy about which McDowell had been sceptical, but it had delivered industrial peace and the PDs recognised and accepted the benefits it afforded.

The key policy areas for O'Malley were the economy, tax reform and Northern Ireland. On all of them Fianna Fáil put up little or no opposition to the PDs' proposals. Fianna Fáil had no problem with the imperative of controlling public spending and was more than willing to sign up to the notion that the annual Exchequer borrowing requirement should not exceed 3 per cent of GNP. The two parties also agreed that the debt/GNP ratio should not exceed 120 per cent of GNP by 1993. (By 2004 it was just 30 per cent—something that was unimaginable in 1989.) On the issue of tax, Fianna Fáil accepted the PD target of two rates, with the lower one pegged at 25 per cent. The top rate, however, was left flexible. The door to privatisation of State companies was pushed ajar, but only through agreement with the social partners. As for the North, there was agreement to conduct dialogue with unionist politicians. There was further agreement on a series of worthy objectives across a range of other areas, from Education to Health and Social Welfare. Among the innovations promised were the establishment of the Environmental Protection Agency, the introduction of competition legislation, the abolition of the death penalty, the liberalisation of bus transport and a reorganisation of the Courts. Throughout all these discussions senior Fianna Fáil figures remained oblivious to the capitulation on fundamental policy. Even those who favoured a deal, like Ahern and Brennan, were fixated on the need not to concede more than one Cabinet seat to the PDs. The actual policies involved did not seem to worry them very much.

When the Dáil met on the afternoon of 12 July, Haughey was duly elected Taoiseach with the support of the PDs. In the short debate prior to the vote, O'Malley and Haughey paid careful tributes to one other and it seemed that the hatchet had finally been buried. 'I want to acknowledge the courage and skill exhibited, particularly by Deputy Haughey, in recent weeks, courage and skill which I know he possesses in abundance and which has been utilised in the national interest during this time,' the PD leader told the Dáil. After his election Haughey responded: 'I want to say about them all, particularly Deputy O'Malley, that I was able to conduct my conversations with them in a way that was always not just courteous but constructive, and I shall always remember that as one of the most important developments in this new Dáil as it went about its arduous and complicated business.'[17] After a visit to President Hillery, Haughey returned to announce his Cabinet to the Dáil. It had taken a full twenty-seven days since the election to put a government together, but in the end the logic of political arithmetic proved irresistible.

There were enormous stresses and strains within Fianna Fáil as the party sought to come to terms with the notion of coalition. Things eventually settled down, but one result was a decisive shift in the balance of power within Haughey's Cabinet. Long-time Haughey supporters, like Reynolds and Flynn, became enemies as a result of the coalition deal and Haughey relied more and more on ministers like Collins, Burke and Ahern.

For the PDs, too, the coalition was traumatic. The party's surviving TDs had all quit Fianna Fáil because of a profound distrust of Haughey —now, they were putting him back into government. Despite winning hands-down on policy, the PDs had also made a few pragmatic decisions of their own which looked a bit grubby. The policy of abolishing the Seanad was abandoned in order to provide a home for some of the defeated party candidates, with an eye to rebuilding the party; Martin Cullen, Helen Keogh and John Dardis were nominated to the Upper House. Michael McDowell couldn't face that prospect and declined to become a senator. O'Malley was furious with all those who had lost their seats and they each got a dressing-down rather than any sympathy for their plight.

Nonetheless, by getting into government and by forcing Fianna Fáil to abandon its last core value the PDs had managed to fashion a victory of some importance from the ashes of defeat. *The Irish Times'* political editor, Dick Walsh, wrote that politics would never be the same again, and he was right. He interpreted Fianna Fáil's decision to share power with the PDs as the most momentous event in the party's history since it abandoned abstentionism in 1927 and entered Dáil Éireann. It was to prove a decision with far-reaching consequences as in the years to come it allowed Fianna Fáil to retain power for far longer than it would otherwise have done. From a PD perspective, it provided the opportunity to participate in government and to dictate the political and economic agenda in a manner that would have seemed utterly incredible on the day the party was founded. It was a vital move in every sense. 'In my opinion, if we had not gone into government after that election disaster, I don't think the party would still be around,' says Harney candidly. 'We wouldn't have been able to sustain the organisation or financially sustain the show if we hadn't been in government.'[18]

Chapter 10 ∿

COALITION CONSCIENCE

T he PDs took to government like ducks to water. With so much
ministerial experience behind them, O'Malley and Molloy knew
how the system worked. Harney embarked on a steep learning
curve as a junior minister, but she made a success of her portfolio at the
Department of the Environment, in spite of the outright hostility of her
senior minister, Pádraig Flynn. The three back-bench PDs, all former
Fianna Fáilers, understood the pressures of being in government and
adapted well to their roles. Outside the Dáil Michael McDowell, as party
chairman, acted as the PD watchdog and kept the two parties in government on their toes with a steady stream of speeches and injunctions
designed to maintain his party's separate identity.

The main reason that the government worked was that Haughey and
O'Malley, despite all their years of conflict and tension, settled down to
business like true, professional politicians. Harney recalls that the coalition
'worked extraordinarily well'. McCreevy pays tribute to both leaders:

'Think how difficult it was for Haughey to go in with O'Malley, the
man who was his true and true enemy, who had formed another
party. Think how difficult it was also for Des O'Malley, and all the
things he had said about Fianna Fáil under Charlie Haughey. To the
credit of both they put it aside and formed a government. People will
say they just did it for power, but that is too glib. For Haughey and
O'Malley, it was more than that.'[1]

O'Malley can identify one of the reasons the coalition worked:

'The government worked reasonably well because I was in a much
better position as leader of another party than I was as a member of
Fianna Fáil. He couldn't walk on me or get his toadies to walk on me.

It was a very different relationship from that I had with him when I was a Fianna Fáil minister. The fact that you were two party leaders gave you status and prevented you being pressurised or undermined. Both of us knew how the system worked and where the limits of the system were.'[2]

Harney recalls one amusing episode in the early days of the coalition. During her initial discussions with McCreevy on coalition she had mentioned the plight of Martin Cullen, who had just lost his Waterford seat. He was said to be in such financial difficulty that he would be forced to sell his car to pay his mortgage. In the event, after intensive lobbying on his part, he was appointed to one of the PD Seanad positions. A few months later Harney, by then a junior minister, got a phone call from McCreevy, who was still on the back benches.

'Harney, do you remember that fellow you said would have to sell his car?'

'Yes,' she replied.

'Well, he has just driven in through the gates of Leinster House in the biggest f***king Merc I have ever seen,' said McCreevy. When Harney checked it out she found that he was not exaggerating.[3]

Once settled in the Department of Industry and Commerce, O'Malley's first priority was to review the operation of the export credit insurance scheme of which he had been so critical in Opposition. He set up a Departmental inquiry into the discrepancies revealed by PD parliamentary questions when in Opposition, which showed that the insurance cover afforded to Goodman Companies for beef exports to Iraq was to a value exceeding the total Irish beef exports in 1987–1988. Once he received the results of the inquiry—which found that 38 per cent of the beef covered had been sourced in Britain and Northern Ireland—O'Malley cancelled export credit insurance policies worth nearly £40 million. Goodman responded by initiating a legal action against the State for £50 million. That action was concluded in 2003, when Goodman effectively dropped his claim.

O'Malley's decision to tackle Goodman was taken after consultation with Haughey; the Taoiseach placed no obstacles in his way. Nor were obstacles raised when O'Malley's inspectors concluded that Goodman was the beneficial owner of Classic Meats and ordered the meat baron to dispose of the company. O'Malley's ability to take independent action surprised many people, but the coalition deal allowed him to operate independently of Haughey. The action of the three PD senators—

appointed as part of the Taoiseach's eleven—in refusing to vote for the Fianna Fáil nominee for Cathaoirleach of the Seanad, Seán Doherty, because of his role in the GUBU controversies of 1982 was also designed to demonstrate that the party could maintain a separate identity in coalition. 'Surprisingly, when the deal was struck the two parties just got on with the job and Haughey dealt with us fairly,' says Mairin Quill.[4]

O'Malley drew a sharp distinction between the way Haughey operated coalition and the *modus operandi* of his successor, Albert Reynolds: 'Reynolds didn't understand how the system worked. He was a deal-maker behind closed doors who had no idea of how a coalition govern-ment should run. Haughey was workmanlike and a hell of a lot better than most people expected. He understood the theory and the practice of government.'[5]

The professional relationship between Haughey and O'Malley helped them to cope with another Goodman-generated controversy in the summer of 1990, when it emerged that the Goodman group was on the verge of collapse. The Dáil was hurriedly recalled on 28 August to pass special legislation to prevent the company from folding immediately as the out-come would have had devastating knock-on effects for farmers. O'Malley informed the Dáil that Goodman International owed a consortium of international banks the massive sum of £460 million. The company was owed £180 million from meat exports to Iraq, which had just invaded Kuwait and was unlikely to be in a position to make repayments. Massive losses of £200 million had also been sustained by Goodman in an ill-fated foray into the British stock market to buy sugar shares. Larry Goodman tried to exert pressure on the government to come up with a rescue package for his operation.[6] He helicoptered into Kinsealy ten days before the special Dáil sitting in an attempt to persuade Haughey to bale him out, but the scale of the losses was so great that the Taoiseach was in no position to attempt a rescue mission. All the government could do was pass the legislation to appoint an examiner to the company so that the debts to the banks could be rescheduled. Considering his close association with Goodman the whole affair was an embarrassment to Haughey, however the decisive handling of the issue by O'Malley helped to calm public disquiet. It was an instance of the participation of the PDs in coalition working to the advantage of both parties in government.[7]

Aside from fire-fighting, the first priority for the PDs in coalition was to ensure that they began to deliver on the tax agenda set out in the government's first Budget. Reynolds was Minister for Finance and he had no ideological problems with following a tax-cutting agenda. In fact, in his first Budget, in January 1989, he became the first Minister for Finance since the 1960s to cut income tax, reducing the basic rate from 35 per cent to 32 per cent. Although Reynolds was happy to cut tax, he was irritated by the PDs dictating this policy to him. He had argued strongly against holding the election in June 1989, and had subsequently opposed the notion of coalition with the PDs. On both issues Haughey had blithely ignored his objections. That remained a source of resentment for Reynolds and was later to have profound consequences for both coalition parties.

Despite his irritation, when Reynolds stood up in the Dáil in January 1990 to deliver his second Budget, he announced a significant step towards the adoption of the PD agenda: the standard rate was reduced from 32 per cent to 30 per cent and the top rate cut from 55 per cent to 53 per cent. The middle rate of 45 per cent remained the same, but the top rate of VAT was also cut, from 25 per cent to 23 per cent.[8] It marked a decisive delivery on a key issue by the PDs at a time when conventional wisdom held that the last thing the country needed was tax cuts. Economists were concerned that the cuts might distract from the need to get the public finances under control, while the Opposition parties pressed for increased public spending as a higher priority.

'We did deliver a cut in the tax rate in our first Budget in 1990. The scope for cutting tax was much less than later on in the decade, but at least we got it started. We got an acceptance of the validity of the strategy,' says O'Malley. 'Of course the tax-cutting agenda was fully implemented after 1997. There was a wider acceptance that this was the thing to do and Fianna Fáil people like McCreevy and Brennan were in favour of it. Without PD involvement, though, they would never have been able to do it.'[9]

The PDs got very little credit for the adoption of the tax-cutting agenda as a central objective of government economic policy in January 1990. The Irish Times' front-page headline concentrated on the positive impact the tax cuts were likely to have in the negotiations on a new round of social partnership deals. The Irish Independent and the Irish Press gave slightly more credit to the PDs for setting the agenda, but the main focus was on Reynolds as the man who had introduced the Budget measures. The second social partnership deal was agreed shortly thereafter and the stable industrial relations environment it created helped to anchor subsequent economic growth.[10]

Once the Budget was out of the way the major political priority in the first half of 1990 was the presidency of the European Community.

Haughey had an opportunity to play a part on the international stage at a time of historic change in Europe. The Berlin Wall had come down in December 1989 and Europe was in a ferment, with the prospect of German unity topping the political agenda. Haughey won the gratitude of Chancellor Helmut Kohl by doing everything possible to facilitate his drive for Germany unity. This political relationship would provide real benefits for Ireland in the longer term because Kohl proved to be an invaluable ally at EU level. All in all, Haughey's handling of the EU presidency was a considerable success, however another presidency—the Irish one—brought him tumbling down to Earth. The Irish presidential election campaign of 1990 became one of the most sensational election campaigns in the history of the State and plunged Fianna Fáil and the PDs into a crisis that came within an ace of wrecking their coalition after barely a year in office.

The presidential election campaign got off to an early start in spring, when Labour nominated Mary Robinson to run for office. Fianna Fáil was expected to run the Tánaiste and Minister for Defence, Brian Lenihan, who had made a good recovery from a liver transplant operation. However, the party didn't get around to actually nominating him until September. Fine Gael struggled to find a candidate and finally Austin Currie was persuaded to run. By the time Lenihan and Currie were in the field, the Robinson campaign had managed to capture the public imagination and the strongly positive response of female voters had become a critical factor.

Just over a week before polling day, in October, the country was rocked by a controversy that sent Lenihan's campaign into a tailspin. The crisis stemmed from Lenihan's denial, on a television programme, that he had ever put pressure on President Hillery not to dissolve the Dáil when Garret FitzGerald's government fell in January 1982. Unfortunately for Lenihan, at the time he had given an interview, on tape, to a post-graduate student, Jim Duffy, in which he had spoken freely of how he had phoned Áras an Uachtaráin on the night in question and spoken to the President. When the tape recording was released, on 25 October, Lenihan's campaign was thrown into turmoil and the coalition was threatened. There followed a sequence of events that mirrored the negotiations on the formation of the government as the PDs imposed on Fianna Fáil their analysis of how to proceed.

The crisis proper was triggered when Alan Dukes moved to exploit the chaos in the Fianna Fáil camp by putting down a motion of no confidence in the government. The move was designed to test the unity of the coalition, and it certainly succeeded in putting immediate pressure on the PDs. The PDs had not come out in favour of any of the presidential candidates, though most of the party's supporters appeared to favour Mary Robinson. However, the parliamentary party felt it would be provocative towards their coalition partners to back her. The PDs stayed out of the campaign as a party, though individual members did campaign for Robinson.

O'Malley flew out to Luxembourg on official business less than two hours after the publication of the Duffy tape, but he was already aware that the government had a political crisis on its hands. Stephen O'Byrnes, who was now assistant government press secretary, received a copy of the Lenihan tape transcript immediately after the press conference. He went directly to consult O'Malley and they were joined by Mary Harney. The consensus among the three was that they would now have a real problem in voting confidence in the government.

The PD leader rang Haughey to express concern at the development and asked him not to say anything that would commit the government as a whole on the motion of no confidence. O'Malley gave a public signal of the PD position by issuing a statement declaring he found the situation 'very disturbing'. Soundings taken by PD headquarters among the membership encountered the strong view that the party should not support Lenihan in the vote of confidence.[11]

When O'Malley returned home from Luxembourg he attended a crucial meeting at Michael McDowell's house. Also present were Harney, Pat Cox and Bobby Molloy, who had flown up from Galway to join them, along with the party's senior officials. After a thorough examination of the issues the unanimous view was that they could not vote confidence in the government if Lenihan remained in Cabinet. 'This is a make-or-break issue for us. A central reason for our existence is our refusal to accept low standards in high places, so there is no way we can go along with Fianna Fáil on this,' said O'Byrnes after the meeting. It was quite an emotional gathering as the younger PDs were very conscious of the sacrifices they were asking their senior ministers to make, and equally concerned at being forced to throw away the potential achievements that could be made in office by implementing PD policy. After so many years in the political wilderness O'Malley and Molloy had come back to government a little over a year earlier, but that night's decision threatened to guillotine their comeback. O'Byrnes paid tribute to the two ministers before the meeting ended.

At 9.00am the following morning, O'Malley met Haughey at Kinsealy before the Taoiseach flew to Rome for an EC summit meeting. O'Malley again emphasised the seriousness of the situation as far as the PDs were concerned, saying it was not a problem of their making but one for Fianna Fáil. O'Malley did not say that Lenihan would have to go, but the clear implication of his remarks was that the PDs could only support the government if Lenihan were no longer a member of Cabinet.

After the Kinsealy meeting, Haughey gave a press conference at the airport before departing for Rome. He said that his earlier meeting with O'Malley was mainly about the current GATT talks, but added that a general election resulting from a no-confidence vote would be 'absolute lunacy'. O'Malley again met with leading PD members in Michael McDowell's house, including his two ministerial colleagues, Molloy and Harney. They were taken aback by Haughey's claim that the meeting with O'Malley had centred on the GATT talks and felt he was not taking them seriously, so they decided to issue their own statement on the meeting between the two leaders.

'The purpose of this meeting was to discuss the implications for the coalition Government of recent events. O'Malley made it clear that these implications were not of the Progressive Democrats making. O'Malley presented to Haughey the PDs' analysis of these events. The parliamentary party of the PDs will meet early next week to consider the matter further in the light of the response from Mr Haughey. That meeting will also decide the parliamentary party's voting intentions on next week's Dáil order of business.'

At lunchtime Pat Cox went on Rodney Rice's 'Saturday View' programme to spell out the seriousness of the situation. For the first time the public was alerted to the fact that the PDs regarded the issue as fundamental to the continuation of the coalition. Cox said his party would decide how to proceed on the vote of no confidence in light of the response from Fianna Fáil. He said the issue had raised questions about the credibility of the government, but that had nothing to do with the PDs: 'A problem does arise which impinges on the credibility of the Fianna Fáil side of the Government.' At this stage the PDs believed it likely that Lenihan would resign to save the coalition.

The following day, 27 October, the Sunday newspapers were full of speculation that the government was close to collapse and that a general election was very much on the cards. It was only at this stage that senior members of Fianna Fáil began to realise that the government's existence was under serious threat. Haughey returned from Rome to find a full-scale political crisis had developed in his absence. O'Malley then travelled out to Kinsealy for another meeting with the Taoiseach, who was now keenly aware of the scale of the crisis that was threatening to bring down his Government. In the early stages of the crisis Haughey had summoned McCreevy to his office and asked him to keep open lines of communication with the PDs. McCreevy—who had not been given any post by Haughey despite his pivotal role in putting together the coalition—worked furiously behind the scenes to ensure each side understood the other and once again carried out a vital job by acting as a conduit for the exchange of information between the two parties. As events moved towards a crunch decision, Haughey relied increasingly on McCreevy to keep him informed of the mood within the PD ranks.

Haughey also convened a special meeting of the Fianna Fáil Cabinet members on the afternoon of 28 October, and shocked ministers listened to Seamus Brennan and Ray Burke spell out what they saw as the threat to economic stability being posed by the political crisis. Brennan, in particular, emphasised the movements on the Dublin stock market, which he believed already indicated that higher interest rates were on the way if an election took place. Neither Lenihan nor his sister, Minister for Education Mary O'Rourke, was informed of that special meeting.

The next day Haughey told Lenihan that the PDs wanted his resignation and he bluntly told his Tánaiste to resign from government. Lenihan headed back out on the campaign trail without giving any response, and then refused to take Haughey's calls. The Lenihan family was indignant at the pressure being put on him to resign and they rebuffed all emissaries from Haughey, including Flynn and Ahern. The PD ministers, who had expected him to step down quickly and quietly, now felt they had no choice but to resign from government when the Dáil met the following morning to debate the motion of no confidence.

O'Malley and Haughey met again that evening at a State dinner at Dublin Castle held in honour of Queen Beatrix of Holland. Both men were now resigned to the fact that Lenihan was not going to step down. Haughey tried to persuade O'Malley to agree to allow the presidential election to run its course, promising that Lenihan would then resign, whatever the outcome, but the PD leader refused to accept this solution. The 9.00pm RTÉ television news carried a report from the Lenihan campaign that confirmed the Tánaiste was not going to step down. O'Byrnes rang O'Malley at Dublin Castle to relay the news and it looked as if the government's fate was sealed. But Haughey was not about to relinquish power easily and he fell back on his former enemies in Fianna Fáil to keep open all possible lines of communication with their contacts in the PDs.

The following morning, 31 October, Harney was woken at 7.30am by a phone call from McCreevy, asking her to tell her colleagues not to take any action until after the meeting of the Fianna Fáil parliamentary party that morning. He hinted that the meeting could change things and advised that there was no need for the PDs to take any decisions until it was over. Haughey met O'Malley and Molloy at 8.30am. The Taoiseach told the PD ministers that there had been no change in the situation and it didn't appear that Lenihan would resign, nonetheless he asked them not to make any immediate announcement but instead to give everybody more time. The PDs met around 9.30am and decided not to make any public announcements, in case the situation changed. However, O'Byrnes got to work drafting letters of resignation for O'Malley, Molloy and Harney and they all mentally prepared themselves to leave office and face into a general election.

Meanwhile Haughey summoned McCreevy and P.J. Mara to his office to discuss the options and both men urged him to do the unthinkable and sack his Tánaiste. Haughey was still agonising over this when the Fianna Fáil parliamentary party met at 11.30am to consider the position. Gloomy deputies and senators listened in silence as the Taoiseach began the meeting by saying, 'As of now there will be a general election.' He went on to delineate how serious was the position facing them because it appeared there was no way they could win a vote on the motion of no confidence. Bertie Ahern induced even more gloom when he outlined the prospects facing the party in both the presidential and a possible general election. Lenihan was not at that meeting, but the word from his camp was that he would not be resigning.

McCreevy suggested to the meeting that Haughey should be given a mandate to ensure there was no election. He didn't have to spell out the implication: Haughey should be given a mandate to sack Lenihan. Haughey then intervened to ask the meeting if he had their approval to take the steps necessary to prevent an election. He pointed out that the last time he had been in this position and had negotiated coalition with the PDs, a number of TDs had gone around the country dissenting from that decision. This time he wanted everyone to be clear about what would have to be done to avoid an election. Kildare TD Seán Power responded by saying that they were now discussing sacrificing Brian Lenihan's head and he demanded to know if the Taoiseach would give the same advice in six months time if his head were the only thing that would save the government. Chairman Jim Tunney summed up by saying that it was the feeling of the meeting that it should be left to the Taoiseach to do his best to avoid an election. Just as in the crisis over coalition, Haughey's TDs gave him a free hand to do whatever he thought fit.

As the Fianna Fáil meeting continued the PD TDs held off making an announcement of their decision to resign. Resignation speeches for all three ministers had been typed up and were ready for release to the media. O'Malley was due to go in on the no confidence debate, but he kept putting off his speech until the position became absolutely clear. O'Malley and Molloy spent most of the afternoon in the PD leader's ministerial office. O'Malley had all his constituency files packed into cardboard boxes, on the assumption that he would have to vacate his office that evening once he had resigned from the government. There was a great deal of embarrassment on the corridors of the Dáil as PDs bumped into members of the Lenihan family, who were in the Tánaiste's office with his private secretary, Brian Spain, during that afternoon. Over at PD headquarters in South Frederick Street the party's new general secretary, David O'Keeffe, rang a number of printers to get quotes for election literature and a number of activists from around the country were summoned to make preparations for a general election.

The atmosphere changed suddenly at 5.00pm. After the Fianna Fáil meeting concluded the Taoiseach rang O'Malley and asked him to come to his office. There he solemnly told the PD leader that he had decided to terminate Lenihan's membership of the government. The meeting between Haughey and O'Malley, like all their meetings since the crisis had started, was correct and formal, with no hint of the emotions seething under the surface. Shortly afterwards Lenihan eventually picked up the telephone and rang the Taoiseach. Haughey formally requested his Tánaiste to resign and Lenihan refused. The Taoiseach then said it was with great regret that he was terminating Lenihan's membership of the government. Brian Spain was dispatched to Lenihan's house with a letter, signed by President Hillery, removing him from office. The crisis was over for the coalition.

After the sacking of Lenihan there was deep hostility towards the PDs in the ranks of Fianna Fáil. O'Malley and his colleagues were accused of looking for 'a head on a plate', an accusation that would be levelled at them again in later years. On the night his father was sacked Conor Lenihan approached O'Malley, shook his hand and said: 'Are you happy now, Des? You got your pound of flesh.'

With the presidential election just one week away, there was a wave of public sympathy for Lenihan. However, another intervention by the PDs put a huge spanner in the works shortly before polling day. During RTÉ's 'Saturday View' programme, Pádraig Flynn raised the subject of how Robinson had remodelled her image for the election campaign, claiming that she had discovered a new interest in her family. His ill-judged comments might not have attracted too much attention in the middle of a radio discussion programme were it not for the fact that PD chairman, Michael McDowell, was a fellow panellist. He pounced on Flynn, called the attack on Robinson disgusting and demanded its immediate withdrawal. Robinson herself later demanded a withdrawal and an apology duly materialised from Flynn, but only after the Taoiseach forced him to do so. McDowell's intervention was decisive in staunching the flow of public sympathy for Lenihan. It was not the first, or last, time McDowell made a decisive intervention at a critical point in an election campaign. The PDs made a final intervention with less then forty-eight hours to go before polling when Minister for Energy, Bobby Molloy, appeared on 'Questions and Answers' to endorse Robinson and in the process took a lot of the sting out of Fianna Fáil's claim that she would be in thrall to the left.

The election took place on 7 November and while opinion-poll findings of a swing back to Lenihan were confirmed, he failed to make it. Lenihan got just over 44 per cent of the vote on the first count, with Robinson following at 39 per cent and Currie trailing badly on 17 per cent. However, the strength of the Currie transfers gave Robinson an easy victory in the end and she won by 86,000 votes on the second count.

The whole episode put considerable strain on the coalition. The resentment Fianna Fáil felt towards the PDs because of the way that party had forced a concession on the core value of coalition was now deep-rooted and festering. However, as in the coalition negotiations, it was Fianna Fáil's instinct for power that was the real motive for the sacking of Lenihan. Looking back with hindsight, McCreevy is blunt about the sacking, which he describes as one of the lowest points of his political career:

'I was as involved as anybody else in that decision. What I always felt was that we all kind of slithered away from it. We blamed Charlie Haughey for doing it and we all knew in the parliamentary party it had to be done. The PDs were saying, "If you don't do this, there is going to be a general election." We would have had a general election with the presidential election and we would have been destroyed. The Fianna Fáil parliamentary party all participated in that decision. It was business and as politicians we all knew that it had to be done and we all participated in it even though afterwards we all tried to get away from it.'[12]

So while the coalition did survive, many people in both parties wondered if they could work together again after such a trauma.

Chapter 11 ～

RADICAL OR
REDUNDANT?

T he PDs had stayed in government on their own terms by calling
the shots on the Lenihan affair. The price of this was a palpable
sense of hostility from a significant segment of Fianna Fáil. Even
before Lenihan was sacked, the PDs had become the whipping boys for
all the resentments bubbling under the surface of Fianna Fáil, particularly
for those growing increasingly restive under Haughey's rule. As early as
February 1990, Albert Reynolds told a Fianna Fáil meeting in Kanturk,
County Cork, that the coalition with the PDs was just 'a temporary little
arrangement'.[1] As often happens in politics, the loyalties of earlier years
were stood on their head and Haughey's future became inextricably tied
up with the success of the PD coalition. O'Malley and Molloy, regarded
by Fianna Fáil as traitors in 1986, were now keeping Haughey in
government, while Reynolds and Flynn, who had helped to drive out the
PD founders, were now snapping angrily at Haughey's heels.

The new anti-Haughey faction grew increasingly vociferous in its
hostility towards the PDs. One sign of that hostility was the contemp-
tuous way in which the Minister for the Environment, Pádraig Flynn,
treated Mary Harney, who was appointed his junior minister. Flynn
insisted that Harney should not be allowed to use the main entrance to
the historic Custom House building on Dublin's Essex Quay. Instead, he
arranged for an old door on the far side of the building to be opened up
for her to use.

'He didn't even want me on the same corridor. He opened up a special
office for me as well as the special door. Traditionally there was an
office for the junior minister on the ministerial floor, but that was set
aside for the use of his media advisor, Terry Prone. She didn't even
work in the Department, but she had an office there.'[2]

Harney managed to confound Flynn with the imaginative way she approached the task of being Minister of State with responsibility for environmental protection. The problem of smog in Dublin had become a serious issue in the 1980s as a result of coal and turf in fires being the primary source of heat in most houses. The Department had initiated a pilot scheme, involving grants and area control orders, with the aim of encouraging people to switch to cleaner fuel, but it was estimated that the process would take twenty years to complete and at an enormous cost. Harney looked at the issue and made up her mind quickly: she decided to ban the sale of smoky coal in Dublin rather than try to ban its use. There was furious opposition from the coal importers and Flynn took their side, but Harney found an unexpected and powerful ally:

'The issue was on Flynn's desk for ages, so I asked Des to raise it directly with Haughey. In fairness, Haughey called a meeting of all the relevant Ministers. I remember some of them raised all sorts of objections about the future of Dublin port and coal importation, but Haughey just cut through it all and said, "I think it makes a lot of sense. We'll do it." So I was delighted with myself and it worked like a dream. To be fair, only for Haughey it would never have happened. I have often acknowledged that. In fairness to Haughey, he was a bit radical, too.'[3]

The PDs were growing in confidence and punching well above their weight in government. In December 1990 O'Malley pushed the Companies Act through the Oireachtas. This voluminous piece of legislation was the most comprehensive reform of company law in the history of the State. It brought the law up to date in relation to business practice and intro- duced a whole range of measures to penalise offenders. The reform did not endear the PDs to the Establishment in the business community, but then they had never been enthusiastic about the party, even though it espoused an ideological, pro-free enterprise stance.

Right throughout that first coalition the PDs were determined to preserve their separate identity. Party chairman, Michael McDowell, who was no longer in the Dáil, acted as the conscience of the PDs and frequently frustrated Fianna Fáil ministers with his pronouncements from the sidelines. There was a degree of calculation in this and the PD members loved it, but there were times when McDowell's own colleagues in government wished he would keep quiet. Harney recalls that, while the steady stream of comments from McDowell on the operation of government was helpful to the PDs, it often created difficulties for the party's ministers: 'Des used often feel embarrassed at having to take on Haughey on issues he didn't regard as that crucial. He was keenly aware of the political risk Haughey had taken with the coalition and he didn't want to put pressure on him unless the issue was really important. I think Des sometimes felt embarrassed at the difficulties we created for Haughey.'[4]

In political circles it was held that the PDs used McDowell to orchestrate rows with Fianna Fáil.

'The truth was, it wasn't orchestrated and Des frequently went berserk,' says Harney. 'I remember Des ringing me quite a few times in the course of those years and saying: "How can I go in and face these people in Cabinet with this in the newspaper?" And there were some fantastic scuds from McDowell. It used to drive Des mad and it used to drive Fianna Fáil mad because they thought Michael was put up to it. Of course, you don't need to put Michael up to anything. He does things of his own volition.'[5]

'Des used to go mad,' says McDowell, recalling the reaction to some of his statements. 'I remember one particular occasion when I was having a drink in Doheny and Nesbitt's with the broadcaster, Leo Enright. We were just having a laugh. There had been an announcement that evening that the Fianna Fáil parliamentary party was having a special meeting to examine the Nineteenth Protocol to the Maastricht Treaty. I remarked to Leo that the Fianna Fáil meeting on the EU Treaty was pregnant with all the possibilities of a band of chimpanzees approaching the back of a television set with screwdrivers. It was a joke, but Leo put it out on air the following morning and Des nearly slit his throat shaving.'[6]

On a more serious note, McDowell's comments and statements did serve to ensure that the PDs were not swallowed up by the coalition. Their separate identity was not only maintained but enhanced by the party chairman's exuberant political interventions. At the 1988 annual conference he coined the phrase that the PDs had to be 'radical or redundant', and he never wavered from that conviction.

Following on from the tax cuts of the first year, the 1991 Budget contained a further instalment of the tax reform agenda. The standard rate was cut again, from 30 per cent to 29 per cent, while the top rate was reduced from 53 per cent to 52 per cent. These modest reductions were overshadowed by the Gulf War, which threatened to undermine the nascent recovery in the Irish economy. Following on from the Budget, Haughey pulled off another three-year national agreement with the social partners; Bertie Ahern acted as his agent in the successful negotiations. The deal, launched with elaborate fanfare in Dublin Castle, was called the Programme for Economic and Social Progress (PESP), and it provided solid pay increases to public servants, sweetened by the promise of further tax cuts. The fact that the trade union movement had signed up to the tax-cutting agenda and had a vested interest in its continuation gave the PDs further leverage.

Just when things were back on an even keel after the Lenihan debacle, Larry Goodman returned to haunt the coalition. It began with the broadcast of a 'World in Action' special on ITV on 13 May, which purported to expose dubious practices in Goodman's meat plants and the complicity of the regulatory authorities. There was a furore in the Dáil the following day, but instead of responding to the Opposition, Haughey stonewalled and the result was uproar in the chamber. The government was forced to concede a special debate on the issue, a debate that almost sank the coalition.

The difficulty related to the wording of the government motion on the issue, which read: 'That Dáil Éireann reaffirms its confidence in the regulatory and control procedures in the Irish meat industry.' Fine Gael leader, John Bruton, waded into the government's record in relation to Goodman and demanded a judicial inquiry. The PDs were caught unawares by the intensity of the debate and started to panic. McDowell and O'Byrnes told O'Malley that, in view of the party's record in highlighting the Goodman issue, it would be disastrous to back the government motion. Even though he had not demurred when shown a copy of the motion the night before, O'Malley went back to Haughey to say his party was deeply unhappy about it.[7]

There followed a day of high drama, which followed a pattern that was now becoming all too familiar. The PD parliamentary party met, took a tough line on the issue and presented Haughey with an ultimatum, insisting that the wording of the motion be changed. The message to Haughey was delivered by O'Malley and Molloy. He asked for some time to consider it and consulted his Minister for Agriculture, Michael O'Kennedy. Despite O'Kennedy's objections, Haughey caved in and agreed to the establishment of a judicial inquiry, although he insisted that it would have to be into the beef industry as a whole and not just focused on Goodman's operations. It was another embarrassing climb-down in the face of PD pressure and it left Fianna Fáil TDs seething, but there was nothing they could do about it. The establishment of the Beef Tribunal was to have fatal consequences for two subsequent Fianna Fáil governments, but at that time, all of that was in the future.[8]

The local elections, which followed shortly afterwards, were the first for the PDs and things went reasonably well. The party took 37 seats nationally, one-third of them won by women—the highest percentage of women elected for any party. One of the women who made the break-through was Liz O'Donnell, while Helen Keogh was elected in Dún Laoghaire. Harney had first met O'Donnell at a conference in Trinity College and the two women immediately took to each other: 'Mary was already quite an icon. I had never even met a Minister before and was quite flattered when she asked to meet me again and then started to persuade me to run in the local elections.'[9] O'Donnell, who was a house-wife at that stage, agreed to run in the Rathmines ward and was the only PD councillor elected to Dublin City Council.

Following on from the disaster of the 1989 general election, the local election result was a sign that the party was not necessarily on an irreversible slide. The party's good performance helped to stiffen nerves ahead of the review of the Programme for Government, due to take place after two years in office. As it turned out, the review coincided with another embarrassing political drama for Haughey.

Haughey's problems began with a court battle between key executives of the recently privatised Irish Sugar Company, called Greencore, over the ownership of a Jersey-based company. The upshot of the case was that the managing director of Greencore, Chris Comerford, and the company secretary, Michael Tully, were forced to resign. Although Haughey had no connection with Greencore, the controversy threw light on the world of the golden circles in which he moved. Hot on the heels of the Greencore resignations came a controversy over the purchase by State company Telecom Éireann of a site at Ballsbridge for £9.4 million. Telecom chairman, Michael Smurfit, stepped down from the board when it emerged that he had an interest in the property company that handled the transaction. Another Telecom board member who resigned during the affair was Seamus Parceir, former chairman of the Revenue Commissioners. The two men tendered their resignations after Haughey suggested publicly that they should 'stand aside' until the issue was resolved. O'Malley appointed inspectors to investigate both Greencore and Telecom.

There were further controversies over Celtic Helicopters, a company owned by Haughey's son, Ciaran, over the installation of an ESB wind-generator on Haughey's island home of Inishvickillane, and over the sale of land at Carysfort College in Blackrock, County Dublin, to a friend of the Taoiseach's. In response to these controversies and Haughey's increasingly shaky leadership position Fine Gael put down a Dáil motion of no confidence, to be debated when the Dáil resumed on 16 October after the long summer break.

Faced with these mounting problems Haughey tried to ensure that the review of the Programme for Government was wrapped up before the Dáil resumed. This didn't happen, however, because he had under-estimated the determination of the PDs to win substantial concessions, or to pull out of government if they did not get them. The PD hardline was reinforced by the view of some senior party members, like McDowell and Harney, that the PDs should get out of government before they were dragged down by the controversies besetting Haughey. On the Fianna Fáil side, Reynolds and other leading members jibbed at PD demands regarding budgetary policy.

These hidden agendas ensured that the Fianna Fáil–PD negotiations were once again pushed to the brink. The talks were far from completed on 16 October when the Dáil resumed to debate the motion of no confidence. The conclusion of that debate, at 4.00pm on 18 October, became the deadline set by the PDs for a deal. The Fianna Fáil negotiating team was Reynolds and Ahern; the PD team comprised Molloy and Cox. Haughey and O'Malley held back to sort out crunch issues.

The final days of negotiation were nerve-wracking. Haughey and O'Malley thought they had an agreement on 16 October, but Reynolds dug in his heels and refused to sign, saying that as Minister for Finance he couldn't accept the budgetary implications of the deal. Many Fianna Fáil TDs were initially delighted that Reynolds had taken a stand against the PDs, and Haughey received a poor response from the parliamentary party when he suggested that he should be given a mandate to conclude the deal on his own terms. However, as the deadline came ever closer and a general election began to look inevitable, the mood of the TDs changed. Haughey wanted a deal because the polls indicated that Fianna Fáil would be hammered in an election. Whatever their attitude to the PDs, most Fianna Fáil TDs agreed with his desire to avoid an election.

Bertie Ahern was the key figure in getting everybody off the hook. Like Haughey, he had been prepared to put his name on the deal put forward on 16 October and was surprised when Reynolds refused to go along with it. In the early hours of 18 October, with the deadline looming, he managed to persuade Reynolds to put his reservations aside and sign on the dotted line. The deal was widely regarded as a victory for the PDs: tax cuts were recognised as the political priority, as opposed to the social spending favoured by Fianna Fáil TDs. Despite the fact that the Department of Finance had argued during the negotiations that further tax cuts were impractical, the PDs got a commitment that the basic tax rate of 30 per cent would be cut to 25 per cent over the following two years, and that the higher rate of 52 per cent and the middle rate of 48 per cent would be merged into one single higher rate of just 44 per cent in the same period. It was also agreed to widen the standard band considerably and to reduce employee PRSI from 7.75 per cent to 6 per cent. Interestingly, the PDs argued that the bulk of the £1.5 billion forgone in tax reliefs and shelters of various kinds for business could be abolished to fund the cuts for ordinary taxpayers. Haughey had maintained that these reliefs were there for very good social reasons and could not be abolished lightly.

In terms of budgetary strategy it was agreed to reduce the national debt/GNP ratio to 100 per cent by 1993, with the Exchequer borrowing requirement not exceeding 1.5 per cent. There was a range of other commitments on Education, Health and social welfare which were more palatable to Fianna Fáil—a light-rail system for Dublin, for example, was just one of the other details agreed. Electronic voting and a reform of ministerial pensions were also to be reviewed and the government committed itself to a higher level of overseas development aid.[10]

It was on the day the deal was struck that Haughey uttered his famous remark about Bertie Ahern to Gerald Barry, Sam Smyth and this author: 'He's the man. He's the best, the most skilful, the most devious and the most cunning of them all,' said the Taoiseach, pointing across to his *protégé* during a briefing on the deal being presented by Ahern in the Taoiseach's Department. (The agreement had been formally launched, with all the principals in attendance, a few hours earlier.) The deal cleared the way for the PDs to vote confidence in the government. While the majority of Fianna Fáil TDs were delighted to have avoided an election, they were sullenly resentful at the way in which their leaders had been outmanoeuvred by the PDs once again.

Over the following few weeks, the sleaze factor continued to dog Haughey. The Beef Tribunal opened in Dublin Castle and witnessed a steady flow of evidence about irregularities in the meat-processing industry which made a mockery of Haughey's statements on the issue in the Dáil in 1989. Against this background Seán Power put down a motion of no confidence in Haughey on 6 November, sparking the fourth challenge to his leadership. It was a difficult position for the PDs, but they stayed out of it and waited to see if Haughey would survive—again. Although his enemies had changed, Haughey's power to mesmerise the Fianna Fáil parliamentary party had not. Reynolds and Flynn, who had been fired from the Cabinet on 7 November when they had declared against Haughey, were routed by 55 votes to 22. A vindicated Haughey set about restructuring his government.[11]

What should have been a simple reshuffle turned into yet another crisis and the PDs were plunged into the thick of it. Haughey, who was usually quite conservative in his ministerial appointments, stunned his own party and his coalition partners by appointing Dr Jim McDaid from Donegal as Minister for Defence. When the Opposition pointed out that McDaid had provided an alibi for a leading IRA man in a high-profile extradition case the year before, there was bedlam.[12]

O'Malley and Molloy went to Haughey to express concern about the appointment. The Taoiseach suggested that the PD leader should meet McDaid in person to discuss his concerns directly with him. After that meeting McDaid defused the potential crisis by going to Haughey and offering to withdraw his name from nomination. Haughey accepted the offer and postponed the appointment for one day. When McDaid announced his decision there was uproar in Fianna Fáil and intense bitterness directed against the PDs; every time there was a political crisis the enemies of the PDs accused the party of looking for 'a head on a plate'.

The PDs appeared fated to be dragged into every internal wrangle in Fianna Fáil, and it was not long before they were embroiled in the biggest one of all: the deposing of Haughey. Haughey's enemies within Fianna Fáil had finally found a weapon with the capacity to breach his defences—Seán Doherty. The ill-fated former Minister for Justice had taken the rap for the phone-tapping scandal during Haughey's GUBU phase, and he had never recovered from the experience. He resigned from the front bench in 1983 and Haughey promised to reinstate him when the fuss died down. In 1989 he tried to follow the MacSharry route to rehabilitation by standing for the European Parliament, but the strategy came horribly unstuck when he not only failed to get elected but also lost his Dáil seat in the simultaneous elections. Doherty eventually made it to the Seanad and managed to get the backing of his Fianna Fáil colleagues to secure the position of Cathaoirleach, with some limited assistance from Haughey.

However, he continued to brood on his misfortune and the more he brooded, the more he blamed Haughey. His pent-up anger found an outlet at the end of 1991 when the Minister for Justice, Ray Burke, published the Phone Tapping Bill. The commitment to the Bill had been contained in the Programme for Government drawn up with the PDs, but Doherty interpreted it as a personal affront. He approached Burke and asked him to withdraw the Bill, or at least to stall its passage so he would not face the embarrassment of having to deal with it in the Seanad. Burke rejected this proposal and also refused to countenance a request from Doherty for permission to examine the files held in the Department of Justice relating to the controversial incidents of 1982.

Reynolds and Flynn continued to plot against Haughey, keenly aware that Doherty was a loose cannon with the capacity to bring down the Boss once and for all. It all came to a head when 'Nighthawks', an innovative television programme on RTÉ 2, decided to do a special edition on Doherty in January 1992. In the middle of an interview the presenter, Shay Healy, asked Doherty about his involvement in the phone-tapping scandal of 1982.

'There was a decision taken in Cabinet that the leaking of matters from Cabinet must be stopped. I, as Minister for Justice, had a direct responsibility for doing that—I did that. I do feel that I was let down by the fact that people knew what I was doing.'

A number of the ministers who had served during 1982, including Des O'Malley, reacted by asserting that the phone-tapping issue had never been discussed at Cabinet: so who else, apart from Doherty, was in on the act?

On 21 January the time bomb that had been ticking for nine years exploded. Journalists were summoned to a hastily arranged press conference at the Montrose Hotel, near RTÉ.

'I am confirming tonight that the Taoiseach, Mr Haughey, was fully aware in 1982 that two journalists' phones were being tapped and that he at no stage expressed a reservation about this action. Here are the details.'

Speaking rapidly, Doherty outlined the circumstances in which he had authorised Deputy Garda Commissioner, Joe Ainsworth, to tap the phones of Geraldine Kennedy and Bruce Arnold. He said that he had done so against a background of ongoing leaks from the Cabinet.[13]

The effect of the Doherty statement was electrifying. A substantial chunk of the press conference was transmitted on the RTÉ television news less than an hour later. Immediately after the press conference senior RTÉ journalist, Shane Kenny, phoned Des O'Malley and played the tape of the Doherty press conference to him. The PD leader expressed his shock and consternation to Kenny and then summoned an emergency meeting of his closest advisors and parliamentary colleagues.

Molloy, Harney and McDowell, along with the policy and press office team of Stephen O'Byrnes and Ray Gordon, were alerted and told to watch the 9.00pm news. Afterwards they all went around to O'Malley's house for a council of war. The composition of the group was identical to that which had advised O'Malley from the beginning of the Lenihan crisis a little over a year earlier, and their advice this time around was exactly the same. They told the party leader that there was no way the PDs could continue to serve in government with Haughey. They knew that by adopting this stance they would be playing into the hands of those in Fianna Fáil who hated the PDs, but they were convinced they had no other option.[14] 'I don't believe Doherty would ever have done what he did had it not been in the interests of getting Reynolds installed as Taoiseach. We knew what was happening, but we still had to act the way we did. We had no choice in the matter,' says O'Malley.[15]

The PDs agreed to hold fire until Haughey had a chance to respond to Doherty's allegations. They met again the following morning, along with the other three TDs and three senators who made up the PD parliamentary party. A statement was again deferred pending Haughey's response, but the PDs gave a clear signal of their intent by refusing to attend a scheduled Cabinet meeting on the Budget. Haughey gave a press conference in response to Doherty's and delivered another of his bravura performances. 'Are the Irish people more entitled to believe me, who has been consistent in everything I have said about this affair from the beginning, or someone who has been inconsistent and by his own words untruthful on countless occasions with regard to it?'[16] Unfortunately for

Haughey, the answer to that question was that the PDs, at least, believed Doherty, and a majority of the Irish people probably did as well. Although this was long before Haughey had been exposed as a liar by the judicial tribunals, most people accepted that Doherty's statement had a ring of truth to it.

Haughey's fate was now in the hands of the PDs. O'Malley and his colleagues held another meeting after his press conference and decided that they had no choice but to act. A statement was drawn up just in time for the RTÉ television news at 9.00pm.

'It is not for the Progressive Democrats to decide as between the conflicting accounts given by both the Taoiseach and Senator Doherty in relation to the telephone tapping affair. The plain fact is that this is but the latest—and almost certainly the most serious—in a long list of unhappy and politically unacceptable controversies, which undermined the capacity of the Government to work effectively. The situation which has now arisen is one which we view with the utmost gravity. It calls for an immediate response in order that the credibility and stability of the Government be immediately restored. While the Progressive Democrats will not interfere in the internal affairs of another party we are anxious to see that the acute dilemma facing the Government is speedily resolved.'[17]

The statement did not spell it out explicitly, but it was clear that the price of continued PD participation in government was Haughey's departure from the Taoiseach's Office. The parallels with the departure of Brian Lenihan a little over a year earlier were uncanny, and the wording of the PD statement bore a striking resemblance to the phraseology employed on the previous occasion. To ensure there was no ambiguity on the issue, Harney and Molloy met Bertie Ahern to clarify what lay between the lines; Ahern passed the message on to Haughey. That night, 22 January 1992, Haughey made up his mind that he would step down rather than dissolve the Dáil and force another election, which was the only alternative course open to him.

Haughey then went into the Taoiseach's office where he met Ahern and the Tánaiste, John Wilson, to discuss the situation. They looked at all the options facing them and the prospect of a general election if the PDs' demand was not met. As the two Fianna Fáil ministers stood up to leave, O'Malley and Molloy arrived in the office to outline their position. They told Haughey they would have to withdraw from government unless he resolved the situation. The Taoiseach told them that he would not be the cause of a general election, signalling clearly that he intended to go. All he asked was that the PDs give him a short breathing space so that he could depart with dignity. Haughey added that this would prevent a complete souring of the relations between the two parties in government—something that would inevitably happen if the PDs were seen to be looking for a sacrificial lamb. There was no animosity between the PD leaders and Haughey, who didn't have to be told there was nothing personal in their ultimatum; it was just business. 'It was a thing you couldn't walk away from. The only way to justify our existence was to insist that he went. He went within forty-eight hours of my telling him he had to go. Our meeting was short and formal. He knew I had to do it,' says O'Malley.[18] O'Malley told one of his PD colleagues after that meeting with Haughey, 'For the first time in my life I felt sorry for him.'[19]

When it came to Haughey's formal resignation in the Dáil, on 11 February, O'Malley was gracious:

'On my own behalf—and on behalf of the Progressive Democrats—I join in the good wishes to Deputy Haughey on his retirement. He has had a long and extremely distinguished career as Taoiseach, as Minister and as a Member of the House. I have, over the years, had disagreements with him on policy matters, but I have come to recognise his outstanding abilities and capabilities. I am happiest of all to acknowledge how positively and how usefully those great abilities were used in this Government, which comes to an end today. I acknowledge, in particular, the way in which something new and different was facilitated by him and how the task of each member of the Government was made easier by his courtesy and concern for every member.'[20]

After all that had passed between them over the years, it was a strange ending to the two leaders' political relationship. There was almost a hint of regret in O'Malley's short speech, perhaps because he knew better than anybody else what was coming next: politics was about to become even more bruising for the PDs.

Chapter 12 ~

IF IN DOUBT,
LEAVE THEM OUT

Des O'Malley was not surprised to find that coalition with Albert Reynolds was a very different affair from coalition with Haughey. A good working relationship between party leaders is essential for the stability of a coalition, but it simply never existed in the doomed government of 1992. Reynolds had become leader of Fianna Fáil by capitalising on the widespread discontent in the organisation stemming from the coalition with the PDs. Yet at the same time he was Taoiseach courtesy of the PDs. The 'temporary little arrangement', as he had insultingly described it, had landed him the highest office in the land. If Fianna Fáil had been alone in government when Doherty made his allegations, Haughey would almost certainly have survived yet again. It was the PDs who forced Haughey out and created the opportunity for Reynolds to become Taoiseach. Reynolds ignored that fundamental fact, however, and ultimately it cost him dearly.

Looking back, O'Malley can remember nothing positive about the 1992 government. 'A short time before, Reynolds had described the Fianna Fáil coalition with the PDs as "a temporary little arrangement" and the way he acted right through the brief turbulent period when we were together in office showed he meant it. I had no option but to get out.'[1]

The only positive aspect of the Reynolds government, from a PD point of view, was the arrival of Charlie McCreevy into his first Cabinet post as Minister for Social Welfare. McCreevy had installed himself in the inner circle that surrounded Reynolds, mainly because of his new-found opposition to Haughey in 1991. As a businessman, Reynolds was sympathetic to the enterprise agenda favoured by McCreevy. In theory that should have translated into an ability to work well with the PDs, but the new

Taoiseach never saw it like that and traded on the hostility felt by many in Fianna Fáil towards O'Malley and his party. McCreevy was never given the opportunity to act as a bridge between the two parties in government, as he had done three years earlier and as he would do again a few years later.

On the day Reynolds took office the news broke that the Attorney-General, Harry Whelehan, had acted to prevent a fourteen-year-old rape victim from travelling to Britain for an abortion. The 'X case' was to bedevil Irish political life for the entire duration of the first Reynolds government. Acting in his role as the guardian of the Constitution, Whelehan took the case to the High Court and secured a court decision that upheld his right to prevent the young girl from travelling for an abortion. The country was convulsed by the case, occurring, as it did, less than a decade after the bitterly divisive referendum that had resulted in the insertion of an anti-abortion clause in the Constitution.

'Nobody is wild about Harry around here,' Sean Duignan recorded in his diary. 'Practically every member of Dáil Éireann is castigating him for not having turned a blind eye. They won't admit it publicly, but that's what they mutter in corners. That is how they want the chief law officer of the State to operate, but not one of them will openly admit it.'[2] Ultimately the Supreme Court decided that the girl was entitled to travel to Britain for an abortion on the basis that she had threatened to commit suicide, which meant there was a threat to her life. In the event, the girl did undertake the journey but suffered a miscarriage before the abortion could be performed.

The abortion issue imposed further strains on the relationship between the two parties in government as they tried to come to grips with the legal and political implications of the X case. The Fianna Fáil grassroots were pushing for a new referendum to copperfasten the pro-life provision in the Constitution; the PDs were instinctively committed to a more liberal agenda that laid emphasis on the right of a woman to receive information about abortion and to travel freely outside the jurisdiction. Conservative and liberal pressure groups tried to make abortion a deal-breaker issue in the referendum to endorse the Maastricht Treaty in June. Following an early scare, the proposal was carried, with the support of the main Opposition parties, after Reynolds attached a protocol to the Treaty recognising Ireland's pro-life constitutional provision. The issue did not go away, however, and after a great deal of agonising the government decided to hold a referendum on the complicated issues involved. The people were asked to vote on three separate issues: first, the right to travel; second, the right to information about abortion; third, a proposal to make abortion illegal except where the life of the mother was in danger. The first two propositions were not that contentious, but a proposal to deal with the so-called substantive issue was opposed by conservatives and liberals alike.

The fallout from the *X* case occupied Reynolds for the duration of his period in government with the PDs. The coalition parties were deeply divided on the issue, with the PDs fundamentally opposed to the government's approach to dealing with the substantive issue. This division compounded the problems the government experienced in dealing with the constitutional implications of the case. Both parties were agreed that it was necessary to change the Constitution to protect a woman's right to travel abroad and her right to receive information about abortion. However, on the advice of Whelehan, Reynolds and Fianna Fáil were determined to proceed with the third clause in the referendum proposal, which reaffirmed that abortion was illegal unless necessary to save the life of the mother. This proposal brought the extreme liberal and conservative fringes together. Liberals saw the amendment as a rowing-back from the Supreme Court decision that allowed the threat of suicide as sufficient reason for abortion. They argued that a threat to the health, rather than the life, of the mother should also be grounds for abortion. On the other hand, conservatives claimed that the amendment would allow abortion in limited circumstances for the first time. Although Reynolds had received the approval, privately, of most senior Catholic Church figures for his wording of the proposal, the zealots were having have none of it and an unholy alliance of pro-life and pro-choice campaigners joined forces against the amendment.

The PDs sided with the liberals on the issue and claimed that the proposed amendment was dangerous for women. For a time the issue threatened the stability of the government, but ultimately O'Malley backed away from confrontation, arguing that to plunge the country into an election on the abortion issue would be unforgivable. O'Malley did consider pulling out of government, but was dissuaded by colleagues who felt that Reynolds was using the issue to try to engineer a split. In the end the PDs retained their own viewpoint but did not block the government from putting all three referendum proposals to the people.

The PDs were wary of open hostility with Reynolds because for much of 1992 he enjoyed broad public support. The new Taoiseach had established a rapport with British Prime Minister John Major, and the two men began the groundwork for an initiative on the North that generated a lot of positive publicity. Reynolds kept O'Malley in the dark about the most important elements of the developing peace process. He also insulted the PDs by refusing to allow Harney to take part in groundbreaking political talks with the unionist parties when O'Malley was unavoidably absent. 'I remember Des wanted me to go to the Northern talks and Reynolds wouldn't let me. He said privately that I was too close to the unionists. Of course that was rubbish, but what he meant was that I was too close to understanding the unionist position.'[3]

Opinion polls revealed a high degree of public satisfaction with the new government. Reynolds had a satisfaction rating of 63 per cent in May, and as late as September it was still a hugely respectable 60 per cent. For most of the year Fianna Fáil was also riding high on support levels of over 50 per cent. By contrast the PDs were stuck in the 5–7 per cent range and the party was being widely written-off. Thus Reynolds and his colleagues were lulled into the false belief that the PDs had to avoid an election at any cost—no matter what the provocation from Fianna Fáil.

That provocation started immediately after Reynolds took the reins. At the Fianna Fáil *ard fheis* in March, Reynolds delivered an unambiguous message to his coalition partners: 'Fianna Fáil does not need another party to keep it on the right track or act as its conscience,' he declared in his conference keynote speech. This was a reference to the PD pressure that had led to the sacking of Lenihan and the resignation of McDaid, but Reynolds seemed to forget that it had also resulted in the departure of Haughey and his own elevation to Taoiseach. His young Cabinet favourite, Brian Cowen, was even more blunt in his warm-up to the leader's address. 'What about the PDs?' he asked rhetorically, before providing an answer the delegates loved. 'When in doubt, leave out,' he declared to great applause. It was good crowd-pleasing stuff, but it was bad politics.[4]

The lack of rapport between the two leaders was mirrored at all levels in their respective parties. Fianna Fáil ministers and TDs who wanted to ingratiate themselves with the party leadership stayed well away from the PDs—even at the level of government advisors there was no fraternisation. Assistant government press secretary, Stephen O'Byrnes, had operated comfortably from the Taoiseach's Department during the PD coalition with Haughey, often giving joint briefings to political correspondents alongside P.J. Mara. All that changed when Reynolds became Taoiseach.

O'Byrnes was cut out of the loop in the Taoiseach's Department and ignored by Sean Duignan, who had come in as government press secretary. There was no exchange of information and no joint briefings to the media. 'There was tension between the parties in coalition all along, but particularly after Albert took over. Sean Duignan came in and he wouldn't talk to me. He wrote me a letter later apologising and saying he was working on instructions,' recalls O'Byrnes.[5] It was just one instance of how the parties in government operated as hostile opponents rather than coalition partners.

The PDs and Fianna Fáil were on an inevitable collision course and it was the tribunal of inquiry into the beef industry and the Goodman group that provided the pretext for the final sundering. The original motivation for the establishment of the tribunal came from a suspicion held by the Opposition leaders and the PDs that Haughey and Goodman had a questionable 'special' relationship. By mid-1992, however, it was clear that the tribunal instead had the capacity to undermine Reynolds and the Taoiseach believed that the PDs were out to get him via the tribunal. 'The PDs set up the Tribunal to get Charlie. He went down before it really got underway. So, now, they've decided that I'm the next best thing,' Reynolds told an associate.[6] For their part the PDs sensed Reynolds' deep hostility and believed that a number of issues were being manipulated by Fianna Fáil in order to embarrass them. They felt that O'Malley was deliberately not being fully informed by his Cabinet colleagues on important matters.

'At every level it was terrible,' says Harney. 'The issue of county enterprise boards was brought to Government without Des O'Malley even being aware it was happening. These were the kind of things that were happening. It was terrible. There was no trust there at all. The remarkable thing is that it lasted as long as it did.'[7]

In June, O'Malley gave his evidence to the Beef Tribunal. The critical issue for the stability of the government was how he would back up his claim that Reynolds had exhibited favouritism towards Goodman in the way he operated the export credit insurance scheme as Minister for Industry and Commerce in 1987 and 1988. O'Malley had first made this claim in Opposition and later in his written submission to the Tribunal. In the early days of his oral evidence O'Malley did not mention Reynolds by name, but he stood over his view that the export credit scheme was abused to benefit two companies: Goodman International and Hibernia Meats. On his fifth day in the witness box O'Malley made a more direct attack on the Taoiseach, describing decisions taken by Reynolds on export credit as 'wrong ... grossly unwise, reckless and foolish'. Reynolds was incensed. Although he did not let it show in public, those around him felt a dread sense of foreboding when they heard him speak of a day of reckoning when he would set the record straight.[8]

Reynolds was not due to be called before the Tribunal until after the summer break and the tension gradually mounted as that day approached. After one briefing session in the Taoiseach's Office Sean Duignan remarked to Tom Savage that the issue was a hundred times more complicated than that of abortion. 'I don't know about that, but it's certainly a hundred times more dangerous for Albert,' replied Savage presciently.[9] His senior civil servants and political advisors urged caution on Reynolds before his Tribunal appearance, but he was implacable. An array of senior Fianna Fáil people—Haughey, MacSharry, Ray Burke, Seamus Brennan and Michael O'Kennedy—had given evidence to the Tribunal and come away unscathed, but Reynolds was spoiling to get even with O'Malley and with some of the Fianna Fáil witnesses who had been notably unhelpful to him.

O'Malley had no doubts about the way the situation was panning out. At a meeting of his party National Executive on 1 October, he reported on developments in government with particular reference to relations between the coalition partners. 'He pointed out that all the evidence was that Fianna Fáil would attempt to force an election before the climax of the Beef Tribunal and therefore requested the selection of good candidates with all speed. He confirmed that the party would not go into a national election with an understanding between the party and any other party.'[10]

When Reynolds came to give his evidence to the Tribunal four weeks later, he did exactly as O'Malley had anticipated. He blustered on the central issue of how he had operated the export credit insurance scheme, but he could not resist landing a direct blow on O'Malley. He described the PD leader's evidence to the Tribunal as 'reckless, irresponsible and dishonest'. There was no way the government could survive after that outburst. Many senior Fianna Fáil people believed that O'Malley would simply have to grin and bear it. Their complacency showed that after all the years of dealing with him, they still had no idea about the true character of the PD leader. O'Malley was on his way out of government—whatever the consequences—the instant Reynolds described him as dishonest. He did give Reynolds a chance to retract, however. On a number of occasions during the cross-examination his counsel, Adrian

Hardiman, offered the Taoiseach the option of modifying his description of O'Malley's evidence from 'dishonest' to 'incorrect'. At one point, Reynolds appeared to waver. Duignan recorded the moment in his diary: 'I kept willing him to say yes, to get back to defending his own decisions, to leave O'Malley out of the damn thing, get the show back on the road. Albert paused for what seemed ages (we all held our breath) and then he said that one word—"dishonest". I think we're bollixed.'[11]

That about summed it up. The PDs took a couple of days to reach the formal decision that they would vote in favour of an Opposition motion of no confidence in the government. When the party didn't respond immediately, hope flickered briefly in Fianna Fáil that O'Malley's nerve would fail. In fact, nothing of the kind was ever going to happen. O'Malley was clear that his participation in government was no longer possible after the attack by Reynolds, although he did strongly consider an alternative to the break-up of the coalition. He went to his colleagues in the PDs and suggested that he resign from government and install Harney in his place at the Cabinet. The PD leader felt this would be an honourable way out, but his party colleagues were aghast at the prospect. After some debate, O'Malley accepted that the effectiveness of the government would be hopelessly compromised if he, as party leader, were to function outside the Cabinet.[12] The PDs decided that the only option was to withdraw from the coalition, but they delayed for two days before making a public announcement in order to keep Fianna Fáil guessing. They also wanted to put more pressure on Reynolds by allowing the evidence of O'Malley's Department head, Sean Dorgan, to be heard by the tribunal before they pulled the plug.

It was not until the night before the Dáil debate on the motion of confidence in the government that the PDs announced the decision to pull out of coalition. In the debate the following day, O'Malley was finally able to go public on the difficulties that had beset his relationship with Reynolds since February. He said that the coalition with Fianna Fáil under Haughey had worked—while it had not been problem-free for either party, neither had it been unduly difficult. He emphasised the point that huge progress had been made on the PD tax-cutting agenda:

'Major achievements of this Government, for which we justifiably claim credit, include the commencement of a total transformation of our tax system to make it fairer, simpler and more employment friendly. Until the Progressive Democrats came forward with our radical programme of tax reform, we had three income tax rates, and a top rate of over 60 per cent. We have made very rapid progress on implementing this programme. There are now just two tax rates: 27 per cent and 48 per cent and the revised Programme for Government, which we negotiated a year ago, envisaged these two rates being further brought down to 25 per cent and 44 per cent. Contrast this rapid progress with the fact that prior to the implementation of our policy, the standard tax rate had stood unchanged at 35 per cent.'

He went on to say that, sadly, the implementation of further reform measures had been interrupted by Reynolds' appointment as Taoiseach and the deliberate way he had attempted to force the PDs out of government from the moment he succeeded Haughey:

'In the last few months it has become increasingly obvious that the cohesion, trust and partnership which underlies all government; and is especially essential in a coalition arrangement, was withdrawn and replaced by a strategy which was the exact opposite—an approach of non-consultation, and taking advantage of deep-seated institutional loyalty. The publicly visible aspects of this reflect only part of the reality.

We accept that even within government there is inevitably a degree of competition and rivalry. With that we could cope, but when ordinary competitiveness gave way to a pattern of dictation, it became clear to me, to Deputy Bobby Molloy in particular, and to our parliamentary party, that the effectiveness of the Government could only be sustained by huge sacrifices on our part. Over the last few months we made those sacrifices because we believed that the national interest required us to maintain the appearance of effective Government even though its reality was ebbing away. So, what now?

We will vote against the motion of confidence in the Government from which I, Deputy Molloy and Deputy Harney resigned last night. We do not have confidence in it. If we did, we would not have resigned from it. We will ask the people of Ireland to give us a mandate to pursue the policy-driven politics which the Progressive Democrats brought about. We fully appreciate that the actions we are taking will be misrepresented by others as unnecessary, self-indulgent or hasty.'[13]

The Fianna Fáil speakers, from Reynolds down, heaped odium on the PDs. Bertie Ahern, normally the calmest of politicians, took a wild swipe at the PDs and at their leader:

'They are addicted to outrage, to annoyance and are hooked on a high moral tone. Consequently, at a time of international economic instability they are prepared to halt progress and stability to pay homage to the outraged feelings of their leader. They do not care about the damage this will do to the country, to Ireland's image overseas, or about the negative effect it will have on our currency. Clearly economic considerations do not matter as much to the Progressive Democrats as does their own status. I do not suppose there is anything I can say which will stop the Progressive Democrats voting against the Government today. They are the victims of their own illusions and they have foolishly decided to plunge the nation into this crisis. Fianna Fáil will break from that stupidity. I do not think the electorate will support the Progressive Democrats.'

Even Charlie McCreevy voiced his disappointment at the decision taken by the party:

'It would be particularly dishonest of me not to state that I profoundly question the motives of some activists of our junior partners in Government since 1989, who have brought about the collapse of this Dáil. I can attest to the qualities of many members of that party. Thus, I am more disappointed than most that perceived party political advantage has been put by some on a higher pedestal than the overall national interest. Other members of our junior partners in Government have been swept along by the personal ambitions of a few.'[14]

The election was called for 25 November to coincide with the referendum on the three strands of the abortion issue.

The confidence expressed by Ahern, McCreevy and other Fianna Fáil speakers that the voters would back their approach to coalition did not last long, however, as the first opinion poll of the campaign, published in the *Irish Independent*, showed a massive drop of 20 per cent in the Taoiseach's satisfaction rating. The voters clearly blamed Reynolds, rather than O'Malley, for the break-up of the government. Some of the old

Haughey gang could not disguise their glee at the fact that Reynolds' strategy had come so spectacularly unstuck, but they did not have much time to enjoy his discomfiture. As the tide of public opinion moved strongly against Fianna Fáil, it was every man for himself in the battle to hold on to Dáil seats.

The deep antipathy between Reynolds and O'Malley had a profound influence on the ensuing campaign. The weekend before the election was called, the political editor of the *Sunday Tribune*, Gerald Barry, asked Reynolds for his reaction to allegations that he refused to speak to O'Malley outside Cabinet. 'You want to know what I think of that? It's crap, pure crap,' said the Taoiseach, adding emphatically: 'I mean that, for the record, it's crap, total crap.' In an interview with Charlie Bird on RTÉ television news the Taoiseach went on to say that O'Malley's arguments regarding the reasons for the collapse of the coalition were 'crap, total crap'. There was a public backlash over the use of such language and Reynolds was forced to apologise. That humbling moment marked the start of a disastrous Fianna Fáil campaign, and a hugely successful one for the PDs.[15]

Throughout 1992 the party had been preparing carefully for an election. Michael Parker, a young business executive who had spent almost a decade in Brussels before returning to Ireland to work for the IAWS, had been appointed director of the PD election strategy committee at the end of 1991. He took over as party general secretary in October 1992. 'I produced an election strategy paper suggesting we could win ten seats and shortly after that I was asked to come in as director of elections,' recalls Parker. He says the critical decision for the party was to take a ruthless attitude to the election and concentrate its resources on the ten target constituencies. 'We had our thinking clear on how we should fight the election before it was ever called.'[16]

Parker was keen to make the issue of trust central to the campaign and he believed that in O'Malley they held the trump card. He devised a poster with a picture of O'Malley accompanied by the slogan, 'Who Do You Trust?' O'Malley, however, was vehemently opposed to this approach. He had always detested the cult of personality in politics and believed it would be wrong to run an election campaign based on his integrity, with the clear implication that other party leaders were less trustworthy than he. The PDs were forced to settle for a more mundane slogan, only to see Labour leader, Dick Spring, appropriate the 'Trust Me' slogan for the Labour campaign. Spring capitalised brilliantly on the anti-Fianna Fáil mood and the polls showed a big swing towards Labour as the campaign progressed.

The PDs did not make the same kind of impact in the polls, but the party had a clear plan of campaign, with almost all resources being concentrated on ten winnable constituencies. Nine other seats were also contested, but the party focused intently on the ten identified as winnable. At this point Pearse Wyse decided to retire, so the party went into the election with five sitting TDs. However, it also fielded some of the former TDs who had unexpectedly lost out in 1989, along with its high-profile senators. Pat Cox came back from Europe to contest Wyse's seat, while Liz O'Donnell generated positive publicity in Dublin South.

Having set his face against a campaign on the issue of trust, O'Malley settled for a stress on the theme of 'leadership'. This issue was highlighted in all the party's campaign literature. Their stated manifesto of 'Getting the Nation Working' was accompanied by four policy documents which focused on PD achievements while in government. The environment, jobs, tax and agriculture were the issues the party highlighted as those where it had shown solid leadership and would do so again.[17]

Martin Cullen, who was battling to regain his seat in Waterford, was impressed that the posters, canvass cards and election literature were designed and printed centrally so that there was a clear message right across the country, in every local constituency. 'The quality of the PDs' material was certainly first-class and gave a good impression to the electorate.'[18]

In the final days of the election the media focused almost exclusively on the downward slide in the Fianna Fáil vote and the dramatic rise in support for Labour, as evidenced by the polls. Other parties were virtually ignored, but when the votes were counted the PDs confounded everybody outside its own ranks by bouncing back to ten seats. The accepted wisdom in the political world that the party was on an inexorable trajectory to oblivion suddenly had to be revised. That the five outgoing TDs contesting the election all comfortably held their seats was surprise enough, but that they were joined in the Dáil by PD faces old and new was a shock. Martin Cullen and Michael McDowell, who had lost their seats in 1989, made it back into the Dáil. Helen Keogh, who had lost out to Geraldine Kennedy in Dún Laoghaire in 1987, also finally made it to Dáil Éireann, while Pat Cox, who had stood in Pearse Wyse's old seat in Cork South Central, added a Dáil seat to the one he held in the European Parliament. After her breakthrough in the local elections, Liz O'Donnell proved that she possessed impressive vote-getting skills by being elected in Dublin South, even though she did not live in the constituency and it was not in her council area and the pundits had assumed with certainty that Fine Gael would get the seat.

The PD success was made all the sweeter by the unmitigated disaster visited upon Reynolds: the Fianna Fáil vote dipped below 40 per cent for the first time since 1927 and the party lost 10 seats into the bargain. Fine Gael also dropped 10 seats. The big winners were Dick Spring and Labour, who gained 17 seats to finish with a record 33, while the Democratic Left took 5 seats and six others were elected. For the PDs, winning 10 seats marked a dramatic comeback from the brink of political anonymity. Those on the election committee received a nice little financial reward too, because Parker had the foresight to collect a contribution from each of them, go to the bookies and place a bet of £600 on the party to win 10 seats at odds of 40 to 1. The result was a spectacular windfall of £24,000 for the election team.[19] Just to put icing on the cake, the abortion referendum also went the PDs' way: the electorate threw out Reynolds' proposal on the substantive issue, which the junior coalition party had so strongly opposed.

However, the euphoria of the result gradually gave way to disappointment when the post-election negotiations revealed that the party was not, in fact, going to be back in government. Spring declined any coalition arrangement involving the PDs. While exploratory talks were conducted into the possibility of participation in a rainbow government with Labour and Fine Gael, the discussions were a complete sham. Although such a government would have had a clear majority, Labour had no intention of going into coalition with the PDs and the negotiations between the parties were torpedoed on Spring's instructions. The bitterness caused between the PDs and Labour as a result of this was to have long-term consequences. The PDs were not surprised that Labour did not want to make a deal with them, given the policy gulf between the two parties; what did surprise the PDs was the insulting way they were treated.[20]

Labour ultimately formed a coalition with Fianna Fáil after prolonged negotiations, which followed the failure of the Dáil to elect a Taoiseach— as had happened in 1989. The Fianna Fáil–Labour coalition was a new experiment in Irish politics and it gave the PDs time to regroup in Opposition. O'Malley tried to warn Spring, privately and publicly, that a partnership government with Reynolds was impossible, but the Labour leader dismissed these claims as petulance. Unfortunately for him, he found out the hard way that O'Malley was right.

Chapter 13 ᵔᵕ

HARNEY TAKES
THE HELM

O nce the euphoria of the election comeback had worn off, the PDs
settled down to the dreary round of Opposition. The PDs and
the other Opposition parties did manage to have a bit of fun at
Labour's expense in the early months of the government's life, during
spring 1993, but Opposition was nonetheless a big come-down after three
years in government. The Twenty-Seventh Dáil was a strange one, with
the coalition of Fianna Fáil and Labour enjoying a massive majority. The
PDs had to carve out a new role for themselves in competition with Fine
Gael and the Democratic Left on the Opposition side of the House. It
was sobering for the PDs to be marginalised by the Fine Fáil–Labour
coalition, despite having had a successful election. During the campaign
the party had debated the pros and cons of another coalition deal with
Fianna Fáil—the main con being Reynolds' antagonism. The other
option, a deal with Fine Gael and Labour, was also discussed but was
never really a runner given Spring's hostility and the incompatibility of
the PDs and Labour on some major issues. What the party had not
anticipated in any of its discussions of possible outcomes was the
possibility of becoming irrelevant in the Dáil arithmetic.

The Fianna Fáil–Labour coalition was installed in office on 12 January
1993, with its huge Dáil majority. It was galling for the PDs to watch as
Bertie Ahern, now Minister for Finance, introduced a Budget in February
1993 that at one stroke undid almost all of the modest tax reform policy
pursued by the PDs over the previous three years. Ahern introduced a
1 per cent income levy on the higher rate of income tax, which was
equivalent to a tax hike of almost 2.5 per cent. The Budget appeared to
signal a return to old-style Fianna Fáil tax-and-spend policies, aided and

abetted by Labour. It seemed that the PD drive to change the direction of economic policy would be completely reversed.

For O'Malley, the failure to get into government was compounded by what he regarded as a series of sinister smears designed to discredit him and executed by elements within Fianna Fáil. Back in May of the previous year, as he was preparing to testify at the Beef Tribunal, he was informed that a senior Fianna Fáil member of the Cabinet had approached a figure in the mining industry seeking to establish that O'Malley had been paid retainers by Tara Mines. In the 1970s he had been a strong supporter of Tara in the row between it and Bula for control of a zinc ore body near Navan in County Meath. O'Malley was also informed that a trawl of all government Departments had been instigated to uncover any information that might be damaging to him.[1] At the Beef Tribunal he was asked whether he had been paid a retainer by Tara Mines; he replied that he had not.

The matter did not end there, however. Just before Christmas 1992, in the aftermath of the general election, a State counsel from the Beef Tribunal, Gerry Danaher, who was also a member of Albert Reynolds' kitchen Cabinet, became embroiled in a verbal exchange in the Shelbourne bar with O'Malley's counsel, Diarmuid McGuinness. Danaher allegedly claimed that the State's legal team had access to O'Malley's private notes relating to his evidence during the Tribunal hearings. He claimed further that Fianna Fáil had the 'dirt' on O'Malley in relation to alleged payments made to him by Tara Mines over the years.[2]

O'Malley requested a meeting with Spring prior to the formation of the Labour–Fianna Fáil government in order to tell him of his concerns about what had transpired, but the Labour leader made it clear that he regarded the affair as an effort by the PDs to upset the coalition negotiations. Instead, O'Malley put his version of events on the record of the Dáil on the day Reynolds was re-elected as Taoiseach.

'Some have sought to trivialise or to dismiss the issues involved but that ignores the gravity of the matter. We are not dealing here with a boast, a jibe, a jest or a jeer. The admission reported to me was clear and unambiguous. Furthermore the contents of the admission were genuine, if foolhardy. It was conveyed to my counsel in the clearest and most unambiguous terms that various drafts of my statement of proposed evidence to the tribunal had been made available to my political opponents and studied. There was a sequence of at least nine drafts of that statement.'[3]

The allegations generated considerable media controversy in the early days of 1993 but dropped out of the public domain after the formation of the government. However, the Bar Council conducted its own investigation into the affair. In the course of that investigation Adrian Hardiman, acting for O'Malley, wrote a letter to the Bar Council outlining the various claims that had been made regarding drafts of O'Malley's evidence being made available to members of Fianna Fáil. Hardiman's letter also referred to the allegations that O'Malley had received money from Tara Mines while he was Minister for Industry and Commerce. O'Malley's brother-in-law, Peter McAleer, at one time a director of Tara, was named as the conduit for the alleged payments. This document was leaked to the *Sunday Business Post* in March, but the Bar Council secured an injunction prohibiting its publication. Of course, that set the rumour-machine into overdrive and unfounded claims that O'Malley had been paid £30,000 by Tara Mines were bandied about freely.

The *Sunday Tribune* brought the story into the public domain by the simple expedient of tracking down McAleer in Australia and asking him if he had paid money on behalf of Tara to his brother-in-law. McAleer explained that he had made personal contributions, ranging from £1,000 to £5,000, to his sister, Pat, over the years to help defray O'Malley's election expenses. He was adamant that the payments had nothing to do with Tara Mines, but were merely his way of supporting his sister and her husband in their political activities.[4]

The payments from McAleer was quite different from the picture painted by the stories that had been circulating, but O'Malley's enemies pounced, claiming there was something shady about his conduct. There was also undisguised delight in some media quarters. 'First we have to stop smirking,' wrote Gene Kerrigan in the *Sunday Independent*. 'Let's face it, the bright side of the O'Malley affair is that a lot of people got a lot of enjoyment from seeing Dessie O'Malley twisting in the wind. There's something in all of us that likes to see stuffy righteousness with egg on its face.' Kerrigan went on to point out that there was not the slightest shred of evidence that O'Malley had done anything wrong, but he speculated as to why O'Malley had not pre-empted the controversy by stating the facts in public.[5]

At the PD annual conference in Cork that same weekend, Harney maintained that her leader had been subjected to a 'cynical, premeditated campaign of innuendo' and she laid the blame at the feet of sources close to the Fianna Fáil leadership. O'Malley received a ringing endorsement from his supporters at the conference, but the episode shook him and led him to question whether he wanted to stay on as leader of the party for the foreseeable future.[6] Some years later Michael McDowell claimed that O'Malley's departure as party leader had been hastened by the controversy, particularly by articles published in the *Sunday Business Post* which contained a 'constant drip of innuendo'.[7]

Although the controversy had died down by the summer of 1993, O'Malley had decided that it was time to step down, even though he was only fifty-four-years-old. He had taken the PDs to electoral triumph and disaster, into government and out of it and back to a qualified electoral success. He didn't feel he had the energy for another long stint in Opposition, working to rebuild the party, and he had in fact thought of stepping down soon after the Dáil had elected the Fianna Fáil–Labour government in January. He postponed his decision because of the Shelbourne bar controversy, but during his summer break in Connemara he discussed the issue at length with his wife, Pat. He made up his mind to step down at the beginning of the autumn Dáil session.

'I was losing my energy by 1993. A lot depends on what a politician has been through. I had been through a very rough time for almost twenty-five years. I was in the eye of the storm in 1969 when the arms crisis developed and from then on through the problems in Fianna Fáil and on to the founding of the PDs I was in the thick of it. I had got a bit worn out. If I had only been in the Dáil ten years it would have been a different matter, but I had been there for twenty-five years through an awful lot.'[8]

Harney recalls O'Malley telling her, around Christmas 1992, that he was thinking of standing down. Her response was: 'You must be joking.' O'Malley told her that he would like her to succeed him as leader. Harney didn't believe he meant it: 'I put it down to the fact that he was in bad form and he was tired. And he needed a break. And then he never said another thing to me until just before he resigned in the following October.'[9]

One of the reasons cited by O'Malley in 1993 for resigning so unexpectedly was his memory of the faction fights that had developed in Fianna Fáil over the succession in 1979, and his determination to ensure that nothing of the kind happened in the PDs.

'It did influence me because it is one of the things I wanted to avoid. Possibly the greatest strength of the Progressive Democrats in the

eight years is that we never had factions. I think I have learned my
lesson from the situation that I saw in Fianna Fáil and I wanted to try
and avoid it. I also thought that resigning quickly and unexpectedly at
a time of calm was the best way to try and hand on an undivided and
coherent party.'[10]

In fact, the manner of his resignation caused a degree of bitterness that
came within an ace of destroying the party because Cox felt that the dice
had been loaded against him. O'Malley told Harney of his plans a few
days before the formal announcement. It was the first she had heard of it
since their brief discussion at Christmas, but it was still not the shock for
her that it was for others because she had been forewarned to some
extent. Some senior party figures heard the news a few days in advance,
but Cox learned about his leader's decision just minutes before it was
announced on RTÉ radio on 5 October. The MEP was in Vienna when he
received a phone call from O'Malley, who dropped the bombshell that he
was resigning that day. As a result, Cox was placed at a disadvantage in
the race to become the next leader of the party and he was the only party
TD not present at the press conference, which was held in Dublin an
hour later.

What made it all the more unpalatable for Cox was that the previous
weekend he had spent three days in O'Malley's company in Helsinki, at a
Liberal party conference, but O'Malley had given no hint of his
imminent departure. The MEP had to make hasty arrangements to
return home immediately as the race for succession developed without
him. He travelled on a small plane in the middle of the night from
Vienna to Munich, where he boarded a scheduled flight to London and
then on to Dublin. He wasn't back at Leinster House until twenty-four
hours after O'Malley's announcement. 'O'Malley dealt badly with it. He
should have told Cox because Cox was never going to win the leadership
in any case,' says Paul Mackay.[11] 'Whatever the reasons, the manner in
which the whole thing was handled was a disaster, because Pat was away,'
says Harney.[12]

While Cox found out only at the very last moment, other key members
of the party had not been in the know for very long either. McDowell
recalls that he was attending a meeting in Northern Ireland with Stephen
O'Byrnes just a few days before the official announcement. O'Byrnes was
called out of the room to take an urgent telephone call, and when he
returned to the room McDowell knew something was up. 'He came back

in and his face was like a sheet.' McDowell had to wait until the meeting was over before he could find out what was wrong. Initially, O'Byrnes would only say that O'Malley had given him a message and he was sworn to secrecy. McDowell countered that as party chairman he was entitled to know something that obviously had very serious implications given the reaction it had provoked; O'Byrnes told him that the party leader was going to resign.

On the evening before the news became public O'Malley travelled to Limerick to tell his constituency supporters of his plans, but most of the party TDs didn't find out until a parliamentary party meeting on the day of the announcement. They were stunned and upset that he had decided to resign, but he was emphatic that he would not change his mind. The wider political reaction to his departure was predictably mixed. Charlie McCreevy, back in the Cabinet as Minister for Trade and Tourism, was characteristically frank:

> 'He liked being a Minister, not for the trappings but because he liked being in charge of a busy brief. He didn't like rows but he was never afraid to respond to provocation. Once he formed an opinion of someone it was hard to get him to change it. This was not one of his high qualities.'

Former Fianna Fáil colleague and fellow Limerickman Gerry Collins was more generous: 'He was a major figure in the political life of the country and he made a tremendous input into economic and industrial development.' Brian Lenihan took a different view: 'I never rated him highly. He was a good debater. Fullstop. His influence on Irish politics has been far too divisive.' Neil Blaney was blunt: 'He should never have been in Fianna Fáil. His background wasn't Fianna Fáil, despite his great worth. He just wasn't Fianna Fáil and should never have been selected.'[13]

The media, too, gave O'Malley mixed reviews, with the case against being put most forcibly by an editorial in the *Sunday Business Post*:

> 'Everywhere O'Malley went divisiveness followed. The politics of *ad hominem* attack were always top of the agenda where O'Malley and his good friend George Colley were calling the shots. The ancient tradition of downplaying personal ambition in the interests of the greater party was forgotten as efforts to undermine the properly elected leader of Fianna Fáil became a way of life. But was the

insatiable desire to unseat Haughey justified? The evidence of history suggests that Haughey was a better economic manager than O'Malley and possessed a greater vision of what he wanted to achieve.'[14]

At the press conference to announce his resignation, O'Malley recalled the scepticism about the party's prospects on the day it was launched.

> 'Founded nearly eight years ago, we have proven to be Ireland's change-makers and the party of the future, forward-looking, agenda-setting and yes, mould-breaking. We can in that short time claim credit for the transformation of Irish politics into a European model in which policy choices are the stuff of politics rather than the arid self-justification of power *blocs* or historical baggage. We have brought many issues to centre stage in Irish politics which our opponents had neglected or ignored, including constitutional reform, tax reform, competition, liberal issues, environmental protection and privatisation, among many others. And our work has scarcely begun.'[15]

While she did not make a formal declaration, Harney was able to effectively launch her campaign for leadership at O'Malley's resignation press conference. She had told RTÉ's Una Claffey a year earlier that she would not be a contender for the leadership because as a single woman she did not feel she would have the emotional and other supports necessary to be party leader, but nobody took that remark very seriously.[16] Harney was not only the deputy leader of the PDs, the public image of the party was almost as strongly associated with her as with O'Malley. There was immediate pressure on her to run from PD members up and down the country.

Harney was straight away installed as favourite by the media and public expectation grew that Ireland's first woman political leader was about to be selected. O'Malley remains unrepentant about the manner of his resignation and the impression it created that he favoured Harney. 'If I did favour Harney, wasn't I right?' he says. He concedes, though, that the small number of people involved in choosing the new leader made it very difficult for all concerned. 'There were only ten of us voting and that created certain problems,' he says.[17]

In fact, regardless of whether Harney was or was not told in advance of O'Malley's decision, there was never any real doubt that she would win the contest against Cox. For starters, she had the support of the three

1. Opposing Haughey. Charlie McCreevy, Des O'Malley and Mary Harney at Leinster House in October 1982, after McCreevy put down a motion of no confidence in Haughey.

2. A new party is born. The PDs are launched on 21 December 1985 by Des O'Malley, Michael McDowell and Mary Harney. (*Photo: Derek Speirs/Report*)

3. PDs at the Marine Hotel, Sutton, Co. Dublin. With O'Malley on the platform are (*from left*) Michael McDowell, Mary Harney and Senator Helena McAuliffe. (*Photo: Derek Speirs/Report*)

4. Billboard campaign for the 1987 election based on the slogan, 'Dessie can do it'. (*Photo: Derek Speirs/Report*)

5. Body language foreshadows doom for Fine Gael–PD election pact, June 1989. Alan Dukes, Des O'Malley, Bobby Molloy and Jim Mitchell.

6. Into office. Press conference to announce the first FF–PD coalition, in July 1989.
Bobby Molloy, Des O'Malley, Charles Haughey and Albert Reynolds.

7. Old enemies relish the deal for power. O'Malley and Haughey adapting to coalition in 1989.

8. Harney stands her ground. Minister for the Environment, Pádraig Flynn, and his two Junior Ministers, Mary Harney and Ger Connolly, January 1990.

9. Coalition strains. Minister for Industry and Commerce, Des O'Malley, and Minister for Transport and Tourism, Seamus Brennan, on the Oireachtas Golf Society prize day, October 1990.

10. Happy days. Stephen O'Byrnes and Des O'Malley take a break from the tension of the Beef Tribunal in the summer of 1992.

11. Old friends. Charlie McCreevy and Mary Harney at the races, Christmas break, 1992.

12. Des O'Malley, with his wife, Pat, and Mary Harney, finds lots to laugh about after announcing his decision to resign the party leadership. Stephen O'Byrnes (*background right*) enjoys the joke.

13. New leader: Mary Harney is overjoyed, as her defeated rival, Pat Cox, looks on.

14. Beef Tribunal report. Michael McDowell, Mary Harney and John Dardis examine the document, August 1994.

15. Election pact. Bertie Ahern and Mary Harney set off on the campaign trail, May 1997.

16. 1997 election tussle. Harney and Dick Spring prepare to debate on 'Prime Time', with Brian Farrell in the chair.

17. A *Darby O'Gill* moment during the 2002 election campaign as Tom Parlon shows his leader the home turf. (*Photo: Collins*)

18. Michael McDowell grabs the 2002 election campaign by the scruff of the neck by clambering up the lamppost near his house in Ranelagh.

19. A second term for the Harney–Ahern coalition. The Cabinet receives seals of office from President McAleese, June 2002.

other women in the parliamentary party—Mairin Quill, Helen Keogh and Liz O'Donnell. With O'Malley also backing her, she already had five out of the ten votes available. By contrast, there was nobody officially in the Cox camp. While he felt he was in with a chance of winning, his lack of visible support was striking. He travelled around the country and called at the homes of all the other PD deputies—except Harney—but no one came forward publicly to back him. Martin Cullen was regarded as being in his camp, but the two had not got on particularly well during Cox's period as general secretary and Cullen was at best a reluctant supporter. A major problem for Cox was that he had spent most of his time since the general election in the European Parliament rather than in the Dáil. Although he was the PD Finance spokesman in the Dáil, he attended only for major Budget and Finance Bill debates and it was obvious to his colleagues that he was more comfortable in Europe. There was also criticism from his constituency organisation in Cork South Central that they never saw him, even though he had given a commitment that, if elected, he would commit himself to national politics rather than European matters.

Cullen and some of the other TDs were not happy with the choice of Harney or Cox and they put a lot of pressure on Michael McDowell to run. He thought about it carefully, but given the precariousness of his seat in Dublin South East, he decided not to let his name go forward. Although he had been involved in setting up the party, McDowell had never envisaged himself as the leader of the PDs. In fact, in the early days he had no ambitions even to be a TD. 'In the early days I had not thought of running for the Dáil. I might have had some idea of getting into the Seanad and playing the kind of role that the late Alexis Fitzgerald played there for Fine Gael in the 1960s and 1970s.'[18]

Some people in the party felt that McDowell's abrasive style was unsuited to leadership, but his uncompromising stance was popular with ordinary party members. 'I am convinced that McDowell would have won,' says one of the key party figures. 'He would certainly have had more votes than Cox and would probably have been ahead of Harney in the first round. Things would have been very different if he had thrown his hat into the ring.' This, though, is a minority view and most senior people in the party were convinced that Harney had both the political record and the temperament required for leadership.

The parliamentary party met in Leinster House on 12 October, the votes were cast and, as everybody except Cox had expected, Harney was declared the winner. The voting figures were never disclosed, but it was widely reported in the media that Harney had won by seven votes to three. Paul Mackay recalls that the vote was in fact eight for Harney and two for Cox.[19] Martin Cullen was the only member of the parliamentary party to vote for Cox, who naturally voted for himself, giving him a total of two. The party was happy to allow the seven–three report to go unchallenged in order to lessen the blow for Cox, but that was no consolation for him. Although the result was no surprise to the PDs or the media, Cox was visibly shattered. He sat alongside Harney on the platform when the result was announced, but to the media it was obvious that he was in agony. It was the first serious setback he had experienced in a hugely successful career that had spanned first media and then politics. In fact, the future held even brighter things for Pat Cox, but on that day it looked as if his political world had collapsed.

Harney, by contrast, was delighted. She announced that she did not intend to change the direction of the party, but wanted to extend its appeal to a broader audience. 'It takes time to change voting patterns, but I hope I can use a different style to sell the message to younger people.' She paid tribute to Cox in an effort to pour balm on his wounds, and she identified unemployment and the North as her priorities. 'To say I am nervous and apprehensive is an understatement, but I will give the job my full commitment and I feel I have the qualities and the toughness to do so.'[20]

The new leader also outlined her political priorities, announcing that she wanted:

'To lead a crusade which will inspire and energise our people to solve the many problems facing us. Part of this crusade means less State interference in many aspects of the economy. It means less confiscation by the State of what people earn; it means less bureaucratic red tape that is infuriating small business people in particular. And it also means less anti-competitive and over-priced State monopolies, which are stifling enterprise. Part of this crusade also means people not always looking to the State to do things for them but getting on with the job themselves.'[21]

This articulation of the main thrust of PD policy since its inception summarises Harney's policy political approach in the years that followed.

However, amidst the joy of her election there was one incident that, in retrospect, can be interpreted as a warning of rocky times ahead. After her election, but before she gave her first press conference as leader in the Davenport Hotel, Harney asked her defeated rival to meet with her in private. In Cox's version of events, Harney said to him, 'I'd like you to be my deputy leader,' and he responded, 'I'd prefer to deal with that another day.' He suggested that if she was asked what position she intended to offer him, she should say, 'That's a question for another day. Pat Cox is an option.' At the press conference less than an hour later, the question duly arose and Harney responded without hesitation that she intended to offer the position to Cox. Asked by a journalist if he would accept, he replied, 'Who could turn down a lady on a day like today?'[22] The reluctant nature of the response hinted at the depth of the wound to Cox's pride, a wound that would not be healed.

Harney, on the other hand, was too excited to read the danger signal— albeit understandably. Her election as the first woman leader of an Irish political party was greeted by a flood of congratulations, flowers and the odd bottle of champagne into PD headquarters in Dublin. And the excitement was not confined to PD members. Harney was greeted enthusiastically by a number of soccer supporters when she turned up at Lansdowne Road for a soccer international between Ireland and Spain the night after her election. The sight of Irish fans surrounding the new PD leader and asking her to autograph their programmes was entirely unexpected, as was the spontaneous round of applause she received when she entered a restaurant for lunch before the match.

In the Dáil chamber Albert Reynolds congratulated her and wished her well, but it was the Fine Gael leader, John Bruton, who paid the most effusive tribute:

'I join the Taoiseach in congratulating Deputy Harney on her election as the first woman leader of a political party in this House. Regardless of her gender, Deputy Mary Harney has, as a member of this House, shown exemplary courage and directness. She has always been willing to stand up for what she believes. I have no doubt that that directness, simplicity and straightforwardness will stand her and her party in good stead and will do good for this House in the years ahead.'[23]

She made good use of her first Dáil set-piece occasion during a debate on the government's national plan, giving free rein to her abilities as a rousing speaker and ignoring much of her prepared script. In the following months she regularly managed to get under the skin of both

Fianna Fáil and Labour ministers, but a particular needle developed between the PDs and Labour at this time. Opinion polls taken within weeks of her succession bolstered Harney's confidence: she immediately won a higher satisfaction rating than Reynolds, Spring or Bruton, while the PD share of the vote rose to an impressive 11 per cent. It seemed that the new leader was capable of appealing to an even wider audience than O'Malley, and by Christmas 1993 the omens for the PDs had never been better.

Chapter 14 ～

CIVIL WAR

Everything seemed to be coming right for Harney in her first few months as leader. In February 1994 a MRBI poll gave the PDs their highest rating in five years, a very healthy 12 per cent of the vote.[1] With the European elections scheduled for the following June, it appeared the party was set to do well in its first electoral contest under its new leader. Then, disaster struck. With the European election campaign in full swing, Pat Cox announced, on the day before nominations closed, that he was leaving the PDs to contest the Munster constituency against the party's own candidate, Des O'Malley.

Cox's decision was a thunderbolt from the blue. While there had been some warning signs, Harney and her colleagues were stunned by the enormity of what Cox had chosen to do. That O'Malley's *protégé*, the young man who had played such a critical role in the party's early success, should turn against his former leader in this way was truly breathtaking. Harney found it difficult to believe and accept. Since the foundation of the PDs in 1985 she had not been merely a political associate of Cox's, she had been personally close to him and to his family. 'I was very friendly with Pat Cox. I am godmother to his child, Grace. We were great old pals and it was never the same after that,' she says.[2]

All PD members concede that the saga of Cox's departure is something that should never have happened. It was a classic story of events spinning out of control in a way that left all the players involved in an impossible position. Through a combination of Harney's inexperience as leader, Cox's refusal to be clear about his intentions and the failure of all the senior members to level with each other, O'Malley ended up running for the European Parliament when he didn't want to, while Cox felt that he was being prevented from running for something he wanted desperately. It was these circumstances that soured the atmosphere within the party and allowed misunderstandings to develop and flourish.

On the night after Harney was elected leader, she invited Cox to her home in an attempt to mend fences and to discuss the political future. In particular, she was anxious to find out about his intentions regarding European elections the following year. During the general election campaign of 1992 Cox had given a commitment to the people of Cork that he would not run for Europe again if elected to the Dáil, so Harney wanted to find out what he planned to do.

Harney and Cox gave somewhat different accounts of what happened at that meeting. Cox maintained that Harney bluntly raised the question of whether he would continue as Finance spokesman in the Dáil, claiming it did not tie in very well with his European mandate. He recalls her saying that McDowell or O'Malley could do the Finance job, if he wished to focus on Europe. 'I was shocked at the suggestion, at her brusqueness. My anger was apparent and I left with nothing resolved. I thought that if the boot had been on the other foot, I would have felt it necessary to keep Mary sweet.'[3] In Harney's version, she asked Cox if he intended running for Europe again and said that if he did, she felt Foreign Affairs would be a more appropriate Dáil brief than Finance. Harney says that Cox 'went bananas' and stormed out. One way or another the meeting sowed the seeds of a misunderstanding that would fester over the following six months.[4]

Harney and Cox discussed the issue again on a few different occasions over the following month or so. Harney remembered Cox saying that the Munster seat would need to be well-defended because the European election would represent her first test as leader. He pointed out that the number of seats in Munster had been reduced from 5 to 4 and that as a slew of new Labour TDs had been elected across the province in 1992, it would take a strong candidate to defend the PD seat there. The possibility of O'Malley running was discussed, but the former leader had emphatically ruled out that option at a press conference on his retirement, so it was decided to put out feelers to see if any other candidates were available. Cox was deputed to seek a replacement candidate and he eventually came up with the name of a charismatic priest, Fr Harry Bohan from Clare, who had been involved in rural housing development. Harney thought it highly unlikely that the priest would be allowed to run by his superiors, so she never established whether he was even willing to run for the PDs.

During one of these discussions with Cox, Harney remembers saying: 'If I were a betting person, I'd reckon 70:30 that you want to run yourself.'

What stuck in Cox's mind was a meeting in the Dáil on 4 November 1993, in preparation for Harney's first visit to Cork the following Monday. The leader and deputy leader were joined at that meeting by Mairin Quill, who represented the other Cork City constituency, and by Stephen O'Byrnes. Cox recalled Quill saying that any prevarication by him on the dual mandate issue would be devastating and she recalled the pledge he had given to the electorate to live in Cork and not to run for Europe again. 'There is no answer and there will be no answer for Monday and that is that,' said Cox. When the visit duly took place and Harney was asked about the issue, she fudged.

However, Cox outlined his own position to a meeting of the Glasheen/Togher branch of the PDs on 24 November. The minutes record him saying that 'he felt that if Des O'Malley could be persuaded to run that the party could retain the seat and that he would be one of the persuaders.'[5]

Looking back, Harney recalls that Cox was the first to suggest that O'Malley should be persuaded to run.

> 'Pat came to me and said that as he had made a commitment in the election that he wouldn't run for Europe again, the only person who could hold the seat was O'Malley. He said, "You're the leader, you should convince him to go." And I said, "Now you know Des told me there was no bloody way he was going to run for Europe." Anyway, we put our backs to the wheel behind Des and had all kinds of people talking to him.'[6]

The PD parliamentary party met in December to decide its strategy for the European elections and there was a quick discussion of three of the four constituencies. John Dardis was prepared to run in Leinster, Bobby Molloy in Connacht–Ulster and Stephen O'Byrnes in Dublin. McDowell queried the feasibility of O'Byrnes' candidature and there was quite a lengthy discussion about this. The issue of Munster was finally reached and Harney spoke about the problem of the dual mandate. Molloy said that the issue could be potentially embarrassing for him. Cox undertook to discuss the issue with O'Malley over the Christmas break. However, on a visit to Limerick a day later, Harney told a press conference that she wanted O'Malley to run in Munster.[7]

In January, prior to the meeting of the parliamentary party to review the European elections, Cox decided to act. He was in Strasbourg for a meeting of the Parliament but he prepared a letter to be distributed to colleagues. In it he stated baldly: 'I wish to seek a nomination to contest the European election at the forthcoming selection convention in Munster.' The letter went on to say that as the dual mandate was an important issue for the party, 'I enclose for your attention a letter of resignation from Dáil Éireann addressed to the Ceann Comhairle, unsigned and not dated.' That second, undated letter, which could be invoked at any time, was enclosed with the first. When the letter was read out at the party meeting all hell broke loose. Nobody was sure what was going on, but the party TDs and senators were adamant that they did not want a troublesome by-election that the party would inevitably lose. Dardis telephoned Cox and demanded that he return from Strasbourg, but the MEP refused. It was Martin Cullen who eventually persuaded him to return for a meeting the next day.

Harney and Cox had a private meeting the following morning, during which she expressed her anger at the 'threat' to the party and insisted that he withdraw the letter. Cox described that meeting as 'tough and bitter', but at a meeting with his parliamentary colleagues immediately after-wards he agreed to a proposal from O'Byrnes that he should withdraw the letter without prejudice to his final decision. He agreed to reflect on what had been said and come back to the party the following week. Back in Strasbourg that night Cox went to dinner with two journalists, Joe Carroll of *The Irish Times* and Ken Reid of *The Examiner*, and he told them he was going to run in Munster. On 24 January his constituency organisation voted strongly in favour of him not running for Europe, and at a parliamentary party meeting the following day his colleagues pleaded with him to honour his dual mandate pledge. He capitulated immediately and announced that he would not put his name before the selection convention. In subsequent media interviews he firmly ruled out the prospect that he might run for Europe: 'I told my wife that the game was up.'[8]

It should have been obvious to everybody in the party that Cox was in despair at the prospect of having to give up Europe, but neither he nor his senior colleagues were able to confront the problem head-on. They were all fixated on the dual mandate and the question of credibility that the party would have to answer if Cox broke his pledge on the issue.

'There was too much uncertainty and lack of clear signals all round,' says McDowell. 'Cox kept saying he would find a replacement candidate himself, but it never happened and Mary had to put huge pressure on Des to run. I wanted the party to put together an appeal to Cox to stay on as MEP. He had given an undertaking to the people of Cork, which was an obvious difficulty for him, but if we had appealed to him publicly to stand in the interests of the party it would have got him off the hook. I thought O'Malley should have run in Dublin and with Cox in Munster we would have won two seats.'[9]

O'Malley is still clear in his own mind that the only reason he decided to go for Europe was that Cox was stepping down.

'Cox had decided not to run and encouraged me to run. He had made a public commitment to the people of Cork South Central when he ran for the Dáil in 1992 that he would step down from the European Parliament. I had told him when he wanted to run for the Dáil that he would have to make such a commitment. I didn't want to run for Europe, but Cox urged me to run. I continued to say no, but Harney prevailed on me saying I had a duty to do it. I went back to Cox and he still said he was not going to run and urged me to go. He later changed his mind, mainly I think because he was not the leader of the party.'[10]

After much agonising about what he should do, Cox appeared reconciled to his position when the PDs held a convention on 6 March to select their Munster candidate. O'Malley met token resistance from a Cork party member, Ben McDowell, but in a secret ballot of the 450 delegates he won an overwhelming mandate. Harney asked Cox to propose or second the candidate, but he refused. He did make a speech extolling O'Malley's qualities as a politician, saying he would make an ideal MEP for Munster. *The Irish Times* ran an editorial commending Harney and the PDs for being consistent on the dual mandate issue, and it looked as if the problem had been sorted out to everybody's satisfaction. Molloy, Dardis and O'Byrnes were also selected during March and the party was confident that it would hold the seat in Munster and also be in with a good chance of taking one of the other three seats on offer.

The PD candidates set out on an arduous and expensive three-month campaign, while Cox concentrated his attention on his final months in Europe. The announcement by Independent Munster MEP, T.J. Maher, that he would not be running again naturally caught Cox's attention because it opened up the race even more, but at that stage he did not think of changing his mind. In early May he went to Strasbourg for what he thought was his final week in the Parliament. 'It was a week when I felt very depressed. I got a great buzz out of Strasbourg and now the whole thing was dribbling away.' On 5 May he hosted his final dinner as MEP for a few friends and colleagues. 'At the end of the meal, while making a speech, I broke down. I cried. I was forty-one. I was good at the job. I thought then, "The people put me in, so they can take me out". He was going to run after all.[11]

Back home, Cox discussed the issue with his wife, Kathy, and his older children as well as with a close Cork associate, Joe McCarthy. Nominations were due to close at noon on Saturday, 14 May. On Thursday, 12 May, Cox and his wife drove to Limerick to explain his decision to Brigid Teefy— she ran his European constituency office for him, but was also O'Malley's director of elections. More than a decade later, Teefy is still haunted by that moment. 'It was the most awful heartbreak. We were like a big family and suddenly we were torn apart.'[12] Returning to Cork, Cox telephoned his constituency officers to inform them of his decision. He then telephoned Harney, who was attending an election fundraiser in Jury's Hotel in Dublin. Not long afterwards he rang O'Malley, who had already heard the news by then. Both phone calls were short and unemotional.

Mairin Quill recalls vividly the day Cox announced his decision to run:

'I was campaigning in Youghal with Des. We had taken a break and were sitting in Tom Mannion's hotel having a cool drink because it was a very hot day. Des' phone rang and something in his tone prompted me to look over at him. His face turned red and purple as he listened to the call. When it ended he immediately called over his wife, Pat, and I knew by the way they were talking that something very serious had happened.'

O'Malley called Quill over and told her Cox was running for Europe. In a daze they drove to Midleton, where O'Malley was scheduled to attend a function at Irish Distillers. 'Des' first priority was to talk to Brigid Teefy. He was terrified she might side with Cox, but he was reassured on that score.' Nonetheless, Quill immediately thought the worst. 'In our hearts we knew the game was up the moment Cox declared. We never thought that something like this would happen to our party. It went much deeper than a mere election contest,' says Quill. 'Something in the spirit of the party just snapped. It divided friends and things were never the same. The PDs were like a family and this was our civil war.'[13]

As in all civil wars, people were torn by conflicting loyalties. In Limerick, the people who had left Fianna Fáil to support O'Malley were torn between their loyalty to the former PD leader and their sitting MEP, who had endeared himself to them with his intelligence and his stunning electoral performances. The 'heartbreaking' position of Brigid Teefy highlighted the divided loyalties with which many party members were struggling to come to terms. While Teefy, like most of the party in Limerick, sided with O'Malley, Cox was able to mobilise a significant number of PD supporters to his cause in Cork. His defection in such circumstances left everybody in the party reeling. Coming after the highs of the party's good election result in 1992 and its revival in the polls after Harney's accession, the loss of Cox was the biggest blow it had ever suffered and one that threatened the very existence of the party.

'It really was a cataclysmic blow to the campaign,' says Liz O'Donnell. 'The local organisation in Limerick and across in Munster was riven out of a sense of loyalty to Des, the former leader of the party, and the obvious talent of Pat Cox. It was clear that Cox was a fantastic campaigner and was going to campaign hard on his track record. That row or hurt lived on and has affected the party in Munster.'[14]

'One of my great regrets is that I didn't see this coming down the tracks. We misread the situation,' says Quill. 'If we had it over again, of course we would do things differently.'[15] John Dardis, who felt his Leinster campaign was going very well, was canvassing in Mullingar when he heard the news that Cox was running and he knew immediately that it spelled disaster for the PDs' national campaign. 'Do we go out now and jump into Lough Ennel?' he asked his election team.[16]

Setting off on his last-minute campaign, Cox initially looked a pathetic sight. People who saw him canvassing outside the Gaelic Grounds in Limerick before a Munster hurling championship match in late May, with just a handful of followers, found it difficult to believe he had any chance of getting elected. But Cox had shown in 1989 that he could get elected against all the odds and he campaigned deliberately and with great professionalism.

Recognising that O'Malley would get the bulk of the PD vote in Limerick, Cox focused most of his attention on Cork. There has always been rivalry between the two leading cities of Munster and Cox began to feel that he could get enough support in Cork to put him in contention, while picking up some support in Limerick as well. In Waterford Martin Cullen gave aid and succour to Cox, publicly canvassing with him and generating considerable media coverage for the Independent candidate.

When the country went to the polls on 9 June, all eyes were on the contest between Cox and O'Malley. The former leader had 31,674 votes on the first count, as against 27,920 for Cox. As the twelve counts wore on and other candidates were eliminated or elected, O'Malley's lead was gradually eroded. Cox picked up transfers from right and left and pulled ahead of O'Malley on the ninth count, eventually winning the last seat on the twelfth and final count with almost 3,000 votes to spare.

It was the stuff of great drama. 'The naked ambition of the protagonist, the Oedipal destruction of a former father-figure, Des O'Malley, gave it an almost archetypal stamp,' wrote Fintan O'Toole in *The Irish Times*.[17] This shattering blow to the PDs was compounded by a disappointing performance in the other three constituencies. 'We could have won two seats in 1994, but instead we ended up with none after a family row,' says Parker. 'It was unfortunate and regrettable. There had been a great sense of camaraderie in the PDs, but a lot of that evaporated in 1994. Harney and Cox both suffered from the way things developed.'[18]

> 'The Progressive Democrats may have to ask themselves if their time in public life is coming to an end. It would not be the first time in Irish political history that a breakaway group has run out of ideas and followers,' declared an editorial in the *Irish Independent*.[19]

In the immediate aftermath McDowell was scathing about Cox. 'I think Cox's behaviour was very destructive. You either have to accept or reject that he told us he wanted Des O'Malley to run. If you accept this, then it is quite impossible to believe his account of what went on. If Cox did in fact suggest O'Malley as a candidate, then his own behaviour was quite despicable and inexcusable. I think Pat Cox abused the willingness of his colleagues to take him at face value.'[20]

'In hindsight it is as well I was not elected, but I didn't think that at the time,' says O'Malley.[21] Harney still feels badly about this episode in PD history. 'The awful thing was it was the only election Des ever lost. It was something I felt lousy about.' She believes that if Cox had been clearer about his ambitions, the whole sorry mess would never have happened.

'If Pat had levelled with people, it could have been worked out. The party took a high tone on the issue of the dual mandate, saying you have made a commitment you can't break, but if we knew how deeply he felt a way could have been found.'[22]

Stephen O'Byrnes, who has remained on good terms with both Harney and Cox, is probably the most objective analyst of all:

'Pat was publicly professing that he was looking for a replacement candidate but I think he never wanted to give up Europe. There is no evidence of Pat saying to anybody, "I'm having second thoughts". Maybe he felt trapped by then. Pat kept his own counsel. The convention was held in Cork and Pat supported the nomination of Des. Then out of the blue he announced he was running himself. Mary persuaded Des against all his better judgment. Pat's decision threw the whole strategy out the window. It was really traumatic, really appalling. It was a dreadful time for the party. Pat let himself down and let the party down.'[23]

'The whole thing had repercussions for Mary as leader,' says O'Donnell. 'When things went bad from time to time under her, some people would say, "Oh we should have gone for Cox". It kind of undermined her in the future and it was such a pity because we were spoiled with talent to have two such brilliant people in the parliamentary party.'[24]

Cox didn't waste any time getting out of Irish politics. He resigned his Dáil seat and committed himself to a political future in Europe. Following the aftermath of the split the PDs tried to have Cox expelled from the European Liberal group, the ELDF, but they refused to countenance this suggestion. Cox had established himself as a senior figure in the ELDF and they were quite happy for him to stay on, even if he was no longer attached to the Irish liberal party that had sent him there in the first place. In the Cork South Central by-election to fill Cox's seat the PDs were again humiliated, receiving just 4 per cent of the vote. It was part of a pattern of by-election disasters for the party that further eroded confidence.

'He was a huge loss,' says Harney. 'After I became leader we were 12 per cent in the polls, but after he left we went to 6 per cent and I don't know when we recovered. We only did from time to time after conferences or big events. It was the internal fight that brought us back down. What really damaged us in people's eyes was that we were supposed to be different. And suddenly all that happened. It was bad, especially in Cork. We have never recovered in Cork from that.'[25]

When Martin Cullen decided to leave the party and join Fianna Fáil a few months after the European elections, the PD obituarists were back out in force. Cullen had been unhappy long before Harney became leader. Back in 1989 O'Malley had given him a dressing-down for not telling his colleagues that he had been employed as a consultant to the private bus lobby (PAMBO) prior to his appointment to the Seanad. While never a fan of Harney, he was not particularly enamoured of Cox either. He threw in his lot with Cox when he saw no other viable option. His disenchantment with the party was obvious on the night of the European election count when he launched a strong attack on the PD leadership. Therefore it was not a huge surprise when, three months later, in response to concerted overtures, he jumped ship and climbed on board with Fianna Fáil, but it was still another bad blow. 'The departure of Mr Cullen raises once again the question of whether the PDs have a future,' wrote James Downey in the *Irish Independent*.[26]

With the loss of two of its male TDs, the party now faced accusations that it was dominated by women. 'A worrying feature for the party is that, knowingly or unknowingly, it has fostered the public perception that it is a woman's party with one man, Michael McDowell, on the side,' wrote Geraldine Kennedy in *The Irish Times*. 'Ms Harney walks into the Dáil with a pack of women for the TV cameras every day. The profile of PD voters in recent opinion polls has changed as a result, with a huge imbalance, unique among the parties, between the number of women and men supporters. This 'womany' perception of the party will be exacerbated by the Cox defection.'[27]

By the autumn of 1994 the party was at a low ebb. The bright hopes that attended Harney's take-over of the leadership a year before were but a dim memory. O'Malley had been humiliated in the European election; Cox and Cullen had departed; and the level of public support had been sliced in half to just 6 per cent. Then, out of the blue, Albert Reynolds and Dick Spring tore their coalition government apart and hope suddenly dawned again that the PDs had a chance of getting back into government.

It began with the publication of the Beef Tribunal report, which generated a great deal of friction between Reynolds and Spring. The Dáil was recalled at the end of August 1994 to discuss the report, and as it happened that debate coincided with the first IRA ceasefire. This helped to take the pressure off Reynolds, but Bruton and Harney made strong speeches criticising Reynolds for the way he had handled the publication of the report and his crowing claims of vindication. The Beef Tribunal was a serious issue for the PDs; O'Malley had played an important role in setting it up. Harney made a strong speech in the Dáil to put the government under pressure on the issue.

Two months later the Reynolds/Spring government collapsed over the appointment of the Attorney-General, Harry Whelehan, as President of the High Court. The reasons for the collapse had as much to do with earlier events, like the Beef Tribunal, as anything else, but the Whelehan affair was the straw that broke the camel's back. The ensuing drama set the political world alight in November 1994. The critical Dáil debates that led to the collapse of the coalition were broadcast live on radio and television, and Harney emerged as a star performer. She had always been a fine public speaker, now the televised debates gave her the opportunity to display her talents.

The PDs got a boost in the polls, but the collapse of the coalition ultimately proved to be yet another political disappointment for the party. Labour's hostility meant that the PDs were never seriously involved in the process of putting a new government in place. Labour conducted negotiations with Fianna Fáil under its new leader, Bertie Ahern, and with John Bruton of Fine Gael about the formation of a new coalition. A rainbow government under Bruton, involving Fine Gael, Labour and either, or both the Democratic Left and the PDs was a possibility. However, one particular meeting between the Labour negotiating team, led by Ruairi Quinn, and the PDs, led by McDowell, made it clear that the PDs were going to be left out in the political wilderness. McDowell felt he was treated with disdain by Quinn, who smoked a cigar throughout the meeting and blew smoke around the room. When Labour eventually threw in its lot with Fine Gael and Democratic Left, having pulled out of a deal with Fianna Fáil at the last moment, McDowell and his PD colleagues came to an inescapable conclusion: with Labour blocking the road to any deal with Fine Gael, the only path by which the party could get into government was in coalition with Fianna Fáil.

Chapter 15 ~

SHOT DOWN IN FLAMES

By the spring of 1997 the PDs appeared to have made a full recovery from the trauma of Harney's first year as leader. The party was bouncing along nicely in the polls, with ratings approaching 10 per cent, while Harney had established herself as the most popular party leader, ahead of Fianna Fáil's Bertie Ahern and the Taoiseach, John Bruton. Although the rainbow government had proved more competent and stable than many had anticipated, the Opposition parties had a slight advantage in the polls going into the election year of 1997.

The PDs prepared carefully for that election. In 1996 Harney made a number of new staff appointments to ensure there was a professional team in place for her first big electoral contest. RTÉ journalist John Murray came on board as her press officer and economist Maurice Roche joined the team as her policy guru. Garvan McGinley, a former Army officer, was appointed as general secretary to replace Michael Parker, who returned to the private sector.

With the rainbow parties of Fine Gael, Labour and Democratic Left bonding well in government and Spring's hostility towards them as strong as ever, the PDs knew that their only chance of power lay in a coalition with Fianna Fáil. As early as March 1995 Harney had told the National Executive that the party was working very well with Fianna Fáil in Opposition. She added that Bertie Ahern's 'preference for Sinn Féin' and his handling of the abortion issue could only be to the advantage of the PDs when it came to carving up the anti-government vote.[1] The second divorce referendum, in 1996, which was carried by a wafer-thin majority, enabled the PDs to emphasise their liberal credentials by strongly backing the campaign waged by John Bruton's coalition.

The party's performance in by-elections continued to be disappointing, however. Some worry was expressed by the National Executive at the poor showing of the PDs in the Dublin West by-election of April 1996, where the party had a good candidate in Sheila Terry. Nevertheless, that didn't dampen the mood of optimism and neither did the massive party debt of £275,000. A series of eleven constituency opinion polls carried out that summer were reassuring, showing the PD vote holding up well and the Labour vote falling significantly. An analysis of the polls found that Harney was regarded as having passion and integrity, but that there was a need for the PDs to distinguish themselves from Fianna Fáil.[2]

An election strategy committee was established in February 1996 and detailed work began in the autumn of that year. The National Executive decided to put the party on an election footing in September 1996, but a note of warning was sounded by Paul Mackay who felt that they didn't yet have the right candidates and needed to seek out candidates with solid electoral prospects. Further polls in the autumn and early winter gave a similar message. 'There were positive results from the polls where we have sitting TDs/senators. However, there is no room for complacency. We must consolidate our present position as well as targeting new constituencies.' In December, O'Malley presciently cautioned the National Executive that the party was considering contesting too many constituencies. 'He feared that we were in danger of spreading our financial resources too thinly.'[3]

The first national opinion poll of 1997, carried out by IMS in the *Irish Independent*, showed the PDs on 11 per cent of the national vote and attracting 16 per cent in Dublin. A subsequent MRBI poll in *The Irish Times* was not quite as promising, but it put the party on 9 per cent and that looked like a very substantial platform from which to gain extra seats. Both polls showed a very high satisfaction rating for Harney, putting her ahead of Ahern and Bruton. These encouraging poll ratings led the PDs into the first of a succession of errors that almost put paid to the party in a matter of a few months. O'Malley's warnings about contesting too many constituencies were ignored and instead there was a frantic search for new candidates to allow the party contest as many seats as possible. With the candidate strategy haring off down the wrong track, the party backroom team and leading members of the front bench prepared a series of policy positions designed to stake out a separate identity for the PDs in the election campaign.

Opinion was divided in the rainbow coalition regarding the timing of the election. Bruton wanted to carry on until the autumn of 1997, but Dick Spring and the Labour party, who had been in government since

1992, were adamant that it should be held before the summer break. Even before the election was called it was clear that the three rainbow parties had decided to campaign as a government seeking re-election rather than as independent entities. That move inevitably forced the PDs and Fianna Fáil together to offer the electorate an alternative coalition, despite the reservations of senior figures in both parties about this strategy. The potential Fianna Fáil–PD coalition had a steady lead over the rainbow coalition in the polls during the spring of 1997, but Bruton was persuaded that his personal high ratings meant his government was in with a real chance.

One good reason for holding off on the election was the sensational evidence emerging from the McCracken Tribunal in Dublin Castle during April 1997, which detailed massive payments to Charles Haughey. The sequence of events that kick-started the era of the tribunals began with the resignation of Fine Gael minister, Michael Lowry. That resignation followed the disclosure that expensive renovations to his house had been paid for by Ben Dunne in what appeared to be a tax scam. It then emerged that Dunne had made substantial cash payments to Haughey during his term as Taoiseach. The upshot was an investigation that led to the establishment of the McCracken Tribunal. These were compelling reasons for Bruton to wait until the autumn, when the tribunal was scheduled to report, but Spring and his Labour colleagues were anxious to get the election out of the way before the summer, and in the end they got their way.

Bruton dissolved the Dáil on 15 May, with polling scheduled to take place on 6 June. It was the first general election campaign in the history of the State in which voters were offered a choice between competing coalitions. The decision of the rainbow parties to campaign for re-election on a joint programme was met by the Fianna Fáil–PD announcement that they would go into government together, if they had the numbers. Despite all the time available to prepare, the two parties had not worked out a joint electoral strategy. At the Fianna Fáil *árd fheis*, less than a month before the election was called, Bertie Ahern had made no reference to coalition or the PDs in his keynote speech. However, government manoeuvrings and pressure from the media to outline what they would do in the aftermath of an election forced the PDs and Fianna Fáil to admit they would form a coalition, if it were feasible.

The PDs had won ten seats in 1992, but they went into the 1997 election with just seven outgoing TDs: Cox had left the party and was becoming a figure of stature in the European Parliament; Cullen had joined Fianna Fáil and was running under its banner in Waterford; while Peadar Clohessy had decided to call it a day in Limerick East. Buoyed up by the high opinion-poll ratings, the PDs were confident that they could beat their performance in the previous election and come back with more than ten seats. The party had difficulty finding high-profile new candidates, but it still went ahead and ran thirty candidates in twenty-eight constituencies; five years earlier the party had twenty candidates in nineteen constituencies. This was just one of a series of fatal errors that would undermine the PD campaign.

The PDs' potential coalition partner, Fianna Fáil, took a very different tactical approach. On the insistence of Charlie McCreevy and P.J. Mara, the party ran the minimum number of candidates in order to maximise its potential haul of seats. The organisation was instructed to give the cold shoulder to an array of candidates who were clamouring for nomination. Selection conventions were held well in advance of the election and the party ended up with 112 candidates in the forty-one constituencies, a reduction of ten from the previous election. 'This is not a three-week campaign for us. We have been working towards this election for the last two years,' the director of elections, P.J. Mara, told the *Sunday Tribune*.[4]

The PDs had been planning for a long time too, but, as it transpired, not nearly as wisely nor as well. One of the difficulties for the PDs was that the party was not sure whether to publicly embrace Fianna Fáil as its partner or to keep its distance until the election was over. In the early days of the campaign there was no all-encompassing agreement between the two parties, although their policies did mesh on major issues—as much because Fianna Fáil wanted to steal the PDs' tax-cutting clothes as anything else. While the rainbow parties had a national transfer pact, the PDs and Fianna Fáil left it to each constituency organisation to work out the best tactics as it saw fit. For instance, in Mary Harney's own con-stituency of Dublin South West the PDs did not recommend that their supporters transfer to Fianna Fáil because they had outside hopes of a second seat. Attempts to forge a working alliance inevitably ran into difficulties. 'The rainbow had two-and-a-half years to get their lines of communication clear; we just had two-and-a-half weeks,' said one Fianna Fáil source.[5]

The PDs thought long and hard about the content of the party manifesto. Harney was concerned that the party's identity should not be lost because of the coalition arrangement with Fianna Fáil, so she was anxious for a 'big idea' that would stake out new ground and attract attention. When the manifesto was unveiled on 21 May it certainly did receive attention, although not of the kind Harney was hoping for. The manifesto, entitled 'A New Deal', contained the anticipated tax-cutting agenda along with a range of worthy social, economic and environmental policies which would have been expected from the PDs. However, all attention at the launch focused on a proposal to encourage young, single mothers to remain with their families rather than set up one-parent homes.

The proposal was not actually terribly radical and might not have attracted much attention if the media had not been prompted by party officials to question Harney about it. Under the heading, 'Supporting the Family', the manifesto stated simply:

'In the longer-term, social habits conform to economic realities, and behaviour patterns are beginning to reflect the diminished value of the family in tax and welfare law. While the State mush cherish all its children equally, that does not mean that it must be indifferent as to whether children are raised in a home founded on a stable relationship. We must refocus the tax and social welfare system in favour of the family. We will bring in new measures to encourage young single mothers to remain with their families rather than set up one-parent homes.'[6]

When the media, on cue, asked Harney about the proposal, she was more than willing to discuss it. 'I am suggesting that an incentive should be given to remain with her family and some of that money should be used to provide back-up parenting assistance that a young mother in that situation requires,' she told the press conference. Harney fielded almost every question from the floor herself. 'With Mary Harney delivering the address and then fielding almost all the questions, Liz and Michael were reduced to just sitting pretty (with different degrees of success) throughout the hour-long event,' wrote Frank McNally.[7]

Other western democracies had been engaged in a debate on the question of whether State policies to assist single parents were in fact contributing to the breakdown of family life and the fabric of society. In the United States, President Bill Clinton had begun to cut benefits to single mothers in an effort to eliminate a poverty trap that was proving to have negative social consequences. The newspaper reports of the PD press conference were largely low-key and even positive. 'The disappointment was palpable when it transpired that the PDs are not actually fixing to drive single mothers from their rented homes with big sticks,' wrote Katie Hannon.[8] However, that was not the way a small number of journalists in influential positions reacted to the PD proposal. The party was attempting to be at the cutting-edge of social policy to prove their distinctiveness, but it inadvertently handed a loaded gun to its enemies at a critical time in the campaign. Harney began to realise this during the press conference when she had to defend herself against a few well-known journalists who accused her of 'going back to the bad old days' and 'stigmatising illegitimacy'.[9]

The issue surrounding young single mothers was incendiary enough, but another proposal in the manifesto probably caused much greater damage, although it was more of a slow-burner.

> 'The PDs propose a new productivity agreement for the public service. This would reduce total numbers through natural wastage and without the need for redundancy payments. Front line areas such as health, education and crime control would not be affected. An annual reduction of 2 per cent would cut the numbers employed in the public service by 25,000 over five years.'[10]

The public service unions naturally reacted with hostility to this proposal and the left-wing parties pounced on the exposed Achilles' heel. Instead of generating a debate, as Harney had hoped, these two proposals enabled the left-wing parties and much of the media to portray the PDs as launching an unsympathetic attack on the most vulnerable in society—keen to rein in single mothers and sack thousands of public servants.

There is confusion and bitterness in the PD ranks to this day about what happened.

> 'I have to take the rap for it because as leader, I did it,' says Harney. 'I wasn't the initiator of the proposal on single mothers. Michael was at me for months about that. He had read an article in *The Irish Times* by Labour TD, Roisin Shortall, about the issue and wanted to tackle it. Anyway, it was my error for doing it in the course of the election. It was a stupid thing to do. You can't raise anything serious in an

election. And I remember Una Claffey blew it up on the news. When I saw the news that evening, I knew we were in trouble.'

She says the proposal on reducing the numbers in the civil service was a genuine mathematical error. 'It was supposed to be 1 per cent of something, but it came out as 10 per cent. I mean, Michael never saw the manifesto. That is actually the truth.'[11]

'I remember the horror of the day the 1997 manifesto was launched,' says McDowell. 'It was bloody awful. The plan to get rid of 25,000 civil servants; nobody to this day will take responsibility for that. I was woken up by an *Evening Herald* journalist who said: "What about the plan to get rid of 25,000 public servants?" I rushed over to the launch. I would never have said that. Nobody has ever admitted responsibility. It was not a good day.'

From the end of January 1997, McDowell had taken time off from the Law Library to concentrate on the campaign.

'I really threw myself into it to ensure that I would keep my seat. From the beginning of February I was in every morning trying to organise the party and get it up and running. The first disaster came early in the year with the issue of water charges. Mary said they should be introduced. It was a millstone around our necks on an issue we should not have become involved with.

Then Easter came and the election was called and there was still no manifesto. Maurice Roche and Martin O'Donoghue were involved in drafting it. I remember the day it was launched. I went into the PD headquarters and saw this utterly bland document. Mary's spin doctor said spice it up; there's nothing in it. Somebody persuaded her to go big on the issue of unmarried mothers. Roisin Shortall had said something similar in an article in *The Irish Times*. A socialist could say it, but a liberal couldn't.'[12]

However, another senior figure in the party blames McDowell for the debacle. 'That manifesto was Michael's,' maintains Liz O'Donnell. 'Michael has a bit of amnesia about this and has rearranged the past. It was his document.' She alleges that McDowell had worked on the policy with Maurice Roche and the team at head office. 'It was his baby. We delegated the responsibility for the finalised document to him. He was always coming forward with policy documents. There is no point in dwelling on it. It was what it was, but he did it under our name.'[13]

Stephen O'Byrnes, who had come back from the private sector to assist the party during the election, gives this analysis of the events of that traumatic day.

'I remember the day of the manifesto launch. I was working on it with McDowell and we produced a solid script about the need for a steady hand at the tiller to ensure that the working people got a fair reward from the economic growth. Then Mary came in and said, "We won't get a single headline from this." She mentioned the unmarried mothers and said that was the issue she wanted to go with to get attention. Una Claffey then went to town on it on the six o'clock news. The combination of the Harney speech and the Claffey report destroyed the campaign. As for the public service numbers, Maurice Roche had done work on the subject but I think a decimal point went in the wrong place and the number turned out way higher than intended.'[14]

Whoever was responsible, there is no doubting the negative impact of the manifesto launch.

'It was a policy disaster that ruined the campaign because we were ready for that election,' says O'Donnell. 'We had five years to prepare for it. We had raised money. We were gung-ho. That mistake in the figure on the cut in the public service just got us off to a cataclysmic start. You don't go into an election promising to cut 25,000 civil service jobs. It is lunacy. It is the sort of thing you do in government with an agreed strategy. It is not something you shout about when you are trying to get votes because with such a huge public service it just hands a cannon into the hands of your enemies.'[15]

The government parties identified the PD manifesto as the weak link in the strategy of the alternative coalition. Senior Fianna Fáil figures were not sure whether to crow at the prospect of picking up PD seats or panic at the prospect of seeing their coalition partner go down the tubes. Bertie Ahern was quick to distance Fianna Fáil from the proposal, saying that if the two parties went into government Fianna Fáil would not support the withdrawal of any existing benefits to single parents. Harney protested that she did not propose to cut any benefits. 'What is more compassionate: a system that forces young single mothers to isolate themselves in council houses away from human contact and support in order to receive benefits, or one which provides them with the option to live with the father of the child or with their own family?'[16]

By that stage, though, Harney was clearly on to a loser. As well as a negative lead story in *The Irish Times*, the newspaper editorial thundered: 'Many will see something odious in what is essentially a proposal for behaviour modification. It reflects a dubious order of priorities while so many aspects of these young girls' lives are fundamentally disadvantaged and when the conditions in which they exist are often cruel and deprived.'[17] Coincidentally, *The Irish Times* was to have one of the most embarrassing episodes in its own history on the very same issue in 2005, but in 1997 its editorial tone reflected the consensus among the opinion-forming class that it was unseemly to mention it at all.

If the Fianna Fáil leadership was taken aback by the PDs' decision to tackle the issue of single mothers in an election campaign, it was dumbfounded by the plan to cut public service numbers. The party's Finance spokesman, Charlie McCreevy, categorically denounced the proposal to cut 25,000 public service jobs as unacceptable to Fianna Fáil. Ahern thought that the plan had the capacity to do serious damage to the prospects of the alternative government and might even rescue the Labour party. He sought a meeting with Harney and they held a summit at the Green Isle Hotel in west Dublin on 25 May to assess the state of the campaign. Ahern told the PD leader of his unhappiness at the way such major policies were announced, without consultation, and they agreed that for the rest of the campaign they would consult each other before making important pronouncements. After the meeting Ahern was positive in public: 'We want people to know that we have an understanding to work together on issues. We can put forward a very comprehensive and satisfactory combination of government right through to the year 2002.'[18]

Aside from the two bombshells in the PD manifesto, the two parties policies actually dovetailed quite nicely. 'The political and personality approaches adopted by both Fianna Fáil and the Progressive Democrats were strongly similar and therefore quite compatible,' observed one political scientist. 'On the policy side they were seeking to concentrate on a very simple message focused on two core issues: tax and crime. The PDs felt that Mary Harney was their most valuable resource and sought to capitalise on her popularity as much as possible. Her face appeared on all posters, prominent next to that of the local candidate.'[19]

The first MRBI poll of the campaign, carried out before the manifesto launch, confirmed the validity of the strategy, with Harney emerging as the most popular party leader with a satisfaction rating of 64 per cent—compared to 60 per cent for Ahern, 55 per cent for Bruton and 47 per cent for Spring. The PDs were attracting the support of 7 per cent of the electorate, which was down slightly on a month earlier but still a reasonable position from which to start. The second MRBI poll, carried out after the manifesto launch, showed the PDs still getting 7 per cent support, but now Harney's satisfaction rating had slipped significantly, putting her back into third place behind Ahern and Bruton.[20]

Harney spent much of the campaign touring the country, attempting to boost support for doomed candidates rather than protecting vulnerable seats or countering the wave of anti-PD sentiment that was rising steadily in the media. It is arguable that the party's seat strategy was not as absurd as it appears with hindsight. After all, at the time the campaign was being planned favourable poll figures and Harney's position as the most popular party leader did give grounds for optimism about extra seats. Nonetheless, experience ought to have taught the PDs that a small party must focus primarily on holding on to what it has because only exceptional candidates can build a seat out of almost nothing. Neither did the party change tack after the manifesto launch, even though it was obvious that a radical rethink was necessary.

The PDs and Fianna Fáil both opted for cuts in tax rates in their manifestos. Both went for a standard rate of 20 per cent, with the PDs opting for a higher rate of 40 per cent while Fianna Fáil pitched it at 43 per cent. The rainbow argued that widening the tax bands and improving allowances was a better way of helping middle- and low-income earners. However, the PD–Fianna Fáil strategy of focusing on tax rates proved more attractive to voters. The problem for the PDs was that as it floundered as a result of the manifesto controversy, Fianna Fáil reaped the benefits.

In the days following the manifesto launch the PDs were riven by recriminations and in-fighting. Before the ill-fated manifesto launch a decision had been taken by the election strategy committee to keep McDowell off the airwaves. 'We wanted a calm campaign and didn't want anybody rocking the boat, so we tried to keep him off the air as much as possible,' admits one strategist. McDowell was convinced he was deliberately being kept off the air, and this added to his fury over the manifesto launch. 'Michael had this notion that he was kept off the airwaves and he still believes it to this day,' says Harney. 'Now if he was, then I knew nothing about it and I doubt if anybody would have taken a decision to try and keep him off. We are always trying to get people on.'[21]

With just two days to go before polling the PDs and Fianna Fáil issued a joint statement offering the electorate a series of tempting morsels. On top of the promise made by both parties to cut the standard rate of tax to 20 per cent, they further pledged specific tax reductions in the Budget later that year, including a 1 per cent cut in the higher rate. A number of pledges were also made to appease the public service unions, including commitments to give Telecom workers a 15 per cent holding in the company on privatisation, to restore the link between the pensions of retired public servants and pay increases for workers in the public service. 'In a strategic attempt to sway working-class and public sector voters, a series of three joint statements was issued by the Opposition parties yesterday to counteract some of the perceived damage inflicted by the PDs' commitment to cut back 25,000 jobs in the public service,' wrote Geraldine Kennedy in *The Irish Times*.[22]

On the day before the election, the country's largest circulation daily newspaper, the *Irish Independent*, published an unprecedented front-page editorial headlined 'Payback Time', urging voters to support the alternative coalition. 'For decades past the draconian PAYE system has bled Irish taxpayers white,' began the editorial, which concluded, 'On any objective analysis it is a vote for Fianna Fáil and the Progressive Democrats tomorrow which offers the better chance of securing our future.'[23] The editorial attracted huge attention and by all the laws of logic it should have been a huge boost for the PDs as the party that had pioneered the tax-cutting agenda. By that stage in the campaign, however, the party had taken such a hammering that it was in no position to capitalise on this unexpected stamp of approval.

The voters went to the polls on 6 June and it was with some sense of foreboding that the PD candidates woke up on the following morning to face the result of the count. The result was even worse than they had anticipated.

'We were just not able to recover from the catastrophic manifesto,' says O'Donnell. 'I survived it because of my own personal vote, even though I live in a constituency inhabited by a lot of public servants, teachers, guards, office workers, but it was a decimation for the party.' She recalls the shock of focusing on the national results after her own election in Dublin South.

'I was the first PD elected and I remember sitting looking at the television with Mary and saying, "I don't want to be the only PD left." Des was struggling, Bobby was struggling. Mary was struggling in Tallaght, she was reliant on Sinn Féin transfers. It looked as if it was the end of the road and I remember the devastation everybody felt. But my feeling was, "Holy God, if I am the last one left, what will happen?" I'll just have to run away leaving a bundle of clothes in Dún Laoghaire. I am not going to go into the Dáil on my own.'[24]

If O'Donnell was shocked at the prospect of being the only PD survivor, others suffered a much greater trauma. O'Malley and Molloy pulled through and, being hardened professionals, made the best of it. Harney also survived, but having led the party to such a disaster, she was shattered. With just four seats in the Dáil and less than 5 per cent of the vote, it was a terrible outcome given the high hopes of just a few weeks earlier.

McDowell was devastated to lose his seat again. He lost by the narrowest of margins, just twenty-five votes, to the Green candidate John Gormley after a series of re-counts that went on for nearly a week. It was not just a cruel blow to McDowell personally but an enormous setback for the party. Since 1985 he had been the intellectual powerhouse of the PDs and even in his first period outside the Dáil, from 1989 to 1992, he had provided a critical element of constructive tension to balance the party's participation in government. The loss in 1997 was far worse. Not alone was there the personal humiliation of being beaten for a second time, the circumstances that gave rise to the disastrous manifesto rankled deeply. McDowell felt bitter towards his colleagues and particularly towards Harney for instigating a disastrous strategy on what he regarded as a whim. He was also furious at what he believed was party policy to keep him off the airwaves during the campaign. Harney, for her part, was disconsolate at seeing one of the party's prime assets removed from the Dáil. McDowell was so angry that he quit the party a few months later.

Arriving at her own count centre Harney was calm and spoke frankly to reporters about the losses. She professed no regret about her controversial election policies: 'I believe in being honest and forthright.' Refusing to be drawn on the formation of the next government she added, 'We are not negotiating tonight and we might not even be negotiating tomorrow.'[25] This was the lowest point of her political career.

'"What can I do? Can I resign? Who can I hand over to?" she asked Maurice Roche. 'It was because I felt hugely responsible for everything. Mairin Quill was gone, so many people just tumbled. It was not that I felt panic because I suppose one of my strengths is that, when things are bad, I cope reasonably well. It was just that I felt a sense of being personally responsible for the way things turned out.'[26]

Chapter 16

VICTORY FROM DEFEAT

O nce they had got over their sense of shock, the PD survivors could see one diamond-hard fact gleaming from the rubble of the 1997 election disaster: the party's four TDs combined with the seventy-seven elected by Fianna Fáil were in a position to form a coalition government, although it would require the support of a number of Independent TDs to be viable. As the two parties had agreed a common set of policies during the campaign, negotiating a programme for government would pose no great problem; and there was none of the drama that had surrounded the formation of the first coalition between the two parties in 1989. The four PD survivors and one of the defeated TDs, Helen Keogh, met a few days after the election and decided unanimously that the only realistic option was to go into government with Fianna Fáil.[1]

Harney and Ahern met for more than an hour on 9 June and worked out the nuts-and-bolts of how many seats each party would get at Cabinet. In view of the fact that the PDs had been pruned back to four Dáil seats, Harney accepted that it would be impossible for Ahern to justify giving two seats out of fifteen at Cabinet to the smaller party. In 1989 the PDs had stood firm on the proposition that one Cabinet position was untenable because a solitary minister would be too isolated. However, a way around this dilemma had been created by John Bruton during the formation of the rainbow government, whereby he allowed Democratic Left to nominate Pat Rabbitte as a 'super junior' minister to attend Cabinet meetings along with Proinsias De Rossa. The PDs were given the same leeway in 1997 to ensure that Harney would not be an isolated figure at the Cabinet table.

Negotiating teams were appointed to work out the details of the government programme. Bobby Molloy and Liz O'Donnell did the honours for the PDs, while Fianna Fáil was represented by Dermot Ahern and Noel Dempsey. There were no serious problems to confront, but the PDs did manage to irritate the Fianna Fáil negotiators to some extent by insisting on the maximum amount of their programme being included. Given that the PDs' controversial policies had nearly cost them the election, the Fianna Fáil negotiators thought this a tad audacious.[2] The programme, entitled 'Action Programme for the New Millennium', was ratified by the two parties on 19 June and contained a hefty slice of PD policy.

Among the key objectives of the five-year plan were: the reduction of the standard rate of tax from 25 per cent to 20 per cent and of the top rate from 48 per cent to 42 per cent; old-age pensions to be increased to £100 a week; public service pensions to be protected; a Green Paper to be produced on a basic income policy in tandem with a national minimum wage; a limit placed on current spending growth of 4 per cent and on capital spending growth of 5 per cent. 'Based on my discussions with Bertie Ahern during the election campaign, and the negotiations we have conducted since then, I am absolutely satisfied that the commitments we have entered into will be fully honoured,' Harney stated.[3]

Joy at returning to government was tarnished by the election catastrophe.

'On the one hand, we in the Progressive Democrats, can reflect on a very successful process of negotiations with Fianna Fáil and the prospect of participation in Government. However, this outcome also comes in the wake of the devastating election result on 6 June, when not only some outstanding members of our parliamentary party failed to be returned but other superb candidates of ours were also unsuccessful,' said Harney.

She added that Ahern had been absolutely fair and honourable through-out all their discussions and negotiations and the necessary chemistry of trust, mutual understanding and give-and-take that they shared was the best guarantee that the government would be stable and effective.[4]

Of course, between them the PDs and Fianna Fáil had only 81 seats out of the 166 seats in the Dáil, so they needed outside support if they were to get into office and stay there. Ahern and Harney were fortunate that three of the six Independents had close links to Fianna Fáil. Mildred Fox, Jackie Healy-Rae and Harry Blaney were part of what became known as the Fianna Fáil 'gene pool' and were more than willing to vote for Bertie Ahern as Taoiseach as long as their local interests were being looked after. The government therefore had three legs: Fianna Fáil, the PDs and the Fianna Fáil-leaning Independents. For some time, though, many doubted whether that combination could provide the country with stable government.

When the Dáil met on 26 June the first task was to elect a Ceann Comhairle. Labour threw in the towel immediately and made it easy for the PD–Fianna Fáil coalition to get one of its TDs, Seamus Pattison, into the plum post. This created a majority of one for the new government and facilitated the election of Bertie Ahern as Taoiseach. Seconding the nomination of Ahern, Harney pointed to her core economic objective.

'I want to be part of a Government that sustains the economic boom through the prudent management of our economy and gives workers a break. I am talking about ordinary workers. Single people earning £11,000 or £12,000 a year should not be paying 55 per cent. They are the people who have created the boom and the time has come to ensure they get their rewards.'

She also referred to her traumatic election campaign and the issues it had generated. 'I remember saying here on 15 May when I set out on the election campaign that politics would be on trial. By the time the election was over I think I was on trial. I intend to prove over the next few years that nurses, teachers and gardaí have nothing to fear. I want to see a dynamic public service serving our country.'

And finally she referred to the effect the election campaign had on her own party. 'Any sense of personal excitement I feel today is somewhat lessened by the fact that three of my colleagues, Helen Keogh, Mairin Quill and Michael McDowell, have not been re-elected to this House. I regret that very much. They were all outstanding deputies and great parliamentarians who worked extremely hard.'

In her nomination speech Harney announced her determination to ensure that the government would not become bogged down by personalities.

'The programme for Government is clearly significant but it is equally important for parties to understand each other's needs. In coalition Governments, things can be achieved by putting guns to people's heads, but where things are achieved in that way they are pyrrhic victories because they damage relationships and undermine the kind of confidence and trust that is essential if a Government is to be stable, policy driven and focused on the issues. We are only interested in participating in a Government that is policy driven, stable from the outset and focused on the needs of our people. That is what we must be determined to do.'

She was clearly trying to lay to rest the PDs' reputation as a party that went looking for 'heads on plates' every time there was a crisis. She did succeed in this during the lifetime of her first coalition, but at a price. On a number of issues of conflict between the coalition partners her own party felt she did not intervene as early as she should have done, for fear of being perceived as gunning for individual Fianna Fáil politicians.

Harney described what she regarded as her bottom-line:

'The Progressive Democrats entered into negotiations with the Fianna Fáil party and concluded a Programme for Government. The spirit in which those negotiations were carried out was refreshing. I welcome that very much and it augurs well for the new Government. In particular, I would like to pay tribute to Deputy Bertie Ahern whom I have known for 20 years. I trust and respect him. He negotiated in an honourable and fair fashion. I want to be part of a Government where people respect each other and where there is mutual trust.'[5]

Given the history of Fianna Fáil's first two attempts at coalition, it appeared the PD leader was being overly optimistic.

Pat Rabbitte summed up the feeling of many on the Opposition benches when he expressed doubts as to whether the new coalition could survive.

'Considering the cohesive and stable reputation of the outgoing Government as distinct from the very unhappy history of the Progressive Democrats and Fianna Fáil, and their inability to coexist, this is a very tentative arrangement indeed. I suggest that Kilgarvan and Kilcoole will have more influence in this Government than will the Progressive Democrats, and in the interests of the country one must ask whether that is healthy.'[6]

Rabbitte was wrong on both counts. The coalition was to prove remark-ably stable and the demands of Kilgarvan (Jackie Healy-Rae) and Kilcoole (Mildred Fox) were modest and workable. One of the reasons why the coalition worked was that Ahern's consensus style of politics was far more conducive to good relations than the attitude of either of the two previous leaders of Fianna Fáil.

The really critical factor, however, was that the Minister for Finance—on whose shoulders rested responsibility for the government's economic programme—was none other than Charlie McCreevy. The two friends who had plotted the foundation of a new party in 1985, and had then gone their separate ways, were now reunited in the top two economic ministries in the land. As well as being Tánaiste, Harney took over as Minister for Enterprise and Employment, with responsibility for the whole area of job creation, while her old pal McCreevy held the purse strings of the State and responsibility for the taxation system. Both had despaired at the state of the Irish economy in the mid-1980s, but now, in 1997, they were in a position to see if the medicine they had prescribed in theory could work in practice.

The relationship between Harney and McCreevy, based as it was òn a shared analysis of the economic system as well as personal friendship, was the foundation-stone of Ahern's first government. In the early days of the coalition one senior Fianna Fáil advisor expressed his astonish-ment that the real axis of this government was Charlie McCreevy and Mary Harney. He expressed his hope that this would never become public knowledge because of the effect it would have on Fianna Fáil.

'We were very fortunate with McCreevy. I think McCreevy would acknowledge that he was able to do an awful lot because the Progressive Democrats were there. To a large extent Charlie helped us to achieve a lot of our agenda and we helped him,' remarks Harney. 'If you think about it, it was a great combination. It was nothing to do with friendship, it was to do with a marriage of policy. And that worked extremely well. McCreevy could understand where we were coming from and he certainly understood the PD view of things,' says Harney. She remembers ringing him up on a number of occasions to say, 'Listen, there is no way we can wear this,' and he immediately understood the problem. 'Nine times out of ten he sorted out whatever problems threatened to arise between the two parties. It never came to a head-to-head with Bertie. It would be taken off the agenda.'[7]

The other PD ministers were Bobby Molloy, who took the 'super junior' position and attended Cabinet meetings as well as having responsibility for Housing and Urban Renewal, and Liz O'Donnell, who went to Foreign Affairs where she had responsibility for Overseas Development Aid. Des O'Malley was the lone PD back-bencher and he acted as party whip.

While Harney and McCreevy controlled economic policy, they had to temper their approach by ensuring it linked in with a more traditional Fianna Fáil method. Ahern continued to rely on the social partnership model, with his priority being to build and sustain good relations with the trade union movement. In this Ahern was greatly assisted by the timing of his arrival in office, which coincided with the early days of the Celtic Tiger, allowing him to indulge the unions through massive public service pay increases. Simultaneously, the boom meant McCreevy and Harney could follow their tax-cutting agenda, which in turn fuelled radical job creation policies. Ahern's preoccupation with Northern Ireland also meant that the Harney/McCreevy axis had the field to itself much of the time.

Three weeks after Ahern took office, the IRA declared its second ceasefire. The IRA's decision was directly linked to Ahern's arrival in the Taoiseach's Office and it got the government off to a good start. An issue that had the opposite effect was the continuing controversy surrounding Ray Burke, a controversial politician whom the Taoiseach had appointed to the sensitive post of Minister for Foreign Affairs. Ahern and Burke had been the two leading members in the Haughey old guard on the Fianna Fáil side of the government. Although they were very different person-alities, they had been close friends for almost two decades. There had been a whiff of scandal around Burke since the early 1970s, and it was widely known that there had been a Garda investigation into his activities. It had long been rumoured that builders Brennan and McGowan had given him his house for free and there were persistent whisperings about his links with the builders. An ebullient man, by times aggressive and by times cynically witty, Burke had a 'tough guy' image that contrasted with Ahern's agreeable and conciliatory public persona.

Burke became an immediate political liability for the coalition and a real problem for Harney. Over the previous eighteen months numerous stories had appeared in the media, mainly in the *Sunday Business Post*, concerning allegations of planning corruption being made by an elderly man called James Gogarty. Gogarty had come forward when a £10,000 reward was offered (by Dublin environmentalists, through a firm of Newry solicitors, Donnelly Neary and Donnelly) for information about planning corruption in the Republic. Gogarty made a statement to the solicitors alleging that he had given Burke a large sum of money to secure planning favours on behalf of the company he worked for—JMSE.

In the middle of the election campaign, at a press conference, Ahern was asked about the allegation by Geraldine Kennedy of *The Irish Times*. Without naming Burke, Ahern replied, 'I have gone to that member and gone through it in detail on four separate occasions as the allegations continued to come up in one newspaper over a period of 17 months. Insofar as I possibly can be, I am satisfied.' Burke was not named at the press conference, but Ahern said pointedly, 'We all know who we are talking about.'[8] The Fianna Fáil leader's apparent denial of the allegation against Burke defused the issue during the election campaign and it merited only a brief mention on page eight of the following day's *The Irish Times*.

After the election was over, but before the Dáil met, Ahern asked his chief whip, Dermot Ahern, to travel to London to meet the CEO of JMSE, Joseph Murphy junior, to find out whether there was any truth in the rumours about Burke. On 24 June, two days before the government was formed, Dermot Ahern met with Murphy jnr, who assured him that no money had been paid to Burke in return for political or planning favours. The relieved chief whip told Murphy that his party leader been questioned about such rumours and had responded by stating that he had spoken to Burke on a number of occasions and Burke had categorically denied there was any truth in them. It subsequently emerged that Bertie Ahern had done more than speak to Burke and send his chief whip to London: he had actually conducted his own inquiry by speaking to Michael Bailey, a builder and one of the key figures in the saga. Gogarty had alleged that Bailey was present when the money was handed over to Burke. However, Bertie Ahern told his chief whip nothing of his contacts with Bailey when he asked him to travel to London to investigate the matter.[9]

Ahern nonetheless went ahead and selected Ray Burke as his Minister for Foreign Affairs. He took the precaution of telling Harney about the rumours before the formation of the government; she agreed to back his selection of Burke. It was a decision that would take the gloss off Ahern and put serious pressure on Harney in the first few months of the coalition. Within weeks of the government's formation the story of Dermot Ahern's trip to London was made public. The Taoiseach gave an interview to Gerald Barry on RTÉ radio's 'This Week' programme, claiming he had gone 'to extraordinary lengths' to resolve Gogarty's allegations before appointing Burke to the Cabinet. Saying he had been 'up every tree in North Dublin' in his inquiries he added, 'I know the circumstances about it and I am quite satisfied with the matter.' Harney then rowed into the debate and publicly defended Burke, to the horror of many in the PDs.

'In reaction to the image of the PDs as a head-hunting party, Mary Harney did not distance the party from Fianna Fáil quickly enough when it came to Ray Burke,' says McDowell.[10] Harney herself now acknowledges this. 'When the Ray Burke issue arose first I was clear in my mind that we could not say to Fianna Fáil, "this one has to go or that one has to go". I was determined that we were not going to start off in Government by looking for someone's head.'[11] Harney's problem was that instead of going away, the Burke issue got steadily worse.

First, Burke was forced to issue a public statement, on 7 August, confirming that he had in fact received a payment of £30,000 from James Gogarty in 1989. Far from ending the controversy as the government hoped, Burke's statement simply fuelled demands for a full explanation. On 10 September—when the Dáil was recalled to debate the McCracken report into the activities of Charles Haughey and revelations about the Ansbacher accounts—Burke made a personal statement about the Gogarty payment:

> 'I have come here today to defend my personal integrity, the integrity of my party, of this Government and the honour of this House. I have also come here to reassure the public and in particular my constituents that I have done nothing wrong.'[12]

The pressure on Burke did not let up and Harney grew increasingly worried about the stability of the coalition. 'I said to Ahern in September, "This can't go on any longer. It will destroy the Government. Burke just has to go".'[13] She didn't have long to wait because in early October *The Irish Times* published a story alleging that, years earlier, Burke had issued 'passports for sale'.[14]

On 7 October, the day of his brother's funeral, Burke resigned, not just from the Cabinet but also from the Dáil. The decision to resign his Dáil seat initially left Fianna Fáil reeling, but the PDs breathed a sigh of relief. Any further pressure could have crushed the coalition before it had even had time to bed-down. As the Burke saga was progressing, PD prodding had prompted Ahern to establish the Moriarty Tribunal, to further investigate the McCracken report findings regarding Haughey and Michael Lowry. As Minister for Enterprise and Employment, Harney conducted her own inquiries into the Ansbacher accounts, which had been uncovered during the trawl through Haughey's affairs. Under the terms of the Companies Act this inquiry led to a full-scale investigation into all Ansbacher accounts.

The resignation of Burke precipitated a by-election the following March, which saw Labour's Sean Ryan win back the seat he had lost to Fianna Fáil in the general election. Importantly, from a PD point of view, it was another disastrous electoral performance for the party. The PDs were not very strong in north Dublin and the candidate, Finian Fallon, polled only 513 votes. It was a far cry from the heady days of a little more than a decade earlier when there were traffic jams on the roads of north Dublin caused by the PD meetings. Following on from the terrible performance in June, it raised questions about the future viability of the party.

Harney put the Burke episode out of her mind as she geared herself for the coalition's first Budget, due in December. A number of pledges had already been made about what would be contained in that Budget, but she wanted to ensure that it set the government on a radical and irreversible movement towards lower taxation. She needn't have worried because McCreevy was equally determined to take this tack. When it was unveiled by McCreevy on 3 December, the Budget proved to be a PD dream. The standard rate of income tax was cut from 26 per cent to 24 per cent, while the top rate came down from 48 per cent to 46 per cent. Corporation tax came down from 40 per cent to 32 per cent, and most surprisingly of all capital gains tax was halved from 40 per cent to 20 per cent. Although the corporation tax cut was actually a result of the rainbow government's agreement with the EU to phase the Irish rate right down to 12.5 per cent, the whole package announced by McCreevy represented a huge step on the road to realising the PD tax-cutting agenda. The Budget did not ignore social needs, providing solid increases in old-age pension and social welfare entitlements.

The media reaction, both positive and negative, stressed the input of the PDs. 'Perhaps the most satisfied person in the Dáil chamber was Ms Mary Harney,' said the disapproving editorial in *The Irish Times*. 'Her party had almost sunk into the embrace of Fianna Fáil without a trace. But the thrust of Mr McCreevy's give-away owes more to the philosophy of the Progressive Democrats than to that of his own party. The PDs live on for a little longer.'[15]

The *Irish Independent* greeted the Budget with a loud headline that echoed its controversial pre-election editorial: 'It's payback time' trumpeted the newspaper, whose business editor, Brendan Keenan, noted that the Budget marked a decisive break with the past as tax concessions were almost twice the spending increases. 'For once in an Irish Government politics triumphed over official caution. The Progressive Democrats needs were too great,' he wrote. It was certainly true that McCreevy, egged on by the PDs, had taken the decision to halve capital gains tax against the strong advice of his officials, who believed tax revenue would plummet as a result. McCreevy refused to accept their arguments, however, maintaining that revenue from capital gains tax would actually increase as a result of increased economic activity. McCreevy would be proved right, in spectacular fashion, in the years that followed. 'If it works in terms of political popularity and economic success, there is no reason not to expect more of the same,' added Keenan.[16] The PDs were hugely pleased with the thrust of the Budget. 'There will be PD babies born all over the country in nine months' time,' joked Liz O'Donnell, reflecting the mood of joy in the party, which was now on the road to implementing its core policies with only four TDs in the Dáil out of 166. Of course, that had only been made possible because McCreevy was every bit as committed to PD economic policies as the PDs themselves. That commitment delivered a succession of Budgets which, as far as their supporters were concerned, justified the very existence of the PDs.

In his second Budget McCreevy focused the bulk of his tax cuts on the lower paid and exempted completely the first £120 of weekly income tax. This measure served to make work more attractive than welfare for people on low incomes and provided real encouragement for the trade unions to sign up to a new national agreement. A truly reforming element in this Budget was a shift from tax allowances to tax credits. This was something that Labour had always wanted to do, but had never been able to implement in government because of the potential cost to the Exchequer. A booming economy allowed McCreevy to implement a measure *The Irish Times* editorial described as 'justified, equitable and overdue'.[17]

For his third Budget McCreevy once again produced a big idea, with Harney's strong backing: the individualisation of the tax code ended the favourable tax treatment of families where one spouse worked in the home and gave significant benefits to those families where both spouses were in the paid workforce. It was a big shift in favour of better-off, double-income families and proved hugely controversial.

There was a great deal of anxiety in Fianna Fáil over the thrust of the Budget, with a succession of back-benchers attacking it publicly. It subsequently emerged that some of its critics had been put up to it by the Fianna Fáil press office, and the Taoiseach was believed to be lurking in the background.[18] McCreevy weathered the storm by promising to increase welfare benefits for families and it gradually abated, assisted by the strong support of the trade unions for tax policies that suited their members. In his next Budget, for 2001, McCreevy pleased everybody in a huge give-away that was widely seen as an election Budget. For example, child benefit was increased by more than 50 per cent in an effort to mollify the critics of individualisation.

With tax cuts making it more attractive to enter the jobs market than remain on welfare, Harney now moved to introduce policies designed to encourage people back into the workforce. The Employment Action Plan, which provoked an incredibly negative reaction from the Opposition, was based around a change in the regulations to ensure that after six months on welfare a person had to undertake a training course with FÁS or else lose their benefits.

Harney had one very important asset in the Department of Enterprise and Employment: the secretary general, Paul Haran, was not only one of the brightest young civil servants in the system, he was also sympathetic to her political perspective. Eight years earlier Haran had applied for and won the post of special advisor to Des O'Malley when he was minister in the same Department. Haran was a firm believer in competition, free markets and the capacity of the individual to better him or herself if given a chance by the State. A committed public servant and a straight-talking Dubliner with a passionate interest in hurling, he defied the stereotype of PD ideologue. His energy and intelligence were a vital asset to Harney as he helped her deliver on an agenda that went far beyond her own Department.

'The individualisation and the tax credits were part of our agenda,' says Harney. 'Ruairi Quinn didn't even bring in the tax credits. On individualisation we had to convince Charlie about it. Paul Haran did a lot of work for me. Those two things were as fundamental as the cuts in the tax rates. Remember capital gains was halved. Finance

calculated a huge cost for it in year one but it brought in a huge amount
of money. All that side of it worked well. That was fulfilling the agenda
and the ethos of the party, but it wasn't getting us any votes.'[19]

There was a wide belief that the give-away Budget of 2001 was designed
as a platform for a general election, but no election was held that year.
Ahern and Harney always maintained that their intention was to go for a
full five-year term, but the outbreak of foot-and-mouth disease in the
spring and the subsequent restrictions on movement necessary to stop
the spread of the disease put paid to any notion that an election might be
held that year. Whether by accident or design, the coalition had no choice
but to see out its five-year term. The result was another give-away
bonanza Budget for 2002.

One electoral contest that the government was obliged to hold was a
referendum on the Nice Treaty, which provided for changes in the way
the EU conducted its business. In the run-up to that election the PDs
and Charlie McCreevy sent mixed signals to the electorate about their
vision for Ireland's future in Europe. In July 2001 Harney made a speech
to the American Bar Association in Dublin and emphasised the things
that Ireland and the United States had in common.

'What really makes Ireland attractive to corporate America is the kind
of economy which we have created here. When Americans come here
they find a country that believes in the incentive power of low
taxation. They find a country that believes in economic liberalisation.
They find a country that believes in essential regulation but not over-
regulation. On looking further afield in Europe, they find also that not
every European country believes in all of these things.'

She then went on to coin a phrase that was to have a considerable
resonance in the years ahead.

'Geographically we are closer to Berlin than Boston. Spiritually we are
probably a lot closer to Boston than Berlin.'[20]

The 'Boston or Berlin' speech had the unintended impact of contributing
to the embarrassing defeat of the government's referendum proposal on
the Nice Treaty. This, in turn, led to even more uncertainty as the curtain
fell on the 2001 political production of the PD–Fianna Fáil coalition. No
one was quite sure what the next act would bring.

Chapter 17 ~

THE PRODIGAL RETURNS

The McCreevy Budgets cemented the coalition with the PDs and ensured that it survived a series of events that in other circumstances might easily have wrecked it. Most of the problems that arose for that first Fianna Fáil–PD government were a direct result of the tribunals of inquiry established in the autumn of 1997, at the insistence of the PDs. From Moriarty and Flood came sensational and astonishing revelations about the activities of senior Fianna Fáil figures in the Haughey era. The potentially destabilising factor was the role played by Bertie Ahern, Haughey's *protégé*. Nor was it just Ahern's actions in the past that counted; his equivocations in the 1997–2002 period were a constant source of tension. Even in the debate on the McCracken report, in September 1997, Ahern displayed an ambiguity in relation to Haughey that the PDs found disturbing. 'In many important areas valuable service by someone of immense ability will be recalled. For the positive things he did he will always be held in high regard by many people,' was Ahern's verdict on Haughey.[1]

If the Taoiseach's residual loyalty to his patron was understandable, his equivocation in relation to his own role in the events being investigated was more worrying. In the same debate on the McCracken report, Ahern gave a hostage to fortune when he referred to the issue of the party leader's allowance. Throughout the 1980s there had been recurring rumours in political circles that Haughey was pocketing a large portion of the State grant allotted to political leaders to run their parties. It was, in fact, one of the factors that had first prompted O'Malley to distrust Haughey and question his motives and his methods. When Ahern was asked about the £1 million paid over to Haughey during the course of his period as leader, he responded, 'Insofar as I could be with little available records I am satisfied, having spoken to the person who administered the account, that it was used for bona fide party purposes, that the cheques were prepared by that person and countersigned by another senior party member.'[2] What Ahern did not divulge to the Dáil was that the other *'senior party member'* who normally countersigned the cheques was none other than himself. At that stage he persisted with his contention that the account was used for bona fide party purposes. He later claimed that he had signed hundreds of blank cheques for his party leader when it emerged that a significant sum of money from the account had ended up in Haughey's personal account, funding his expensive shirt-buying and wining-and-dining habits.

On foot of tribunal discoveries in relation to the infamous Ansbacher accounts, Harney, through her Department, had instigated an inquiry under the Companies Act. That investigation would bring her into direct conflict with some of the most powerful business interests in the country, but she refused to be bullied into restricting the scope of the inquiry, even though it took years to reach a conclusion. It was the presence of the PDs in government that led to the establishment of the various tribunals and the consequences resulting therefrom; elimination of corruption had always been a key element of the party's programme and its political philosophy.

With the government's first Budget out of the way, the increasing tempo of events in the North demanded more and more of the Taoiseach's time. Just weeks after Ahern was installed as Taoiseach a new IRA cease-fire duly followed and Sinn Féin was admitted to talks with all the other Northern parties, chaired by former US senator, George Mitchell. This process continued until Easter 1998 when the Good Friday Agreement was signed. Liz O'Donnell represented the PDs at those talks and found it uplifting to be involved in the process. 'The Good Friday Agreement was negotiated in different strands. I did strand two dealing with North–South issues. When the whole thing came together I was shocked at the totality of it. It was a fundamental change, like starting Northern Irish society right from the beginning again. It was a unique model of sharing power.'[3]

Part of the deal hammered out was that the territorial claim to the North in Articles 2 and 3 of the Irish Constitution would be abolished and replaced with provisions expressing an aspiration to unity. This was a change the PDs and the Opposition parties had long been campaigning for, but Fianna Fáil, the Republican party, was reluctant to contemplate such a move outside of an over-arching agreement. Ahern skilfully steered the requisite changes through his parliamentary party and secured the endorsement of the Fianna Fáil National Executive. In the subsequent referendum, over 90 per cent of voters supported the constitutional change. All the Dáil parties—with the obvious exception of Sinn Féin— supported a Yes vote, but the PDs notched up another item of long-standing party policy.

The referendum was barely completed when Fianna Fáil's past returned once more to rattle the coalition. Vincent Browne reported in *Magill* magazine that Fitzwilton plc had paid £30,000 in cash to Ray Burke in June 1989, within a few days of the £30,000 payment allegedly made by James Gogarty. It emerged that the Flood Tribunal was investigating the Fitzwilton payment, said to have been made through a subsidiary called Rennicks, and that Fianna Fáil had already made statements and handed in documents in relation to it.[4] A political row immediately erupted about non-disclosure of this payment to the PDs, not least because it emerged that Ahern had not kept Harney informed about the development when it had first come to his attention. Amid the political uproar that attended the revelation, the government—at the insistence of the PDs—decided to widen the terms of reference of the Flood Tribunal to allow it to investigate *all* payments made to Ray Burke or any other politician and not just those concerned with the planning process.

Over the following two years the same pattern was repeated many times: the coalition achieved high popularity ratings as the economic boom went from strength to strength, but periodically another skeleton would clatter noisily from the closet and give the coalition a dose of the jitters. Later in 1998 the 'skeleton' was the issue of Haughey's tax liability for the payments made to him by Ben Dunne. Haughey was served with a tax assessment of £2 million by the Revenue Commissioners, but on appeal to the Tax Appeals Commissioners the bill was reduced to zero. There was a furore in the Dáil when it emerged that the Appeals Commissioner who had made the decision was Ahern's brother-in-law, Ronan Kelly. Not only that, but Kelly had been appointed to his position by Ahern in 1994. This damaging information was sprung on the Dáil by Pat Rabbitte and, for once, Ahern was caught on the hop.[5]

In January 1999 another voice from the past spoke up. Intermittent stories had appeared in the media in the autumn of 1998 about property developer Tom Gilmartin, a Sligoman living in Luton, who had reportedly talked to the Flood Tribunal about a payment of £50,000 he had made to Pádraig Flynn in June 1989. It seemed, however, that Gilmartin was unwilling to give evidence at the tribunal—until he was provoked into doing so by Flynn himself. In a startling performance on 'The Late Late Show' in January 1999, Flynn dismissed Gilmartin's allegations and said that the developer was unwell. That prompted an immediate and furious reaction from Gilmartin, who said he was now willing to give evidence at the tribunal. He also claimed that he had informed Ahern about the £50,000 payment to Flynn during one of a number of meetings.[6] In response, Ahern said he had met Gilmartin only once, but as political pressure mounted he revised his statement and conceded that he had met Gilmartin on a few occasions. Ahern was then forced to submit himself to a long question-and-answer session in the Dáil about the matter, but again he came through without suffering any serious embarrassment.[7]

Harney managed to live with Ahern's amnesia in relation to the blank cheques and the meetings with Gilmartin, but she was presented with a more difficult problem a couple of months later during the so-called Sheedy affair. This was a complicated sequence of events that led to the unprecedented resignations of a Supreme Court judge, a High Court judge and a senior judicial officer. It began with the release from jail of a young architect, Philip Sheedy, who had received a four-year sentence for dangerous driving causing death. However, Sheedy was released nearly three years early by Judge Cyril Kelly; Kelly was not the original sentencing judge. It then emerged that Supreme Court judge Hugh O'Flaherty had asked the county registrar to put the case back into the list for hearing. In the resulting furore, O'Flaherty and Kelly were effectively forced into resignation by the government. In the dramatic twenty-four hours before he resigned, Ahern's then partner, Celia Larkin, visited O'Flaherty at his Ballsbridge home along with a number of other well-wishers. To crown it all the *Sunday Tribune* security correspondent, Catherine Cleary, uncovered the fact that Ahern had made representations on Sheedy's behalf, asking that he be released early.[8]

Luckily for Ahern he had informed Harney about the matter a few days before the news broke, but a row developed between Taoiseach and Tánaiste when he publicly dismissed her concerns and denied that she had asked him to make a statement to the Dáil on the issue. Harney refused to attend a Cabinet meeting and for twenty-four hours it looked as though the coalition would crack.

'Mary really felt let down by Bertie on the Sheedy issue,' recalls Paul Mackay. 'She was really upset, so she phoned McCreevy to tell him the coalition was in trouble.' McCreevy's response was immediate. "For God's sake don't do anything foolish. I'll come straight over to you," he said.' McCreevy then hot-footed it around from Merrion Street to the Department of Enterprise and Employment in Kildare Street. 'The two of them had a long chat in her office while the rest of us waited outside. McCreevy then went off and sorted it out with Bertie and got him to agree to deal with the issue in the Dáil.'[9] Ahern went back into the Dáil and answered questions from the Opposition about the affair. It was a typical Ahern performance in which he maintained that he had merely made representations on behalf of Sheedy, as he would for anybody else who asked him. 'The closest the coalition came to breaking up was over the Sheedy issue,' says Harney. 'He told me he was going to go in and tell the Dáil all about the representations that had been made to him. When he didn't do it, I was bloody livid.'[10] It was a close shave, but the government survived.

The Gilmartin story scuppered any chance Flynn might have had of remaining on as a European Commissioner. It also put his daughter, Beverley Cooper-Flynn, in an embarrassing position in the Dáil. She was already under something of a cloud because of unanswered questions about her role as a financial advisor with National Irish Bank before she entered politics. The bank had facilitated a tax-evasion scheme based in the Isle of Man, which was the subject of a Department of Enterprise and Employment investigation and a number of court cases. When Fianna Fáil accepted an Opposition motion censuring Pádraig Flynn for refusing to give any explanation for the Gilmartin donation, Cooper-Flynn refused to vote for the motion and lost the whip for a period as a result. In a debate on 10 February, Des O'Malley took the opportunity to make a few observations on standards in political life. He referred to the climate under Haughey and pointed out that many people had left Fianna Fáil because of it. 'However, there were many who did not leave, many who felt totally comfortable in the kind of party which Charles Haughey had created. Among them was Mr Pádraig Flynn.' O'Malley recalled that when he had been drummed out of Fianna Fáil in 1985, Flynn had 'addressed the nation through an RTÉ camera and pronounced that my conduct was "unbecoming a member of Fianna Fáil". Now it is Mr Flynn's turn to be dumped upon.'[11]

Flynn was not the only one being dumped on at this juncture. The PDs may have had an influence on government policy out of all proportion to their numbers, but the party was still smarting from the 1997 election disaster. Just after McCreevy unveiled his 'PD Budget' in

December 1997, the party was rocked by a short-lived controversy over its finances. It arose when sensitive financial documents from Des O'Malley's old files, which listed donations to the PDs in their early years, were inadvertently thrown into a skip outside party headquarters. The documents were found and passed on to the *Sunday Business Post*, which, naturally, made a song-and-dance out of the information.[12] The juiciest detail was that the party had received a £12,000 donation from the Smurfit Group in 1992. The controversy did not amount to much—all parties sought and obtained donations from the business sector—but it was deeply embarrassing nonetheless. The fact that such sensitive files of a former party leader had been dumped in a skip reflected the disorganised state of the party.

> 'Des was devastated by the episode. He felt he had let down people who had given donations in confidence,' says Mackay. 'He wrote to all the people on the list apologising for the incident, but in fact a lot of them replied to say they were honoured to be included among the party supporters. A few were upset about it, but it was one of those things that was not nearly as damaging as we all thought at the time.'[13]

Things went from bad to worse the following year. At a by-election in Cork South Central in October 1998, the party polled just 971 votes. To win just 2 per cent of the vote in a constituency where the party had previously won a seat in three successive general elections (Pearse Wyse; Pat Cox) caused a lot of soul-searching. The media once again began to question whether the PDs could survive as a separate political entity and some within the party even began to contemplate a merger with Fianna Fáil.

A meeting of the PD General Council was held in the Green Isle Hotel on 10 November 1998 to consider the party's future. Almost 170 members turned up, shook off the mood of depression and expressed a determination to soldier on. Harney emerged from that meeting in a fighting mood and declared: 'If the Progressive Democrats go under, I will go under with them.' She certainly had no intention of allowing the party to wither away or merge. 'This party has no intention of merging with any other party,' she stated.[14]

A few months later the Flynn saga gave Harney an opening to explore a bold long-term strategy to inject new life into the PDs. When Flynn was ruled out from reappointment as European Commissioner, there was a tussle among senior Fianna Fáil people for the coveted job. Brian Cowen, then Minister for Health, had his eye on it, as did Minister for Agriculture, Joe Walsh. However, there was a strong argument for not giving the job to a TD, for fear the government might lose a vital seat in the resulting by-election. Ahern was urged to consider former minister Máire Geoghegan Quinn, who had retired from the Dáil, but in the end he opted for his trusted Attorney-General, David Byrne. That was the decision Harney wanted, and had manoeuvred for months to achieve. She then insisted that as Fianna Fáil had taken the Commissioner's job, it was the turn of the PDs to appoint the Attorney-General. The game-plan was that through this mechanism she would be able to install Michael McDowell into the Cabinet and attempt to heal fully the old wounds of the PDs.

Of course, everything hinged on Ahern offering the EU post to his Attorney-General. David Byrne was highly respected both inside and outside Fianna Fáil, but he was not a powerful party figure with claims on the post. 'To make the Attorney-Generalship vacant required David Byrne to go to Brussels. Harney and McCreevy were conspiring at this outcome for ages. After Flynn imploded on 'The Late Late' the thing gradually became clear,' says one insider.[15]

At this stage McDowell was still smarting from the debacle of 1997 and had no involvement with the PDs. 'I said to Niamh in 1986 that I'd do ten years. Perforce in the tenth year I was out and I had no thought of coming back,' says McDowell. He had formally left the PDs a few months after his election defeat, bitterly disappointed with the party for the way he lost his seat and feeling disillusioned with politics. Losing his seat twice was a traumatic experience—particularly as each time he lost, the party he had helped to create got into government. Harney, though, never gave up trying to lure him back. In 1998 she asked him to chair a committee on company law, which led to the establishment of the Office of the Director of Corporate Enforcement. Then he was asked to do a report on the Central Bank and the issue of compliance in the financial services industry. He took on both tasks as an interesting challenge, but had exhibited no desire to return to the political fold.

'In May 1999 I was approached about rejoining Fine Gael and I agreed to meet John Bruton and Mark FitzGerald for dinner. Amazingly, on the very evening I was to have dinner with them, I got a phone call from an intermediary raising the question of my taking the Attorney-Generalship,' says McDowell.[16] It was an offer he simply couldn't refuse. The position is one that any barrister would covet, but for McDowell in particular, with his passion for political life and ambition to reform the legal system, it was utterly irresistible.

'I was keen to get Michael back, very keen. From my own point of view and also from the party's point of view, I knew his presence at Cabinet would make a big difference,' says Harney.

Senior PD figures consulted by Harney before she made the offer encouraged her to obtain a commitment from McDowell to rejoin the party and run in the next election, but the party leader had her own ideas. 'I didn't do it like that. I wanted to do it in the spirit of friendliness because things had been bad between us after the '97 election. Paul Mackay and others said to me, "That was foolish. You should have done a deal." But I think I was right not to.'[17]

The political impact of McDowell's return was to stabilise the coalition, steady nerves after the Sheedy affair and boost morale in the PD camp. 'The prospect of an early general election has receded because of the political horse trading engaged in by Bertie Ahern and Mary Harney,' wrote Denis Coghlan in *The Irish Times*. 'The Progressive Democrats were cock-a-hoop at Leinster House. They had pulled off a double whammy: getting Michael McDowell installed as Attorney-General while blocking Máire Geoghegan Quinn as European Commissioner. Ah, the sweet smell of success. A former minister and critic who had dismissed the Progressive Democrats as a threat to democracy was elbowed out of the way. And a new and powerful voice was secured in Cabinet.'[18]

Coghlan correctly forecast that McDowell's promotion in mid-July would be followed by a successful review of the Fianna Fáil–PD Programme for Government. That paved the way for a new National Plan, with an unprecedented level of infrastructural investment, which was in turn followed by another national wage agreement, underpinned by further tax cuts in the Budget for 2000.

McDowell was clearly delighted to be in a senior, if unelected, government position for the first time in his political career and he threw himself into the job with gusto. The fact that Harney had brought him in from the political wilderness did not prompt an early return to the PDs, however, and his relationship with the Tánaiste remained strained. 'My biggest aim was not to be sucked back into a 1997 debacle. Effectively I had to say to the PDs, "I won't go back into politics unless I have a clear guarantee that what happened in 1997 would not happen again." So I didn't go back at that stage.'[19]

As time went on there was even some speculation that he might join Fianna Fáil. McDowell was considering no such thing—he was instead working on another political blueprint. In the autumn of 2000 he produced a policy document that suggested the PDs should transform itself into a new political entity, with him in a key position to help direct its fortunes. For a start, McDowell proposed dropping the name Progressive Democrats, which he had disliked from the very beginning. 'To create the new wave, there has to be a break with the past. The PD label is dated and carries a lot of negative baggage of economic élitism, Fianna Fáil factionalism, niche ambitions, revisionism and smallness. On the positive side, its image is liberal, honest and straightforward—and as having had many of its good ideas stolen.' He then went on to propose a rebranding. 'The new name has to be catchy and punchy. Rather than have a vague and meaningless double-barrelled adjectival name, it is suggested that a single, strong word be adopted. The name Radical Party is suggested. It connotes change, strength, thoroughness, youth, vision, vigour, rigour and vitality. It is a label which attracts youth and reformers. It suggests a strong agenda.'[20]

On top of that he suggested a novel concept of political flexibility.

'Local and regional politics demand the capacity to set up an alliance of sister parties to contest elections. For instance, the Radical Party could have as a sister party in Dublin city and county, a Dublin First party with membership overlap and the potential for different memberships. The same could apply to other regions. Flexibility could also include European-constituency parties. Pat Cox could have a Munster Euro-party with common membership with the Radical Party in that region. Marian Harkin could organise a political movement in Connacht–Ulster and combine with the Radical Party to fight a Dáil seat. Separate local sister parties could organise at the same time in Galway and Sligo to fight the local elections, and combine, say, for BMW regional purposes. By introducing a new variable geometry to Irish politics, the Radical Party could be the anchor-point for a much broader base. One of the features of the existing larger parties is the extent to which they have become a political franchise operated locally by independent organisations and figures. By concentrating the efforts of the Radical Party as a franchise for general elections and creating flexibility for European, local and regional politics, a new set of opportunities could be created.'

As if all that was not jaw-dropping enough for the PDs, McDowell went on to propose that he should be appointed as president of the party, with responsibility to control and direct the other officers and employees. He also proposed that the party president would be responsible for the transformation, development and expansion of the party into an 'effective political movement'. Harney would remain as party leader and its main representative in the Oireachtas and government, but the party president would have the key role in shaping its policy and its image.[21]

The McDowell initiative had been encouraged by Harney, but other senior figures in the party were dubious in the extreme. Des O'Malley and Liz O'Donnell were not prepared to accept the core proposals in the McDowell plan and accordingly recommended its rejection. A special meeting of the parliamentary party and the National Executive endorsed that view and, to the disappointment of many party members, McDowell refused to return for the party's annual conference in November of that year.

'Michael wanted to take over. I was dead against that,' says Liz O'Donnell. 'It was a grab for power. I always saw the value of Michael, but the notion of changing the constitution of the party to make the leader a leader only in name and effectively making Michael the leader was just not on.' O'Donnell recalls that McDowell was 'still quite offside' with the party for most of his period as Attorney-General.

> 'At times he seemed to be closer to Fianna Fáil than he was to us. He was bruised and blamed everybody else for 1997 and erased his own involvement as the author of that document which sank us. We have never had this out but some things are too painful to revisit, obviously. It was a massive disappointment and we were devastated to lose him. Nobody took any pleasure in that because he is a great strength.'[22]

'I wanted to encourage Michael to come back so he produced a document,' says Harney. 'He wanted a regional party with people like Pat Cox and Marian Harkin being associated with the party in Dublin. When news of the plan leaked out to the media it caused a lot of problems. I remember Des got his eyes on it and went berserk. Anyway it didn't go anywhere.'[23]

There was deep disappointment among PD members that McDowell had not returned to the party and it seemed as if the party would have to reconcile itself to managing without its intellectual driving force. Two PD government advisors, Maurice Roche and Oliver O'Connor, expended a lot of effort talking to McDowell to try to persuade him to come back. 'There was some tension between Maurice and McDowell over the 1997 manifesto debacle, but Maurice always maintained that McDowell's return would electrify the party and jump-start it into recovery,' says O'Connor. In the summer of 2001, Harney was prepared to accept that it was unlikely he would be a PD candidate in the next election. Her admission on RTÉ's 'The Week in Politics' came after reports that a constituency convention in Dublin South East had been postponed and possible candidates had been dissuaded from establishing a base there in the hope that the Attorney-General would change his mind.[24]

As 2001 drew to a close the future of the PDs looked decidedly bleak and the media was happily engaged in its traditional sport of predicting the party's demise. To be fair, there was every reason to believe that the party might not survive the election in 2002. For a start, Des O'Malley had announced his intention of retiring and Bobby Molloy was anxious to do the same. That would leave the party with just two sitting TDs— O'Donnell and Harney—going into the campaign. On top of that the party had slipped down to a paltry 3 per cent in the polls. It was therefore understandable that the party faithful were bracing themselves for the worst.

Despite everything, Harney did not give up and was even searching for new candidates. In particular, she set out to woo the leader of the Irish Farmers' Association, Tom Parlon, who had let it be known that he was interested in a political career. On a personal level things were going very well for Harney and in November 2001 she married Brian Geoghegan, a director of IBEC and chairman of the State agency FÁS.

'I had made up my mind if we could get Bobby, McDowell and Parlon to run, even if we could get two out of three, we'd have a reasonable platform going into the election. Des wasn't going to be running and there were huge doubts over Bobby. We didn't have McDowell and everybody was forecasting we would only get two seats. There was a stage when I wondered would Liz bloody well even go. So I said to Brian, if we could get two out of Bobby, McDowell and Parlon, I'd be really happy.'

The tide turned when Parlon unexpectedly decided to give it a go.

'We were away on our honeymoon when Tom Parlon rang me to say he would run for the PDs. I honestly didn't think we would get him. A few weeks earlier he had come to my house one Saturday for about five hours. I told him that Fine Gael would be in Opposition in the next Dáil and he would be a nobody in a big party. I didn't have huge hope. I thought at most it would be 40 per cent. And then he rang me when I was on my honeymoon in Kenya after Christmas. I was amazed as I actually thought he was going to go for Fine Gael.'[25]

Over the Christmas break Molloy also agreed to Harney's entreaties to run one more time rather than leave the party in the lurch. Then in January 2002 the party's fortunes took a decisive turn for the better when the prodigal McDowell returned.

'Parlon's decision was a great stroke of luck that helped the McDowell thing along. McDowell had wanted to do a joint pact so that the two of them would come together. He even arranged a meeting with Parlon in Doheny and Nesbitt's to discuss it. Of course, Parlon didn't want anything to do with that kind of arrangement. He wanted to be his own man. So Parlon formally joined on a Sunday in January 2002, and on the following Tuesday evening Michael came to see me in the office in Kildare Street in the Department of Enterprise, Trade and Employment and that was that.'

At that meeting, which was also attended by Mackay, Molloy, O'Donnell and Gerard Hogan, a barrister, it was agreed that McDowell would come back as president of the PDs with responsibility for the organisation. Critically, though, the party president would be appointed by the leader and not elected by the organisation. That arrangement meant there was no doubt about who was leader of the PDs.

Chapter 18 ⌒

UP THE POLE

T he return of the prodigal McDowell and the arrival of Parlon gave the PDs a huge lift for their annual conference in February 2002. With an election looming in a matter of months, Harney tried to capitalise on the positive mood in her televised keynote address. 'Tonight I say to the Irish people. Give us your support. Give us the chance to work for you in government. We have shown what we can do with four seats. Let us show you what we can do with eight.'[1] People in the political world gave Harney full marks for bravura, but nobody outside the party believed there was any chance that the PDs could actually win eight seats. In fact, the prevailing consensus in political circles and in the media was that on foot of O'Malley's decision to retire, the party would struggle to hold its four seats; many commentators felt that the PDs would be reduced to two seats or less.

However, the target of eight seats was not a figure plucked from the ether. The PDs were already planning carefully for the election everybody knew would have to take place in May because the coalition's term of office expired in early June. Bertie Ahern and Mary Harney had pledged their government would last for five years, so everybody knew the approximate date of the election far in advance. Acutely conscious of the election disaster of 1997, the PDs were determined to run a smooth and well-planned campaign. One decision that had been taken very early on by the parliamentary party and the National Executive was that the PDs would fight the campaign as an independent party. The party would not participate in a pact with Fianna Fáil, or anybody else. Harney and her advisors were sure that one of the contributing factors to the party's disastrous performance five years earlier was that it had been marginalised after agreeing to a pre-election pact with Fianna Fáil.[2]

Even though relations between the two parties had been exceptionally good and robust enough to survive a number of crises during the coalition's term of office, the PDs decided that the only way they could succeed in holding on to what they had, never mind increasing their number of seats, was to fight the election as a distinct and separate entity. In terms of a campaign platform, the economic record of the government was the obvious trump card for both Fianna Fáil and the PDs. The country had experienced an unprecedented economic boom for the previous five years and even though there had been a slight downturn at the end of 2001, it was a remarkably healthy position from which to fight an election. Therefore the pressing question for the PDs was how to make a well-defined appeal to the electorate.

On the organisational front a number of new key personnel had joined the party over the previous four years. A new general secretary had been appointed at the end of 1998. He was the former chief executive of Western Development, John Higgins, a Mayoman and brother of Fine Gael TD, Jim Higgins. He arrived in Dublin in December 1998 to find a skeleton staff at party headquarters and no candidates in place for the local elections, due just six months later. 'I spent six months pleading with people to run and eventually we got 66 candidates into the field and won 32 seats.' Still, at the end of 2001 he was acutely conscious how difficult things could be for the party with an election imminent. 'Before Christmas 2001 we were facing the prospect of an election with just two outgoing TDs, Mary Harney and Liz O'Donnell. Then the Parlon thing happened, McDowell came back, Kate Walsh joined in Kildare and Bobby Molloy announced he would run. We were back in with a chance.'[3]

In the spring of 2002 Stephen O'Byrnes and another former party press officer, Ray Gordon, were brought back to provide advice in their new role as public affairs consultants. On the suggestion of O'Byrnes, market research was commissioned to measure how voters viewed the party's standing in the outgoing government, and to test-market the best way of positioning it for the election ahead.

A series of focus groups was set up involving people who were not necessarily PD voters, but who were not hostile to the party; 'non-rejectors' was the term used by the market researchers to describe them. The focus groups perceived the government as overwhelmingly Fianna Fáil, but the junior partner was seen as making a vital contribution to job creation and cutting tax, and Mary Harney was identified as one of its key ministers.

With the economy beginning to slow down in late 2001 and early 2002 another view to emerge strongly from the focus groups was that the

FF–PD team was seen as best qualified to navigate the country through the uncertain waters ahead. According to O'Byrnes, these two key findings provided the genesis of the party's electoral strategy in early 2002. A national billboard campaign, launched in the run-up to the party's annual conference in early February, portrayed Harney declaring confidently: 'Last time just 4 TDs . . . think what we could do with 8.' It was a theme she returned to in her conference speech and it was one that dominated the conference weekend in Limerick and was to dominate the party's election campaign. However, it had been adopted only after much debate.

> 'Mary resisted the 4 to 8 slogan for a while,' recalls O'Byrnes. 'She thought it was too specific, but more importantly she wasn't happy about drawing attention to the smallness of the PD parliamentary party. There is a natural inclination among all politicians to try and pretend they are bigger than they actually are. Anyway I thought it was a saleable proposition because it gave the public a very particular message and in the end Mary agreed to run with it.'[4]

O'Byrnes was delighted that the billboard campaign and the conference had given the party a good lead-in to the campaign. In an analysis of the campaign he wrote:

> 'Now all the elements were in place: a target of eight seats in the upcoming general election; a sound-bite that reflected the party's key achievements in government but looked to the future ('keep taxes low and employment high') and an election slogan ('Value for Your Vote') that said you got bang for your buck when you voted PD. The plan was to cite these mantra-like, emulating the Sky News weather ad, 'Ryanair. com . . . the low fares airline.' But intelligent politicians don't like parroting stock lines *ad nauseam*. However, given the party's meagre Budget, it was essential to stick with simple, ultimately memorable messages.'[5]

One issue that caused some controversy at the conference was that of abortion. Bertie Ahern had been anxious to agree a formula to deal with the so-called 'substantive issue', which had been left unresolved by the 1994 referendum. The No vote in 1994 meant that abortion would be legal in Ireland in circumstances where a pregnant woman threatened to commit suicide. Through the All Party Oireachtas Committee on the

Constitution, Ahern set in train a long consultation process and by early 2004 he believed he had a formula that would be broadly acceptable.

That formula ruled out the suicide loophole and was essentially not all that different from the proposal rejected in 1994. It had the support of the Catholic hierarchy, the Pro-Life movement and the moderate middle ground. However, just as in 1994, it was denounced by liberal and ultra-conservative groups who mounted an aggressive campaign against it. The issue proved an embarrassment to some PDs, who would have felt an instinctive inclination towards the liberal side in favour of a No vote. The party's candidate for Dún Laoghaire, Fiona O'Malley, daughter of the former leader, stated at the conference that she would be voting No. Junior Minister Liz O'Donnell refused to say where she stood on the issue, but she, too, was clearly in sympathy with the No position.

Harney, on the other hand, stood by the government's decision to hold the referendum and she called for a Yes vote. In the event the proposal was defeated narrowly, with 50.4 per cent of the voters saying No. It was a real setback for Ahern, whose personal commitment to dealing with the issue was the only reason the referendum had taken place. Although the result did not really matter to the PDs, coming hard on the heels of the defeat in the Nice Treaty referendum it was a setback for the coalition. It gave the Opposition parties some hope, if only for a brief period, that the coalition could be vulnerable, particularly as the economic downturn was beginning to bite.

Buoyed up by a successful conference the PDs were confident that they could confound the sceptics once again and put in a good election performance. Then came another upset that threatened to unravel all the careful preparatory work. Two weeks before the Dáil was dissolved Bobby Molloy was caught up in a controversy that forced his resignation as a junior minister and led him to decide not to run for the Dáil. The episode was a sad way for Molloy to end a successful and respected political career. His position was compromised because of representations he had made on behalf of a constituent whose relative was charged with incest. The judge in the case announced in court that improper contact had been made with him, following letters written by Molloy to the Minister for Justice. Molloy resigned immediately. There was widespread sympathy across the political spectrum for his plight because TDs routinely make representations on behalf of constituents who come to their clinics. Nonetheless, it was a bad blow for the PDs just as the election campaign was about to begin and it bolstered received wisdom that the party would be lucky to win two or three seats.

A number of constituency polls published in the run-up to the election appeared to show that the party was in real trouble. An IMS/*Irish Independent* poll, which was also broadcast on RTÉ's 'Prime Time' programme, showed Michael McDowell trailing in sixth place in Dublin South East, on the same share of the vote as Sinn Féin. 'Having decided to run again I vividly remember being on RTÉ one night with Eoin Ryan of Fianna Fáil. A 'Prime Time' poll showed me on just 7 per cent, level with Sinn Féin. Chris Andrews was topping the poll,' says McDowell. Other polls showed the party faring badly in places like Limerick East and Galway West, reflecting the absence of Des O'Malley and Bobby Molloy. 'In the run-up to the election the PDs did not appear to have a winning gloss. The fact that only three of our outgoing Oireachtas members were contesting seats made the task even more difficult for us. We appeared to be sunk, even before we got started,' recalls Fiona O'Malley, who was running in Dún Laoghaire.[6]

The other difficulty was that public and private polling market research was producing evidence that an overall majority for Fianna Fáil was on the cards. Oliver O'Connor recalls that his late colleague, Maurice Roche, began to refer to the prospect of 'SPG' (Single Party Government) as early as March 2002. 'Maurice got the notion that Fianna Fáil was in with a real chance of an overall majority and he kept referring to SPG and what we could do to avert it well before the campaign began.'[7] Fianna Fáil strategists were keenly aware that they were in with a real chance of winning a majority of seats, but they consciously damped down speculation about that prospect because they knew it would have a negative impact on their campaign.

When the Taoiseach dissolved the Dáil on 25 April, just two weeks after Molloy's hasty resignation, and set an election date of 17 May, all the omens suggested that Fianna Fáil was on course for a good result, but that its coalition partner faced wipe-out. 'It's showtime,' declared the Fianna Fáil director of elections, P.J. Mara, at the launch of its manifesto, reflecting the party's buoyant mood. At that same press conference Ahern and McCreevy stoutly maintained that no spending cuts, secret or otherwise, were being planned. It was pledge that worked wonderfully as a campaign tactic, but it was to have long-term consequences for the government.

Fianna Fáil and the PDs certainly had plenty to boast about going into the election campaign. The Irish economy had out-performed all others in the developed world for the previous five years, with growth of close to 10 per cent per annum. Unemployment had fallen from 10 per cent to just 4 per cent, while the debt/GDP ratio was below 35 per cent. Income tax had been cut from 26 per cent to 20 per cent on the basic rate and from 48 per cent to 42 per cent at the higher rate; capital gains tax had been halved and corporation tax slashed to 12.5 per cent. It was an astonishing record to go to the country on, but would the PDs get any credit for it? The media had long been predicting that Ahern would find an alternative coalition partner in Labour should the numbers fail to add up for a new coalition with the PDs. At that point, few believed that the PDs would get the required numbers and a FF–Labour alliance was touted as the likely outcome.

The first national opinion polls showed Fianna Fáil storming to victory, and while they grossly overestimated the strength of the party vote the polls did dictate the nature of the campaign. The prospect of an alternative government evaporated immediately and the question now became whether Fianna Fáil would have the numbers on its own. The junior coalition party was left with big decisions to make on how to respond.

In early April the PDs had briefed a marketing company to come up with a visual message for a newspaper advertising campaign for the final two weeks of the election. 'It did not take a political genius to anticipate that in the continued absence of a coalition pact between Fine Gael and Labour, and Fianna Fáil campaigning on the most successful term of office of any government in the history of the State, the real threat was that the PDs would be overwhelmed in the tidal wave of support for its much larger government partner,' concluded O'Byrnes.[8] However, the ploy devised by the marketing company to counter the prospect of a Fianna Fáil landslide was met with uncertainty in the PD camp. Fianna Fáil's single party government was dramatically portrayed as a headless chicken. Harney, McDowell and the backroom team were somewhat unsure whether it would be feasible to run with this image of their coalition partners. In the end they decided to bide their time on a decision.

They had more pressing matters to attend to at that stage, particularly the media's curt dismissal of the party after Molloy's resignation coupled with a unanimous prediction of the party's fate in the upcoming election, which generally ranged from two seats to none. In an effort to maximise publicity the PDs' manifesto was launched the weekend before the election was formally called. Entitled 'Value for Your Vote', it stressed the need to keep taxes low as a means of keeping employment high. It also promised prudent economic management and investment in roads and railways to tackle the country's developing transport crisis. The PD campaign proper was launched in Prosperous, County Kildare. It was the first in a series of carefully planned photo opportunities that focused on Harney. The campaign was conceived to reflect a confident, upbeat party and it generated a fair amount of media coverage. 'Prosperous had its media critics, but it was a deliberate, self-confident statement about the new Ireland, and the party's role in bringing it about,' maintained O'Byrnes.[9]

The deliberate emphasis on photo opportunities was consciously designed for a media that had no real interest in issues but was instead dominated by coverage of opinion polls and photographs. (Mind you, there was one gloriously inappropriate, but brilliant, photograph that ran counter to all the carefully choreographed shots set up by O'Byrnes. It was a shot of Harney and Parlon in a pony-and-cart in County Offaly and it evoked *The Quiet Man* more than the Celtic Tiger.) 'Reliance on photo ops can be criticised, but the reality is that a succession of morning press conferences featuring policy launches on important issues like crime, health, insurance, older people and so on received scant to nil coverage. And there was also the RTÉ stopwatch, which inevitably meant some days of no coverage whatsoever on that vital medium,' said O'Byrnes.[10]

At the beginning of the campaign Harney faced a series of ludicrous allegations published in *Magill* magazine, but a prompt court action showed the magazine's claims to be completely bogus. Harney received legal advice that she could win massive damages if she waited until after the campaign and mounted a full-scale libel action, but she instead took the correct political decision to go for a quick hearing and got a settlement in her favour, which she donated to charity. 'She said at the time that she owed it to PD candidates around the country to have the matter sorted out immediately. She did not want it on her conscience that people might lose their seats because she acted too slowly or was more concerned with winning damages than getting the truth out in the open,' says one advisor.[11] It was a distraction that could have been very damaging, but prompt action coupled with Harney's public image thwarted the attempted character assassination.

As the campaign developed the polls got better and better for Fianna Fáil, while the PDs barely registered with just 2 per cent or 3 per cent support. As it dawned on people that Fianna Fáil might be heading for a landslide, Ahern stated publicly that he was in favour of going into government with the PDs, even if his own party won an overall majority.

Harney was quick to say, 'Thanks, but no thanks', asserting that the PDs would not go into office in a situation where they had no leverage. 'I remember the way Bertie announced that even if he had a majority he wanted the PDs in government anyway. Of course he wasn't serious. That was just to reassure the public. In fairness to him, Fianna Fáil nearly pulled it off. It was a great performance,' says Harney.[12] From the beginning the PDs knew that the prospect of a Fianna Fáil majority threatened their future in government, but they were not sure how to react. Just before the beginning of the campaign Des O'Malley had made a speech to the Association of European Journalists, warning obliquely of the dangers posed by a Fianna Fáil majority. He pointed out that coalitions were the norm in Europe and had worked well to date in Ireland.

With a little over a week to polling, Harney announced that a Fianna Fáil Cabinet colleague had told her that an overall majority was on the cards. She never disclosed who had briefed her, but close colleagues assumed the informant was her long-time confidant, Charlie McCreevy. It became abundantly clear that Fianna Fáil was heading for a potential landslide; the PDs knew they had to up the tempo. The party put its entire focus on the need to prevent Fianna Fáil from getting an overall majority and assuming full control of the country's affairs. Harney kept highlighting the matter at PD press briefings, forecasting that on the basis of the polls Fianna Fáil was on course to win more than 90 seats. 'When Mary began to sound this warning from the start of week two of the campaign, journalists were openly sceptical and regarded her as crying wolf,' says O'Byrnes.[13]

The backroom team decided it was time to confront the voters with this message in its key target constituencies. At McDowell's suggestion, a planned media advertising campaign was abandoned in favour of a series of lamppost posters that highlighted the need to avert a Fianna Fáil overall majority. From the very beginning of the campaign McDowell had targetted his attacks on Fianna Fáil and the dangers of 'SPG': he had strongly denounced the Taoiseach's plan for an expensive national sports stadium at Abbotstown, the famous 'Bertie Bowl', saying it had echoes of the Ceausescu regime in Romania. He had also landed some body blows on Sinn Féin, warning voters of that party's Fascist tendencies.

With the election campaign entering the final straight, McDowell staged a publicity stunt that has gone down in political legend. He climbed a lamppost near his home in Ranelagh and stuck up a poster with the message: 'One-Party Government? NO thanks.' The stunt generated huge media coverage, dominating the RTÉ television news that night and featuring on the front pages of the Sunday newspapers the following day. The poster had a profound effect on the campaign, focusing debate in the final week on the question of whether Fianna Fáil ought to be in government on its own, or with the PDs. A leaflet distributed by McDowell spelled out the message that one-party government was undesirable for a host of reasons. One of these was that a one-party government could more easily cover up scandals and policy errors, a sobering thought considering that the worst excesses in political mis-behaviour had occurred during periods of single-party government. 'McDowell's genius was to take the concept of the danger of "SPG" and project it as the key issue of the campaign,' says Oliver O'Connor. 'I can't think of any other politician who would have done what he did and there is nobody else who could have generated such publicity from a simple stunt like climbing a lamppost.'[14]

McDowell's plea to the electorate not to give Fianna Fáil an overall majority struck a chord with a significant number of voters and catapulted the PDs into a pivotal position during the final stages of the campaign. What McDowell's *démarche* showed was that even in the era of meticulously planned campaigns based on focus groups and con-tinuous polling, it was still possible for a politician with flair and courage to take a campaign by the scruff of the neck and have a decisive impact on the final result.

Of course he was not sure of this at the time, and in fact was seriously worried that he might have pushed the party into a disastrous mistake on the same scale as 1997. However, his unerring instinct for publicity and controversy catapulted the PDs centre stage at a critical juncture, when Fine Gael and Labour were floundering. Shinnying up the lamppost was an undignified gamble, but it paid off.

'When Michael McDowell climbed the pole and hung up the "One-Party Government? NO thanks!" poster, the fear of an overall majority for Fianna Fáil—palpable on the doorsteps up to this—crystallised. It spoke to the general public of the very obvious relevance [of] the Progressive Democrats,' said Fiona O'Malley.

She added that for her own part, while 'We had initially agreed to this poster in Dún Laoghaire . . . in the light of the Fianna Fáil annoyance over it and my dependence on their transfers, I opted for the more subtle 'Coalition Works' poster. The point, I decided, had been made.'[15]

McDowell offered his poster to other party candidates, but some felt the approach was too strident. Most of the PD candidates in Dublin followed his lead, however. On televised discussions, McDowell and Harney kept hammering home the message: vote for the PDs to prevent an overall majority for Fianna Fáil. In a televised debate with Ruairi Quinn two days before the election, Harney kept repeating the message and pleaded with viewers to vote for her candidates if they wanted her and her party back in government to provide a counterbalance to Fianna Fáil.

The voters went to the polls on Friday, 17 May and the big issue in everyone's mind was whether Fianna Fáil would have an overall majority.

'I vividly remember the night of the last election,' says Harney. 'It was a very wet day and John Higgins rang me up and said he was going to bring the people who worked with him in head office out for a meal so I asked him to ring Michael and Liz and see if they would come along. But it was like a feckin' wake. It was going grand until Michael arrived. He was in a state, thinking he wasn't going to get elected and worrying about the rest of us. It really was like a wake. I was so sorry we had it and we went home that night totally depressed.'[16]

Oliver O'Connor recalls that meal in the Old Dubliner restaurant, in Francis Street, a little differently.

'There was a bit of a Last Supper atmosphere about it. People made speeches recalling the high points of the PDs over the years and agreeing that it had all been worthwhile, even if it was now going to end in electoral wipe-out. People were preparing themselves for the worst.'[17]

John Higgins has a similar memory.

'I had to leave the Old Dubliner to do an interview on the Vincent Browne programme as the three electronic counts were coming in that night. As I was going out the door somebody shouted, "At least we had a good Last Supper." I replied, "Let's hope it's more like the Resurrection." To be honest, I would have been happy that night if I thought we were sure of four seats.'[18]

The following morning it soon became evident that not only had the PDs held their four seats but they were on course for the target of eight.

The early tallies showed McDowell storming to victory at the head of the poll in Dublin South East. He most certainly had not blown it for the PDs by climbing the pole: his tactics were thoroughly vindicated. The tallies showed other leading PDs, like Harney and O'Donnell, also being comfortably re-elected, but that was not all. Tom Parlon romped home in Laois–Offaly and Tim O'Malley held the former leader's seat in Limerick East. Another O'Malley, Fiona, was on track to take a seat in Dún Laoghaire. Good and all as the news was for the PDs, the predictions during the Saturday of the count and right into the evening still pointed to Fianna Fáil getting its overall majority and the PDs being routed into the political wilderness. It seemed that McDowell was fated to win a Dáil seat when his party was in Opposition, but never when they were going into government.

Then, in the early hours of Sunday morning, two extraordinary results emerged. Mae Sexton took a seat for the PDs in Longford– Roscommon that Fianna Fáil had been counting on. Bertie Ahern was actually on his way to Longford to be present for the announcement of the Fianna Fáil victory that would deliver an overall majority, but he had to turn back at the last moment when the PDs won the seat. There was another, even more astonishing *coup* when Noel Grealish pulled off the win of the election by taking a seat in Galway West.

The final two PD seats brought the party's total to the target figure of eight but, more importantly, the victories deprived Fianna Fáil of the two seats that would have given the party its overall majority. It was a damn close-run thing, but it amounted to an extraordinary success for the PDs. Incredibly, the PD share of the vote, at around 4 per cent, was actually down on its 1997 showing, but a policy of careful constituency targeting and an astute campaign strategy plucked victory from the jaws of defeat. Eight seats was a remarkable yield for the party's first-preference total. 'We had the wind at our backs and we got every lucky break going,' says John Higgins.[19]

'I suppose there was a lot of luck involved,' agrees Harney. 'We had nearly gone down and just survived and been in government and come back again. Certainly luck played a part in getting Michael back and Parlon in at the same time. It created a good momentum. Luck is as important sometimes as strategy.'[20]

Chapter 19

THE PARTY
GOES ON

The PDs could hardly believe their luck. For the first time in the party's history they had combined the twin political objectives of a good election result and participation in government. Bertie Ahern could have got enough support in the Dáil to put a minority Fianna Fáil government into office, but he chose instead to do another deal with the PDs and go into government jointly. A continuation of the Fianna Fáil–PD coalition was clearly the electorate's preference and Ahern preferred to take that option rather than attempt to navigate the uncharted waters of a Fianna Fáil government dependent on a group of Independents. It was the first time since 1969 that an administration returned to office in the same form in which it had left.

> 'To be honest, I didn't expect that we were going to be back in government after the last election,' recalls Harney. 'No coalition had ever been re-elected in Ireland and no government had been re-elected since 1969, so it was a very pleasant surprise when we pulled it off.'[1]

There was one significant change, however. With eight seats the PDs were now in a slightly stronger bargaining position. Harney insisted on two Cabinet posts and Ahern agreed without any equivocation. Nor was there any argument about who should get that second Cabinet post: it could only be the party president, Michael McDowell. His role in getting the PDs back into government was widely acknowledged. Better still from McDowell's point of view, Harney was able to persuade Ahern that he should be appointed Minister for Justice.

Many in Fianna Fáil were nervous about McDowell taking charge of the Justice portfolio, particularly given the Department's key role in the sensitive, complex and ongoing talks about the future of Northern Ireland. However, as Attorney-General McDowell had established a good working relationship with Ahern, so the Taoiseach diplomatically ignored the stinging comparisons with Ceausescu made during the campaign and agreed to appoint McDowell Minister for Justice. Fianna Fáil TDs took some pleasure from contemplating how he might cope with a range of contentious issues in the Garda Síochána, which they expected would keep him fully occupied during his term in Justice.

There was some disappointment within the party that McDowell's return had effectively prevented Liz O'Donnell from being promoted to the Cabinet. She had been a star performer for the party in the dark days after the 1997 debacle, playing a high-profile role in the Northern talks as well as fighting her corner as Minister with responsibility for Overseas Development Aid. But there was no argument about McDowell's entitlement to the post. As O'Donnell did not want another junior ministry, she dropped to the back-benches.

As well as getting two Cabinet posts the PDs also secured two junior ministries. Tom Parlon got the Office of Public Works—the only really independent Minister of State post—while Tim O'Malley was made a junior minister at the Department of Health.

In policy terms the new Fianna Fáil–PD coalition promised more of the same, but it was only in office a matter of weeks when a fierce controversy developed about the way the election had been fought. At the launch of the Fianna Fáil manifesto in April, Ahern and McCreevy had been asked if public spending cuts were in the pipeline to deal with a slowing economy. Both had maintained that no cuts in public spending would be required to tackle that situation. McCreevy then went one step further and in a letter to Fine Gael leader, Michael Noonan, just four days before the election had declared: 'I can confirm that there are no significant overruns projected and no cutbacks whatsoever are being planned, secretly or otherwise.'[2] It was a guarantee that would come back to haunt him.

Just weeks after the election the *Sunday Tribune* reported that McCreevy was going to propose a range of cuts to the Cabinet in view of a combination of higher-than-expected public expenditure and a slowdown in tax revenue. Two months later the same newspaper published a Department of Finance internal memo, which showed that serious cuts were being devised during the election campaign itself.[3] The disclosure was a severe embarrassment for the government, but McCreevy brushed it aside, maintaining that decisions not to spend as much money as previously planned were not the same as spending cuts. He made light of Opposition claims that he had misled the public during the election: 'Look, it was my job to win the election for Fianna Fáil—not to do it for Fine Gael, Labour, or anybody else,' he told reporters after a Fianna Fáil parliamentary party meeting in September.[4]

There was public outrage at McCreevy's flippant attitude and privately many Fianna Fáil TDs came to regard him as a liability. The fact that his economic policies had won the election for them was quickly forgotten as the controversy over 'cuts' raged. McCreevy and the PDs were united in the belief that whatever had been said during the election campaign, the important thing was to sort out the public finances as quickly as possible. A short, sharp dose of hard-to-swallow medicine actually worked in just a little over a year, but many voters now felt they had been conned during the election campaign.

The strange thing about the pledges made during the campaign regarding spending cuts was that focus-group research had shown that most people wanted firm decision-making to ensure the continuation of the Celtic Tiger economy. One of the main reasons they had voted for both government parties was that they were regarded as more likely than the Opposition parties to adopt a tough stance and do whatever was necessary to protect the economic gains of the previous eight years.[5] There was therefore no need to con the voters on this issue, but McCreevy and Ahern just could not resist over-selling their case during the campaign. This political manoeuvring for its own sake would exact a large price from McCreevy in the long term.

The PDs had no hesitation weighing in behind McCreevy in his battle to control the big-spending ministers, particularly the Minister for Health, Micheal Martin. McCreevy had a series of public jousts with Martin over the minister's failure to deliver a better service from the rapidly escalating budget for his Department. Harney and McDowell made no secret of their view that Martin and his Department were not capable of getting to grips with the massive problems in Health. As expenditure increased and employment in the health service mush-roomed, complaints from the public about the shortcomings of the service seemed to multiply with each passing day, and very soon it became the biggest problem facing the government.

McDowell made reform of the Garda Síochána his first priority in Justice. The image of the force had been tarnished by a scandal in

Donegal that became know as the McBrearty affair. This related to the death of the Donegal cattle-dealer, Ritchie Barron, apparently killed in a hit-and-run road accident outside Raphoe in October 1996. Local publican, Frank McBrearty, was treated as a murder suspect by the gardaí, but charges were not proceeded with and it emerged that the Garda investigation was deeply flawed. In March 2002 the Morris Tribunal was set up to investigate the affair, as well as a range of other complaints against the gardaí in Donegal. As the evidence was heard, between 2002 and 2004, the public was shocked by the practices revealed.

On 15 July 2004 the Tribunal issued its first report into explosives finds in Donegal, and it was a damning indictment of the way in which certain elements in the force had been allowed to operate for years.[6] The report galvanised the Department of Justice into producing reforming legislation in several key areas. The Garda Síochána Bill 2004 provided for the most comprehensive reform of the police force since its establishment in 1922. Among the key elements of the Bill were an independent Ombudsman Commission and a Garda Inspectorate, as well as the establishment of local policing committees.

Harney continued to preside over a very healthy jobs market, which held up remarkably well during the brief downturn in the economy. One major item on her agenda that had not been delivered during her first period as minister was the issue of exorbitant insurance costs. The combination of a growing compensation culture, a supine insurance industry and enormous legal fees drove premiums ever higher for individuals and businesses. After a great deal of struggle and intense opposition from the legal profession, Harney eventually got the Personal Insurance Assessment Board (PIAB) off the ground. It was designed to reduce insurance costs by cutting down considerably on legal fees. Apart from the PIAB, Harney did not have any major reforms to pursue in her Department and she began to consider her options in terms of the reshuffle promised by the Taoiseach in two years' time.

That proposed reshuffle became a political imperative in June 2004 when the government got a kick in the teeth from the electorate in the European and local elections. Fianna Fáil expected to lose some ground in the contest, but the party was not prepared for the thrashing it received from the voters. The PDs also did badly in the local elections, winning just 17 seats—a drop of eight since 1999. The party didn't contest the European elections, although serious efforts were made to get at least one high-profile candidate on board to fly the PD flag. Negotiations took place with Mairead McGuinness, the farming editor of the *Irish Independent*, who was very well-known in rural Ireland as the presenter of 'Ear to the Ground', a popular television programme aimed at the farming community. McGuinness did seriously consider running for the party in Leinster, but in the end opted to run for Fine Gael instead, even though it already had a sitting MEP in Avril Doyle. In the event, McGuinness topped the poll and Fine Gael won two seats out of three in Leinster. McGuinness' decision to run for Fine Gael rather than the PDs was an exact reversal of the Parlon story of two years earlier.

Fine Gael, which had come close to meltdown in 2002 and had been written-off by most media commentators, made an astonishing come-back. The party won almost 28 per cent of the vote. This was in stark contrast to opinion polls, which had consistently showed the party hovering around the 20 per cent mark. Fine Gael came within 9 seats of overhauling Fianna Fáil in terms of the total number of county councillors, and it actually overtook its great rival in the European contest, winning 5 seats out of 13 in comparison to Fianna Fáil's 4.

Fianna Fáil was stunned by the results. The party vote dropped close to 30 per cent in both contests, a fall-off that no one had seen coming. Fine Gael took one slice of the Fianna Fáil vote, and Sinn Féin took another. Sinn Féin did well in the local elections, more than doubling its number of councillors and pulling 8 per cent of the vote, as well as winning one European seat, in Dublin. Fianna Fáil strategists had complacently assumed that the rise of Sinn Féin would hurt the Labour party, but instead it impacted directly on Fianna Fáil. Of the 32 new seats won by Sinn Féin, a total of 24 came off Fianna Fáil and just one from Labour, with the rest being won at the expense of Independents. The penny finally dropped that what Sinn Féin had done to the SDLP in the North it could repeat in the South, at least to some extent, and the victim this time around was going to be Fianna Fáil.

In many ways the person who should have taken most responsibility for this development was Ahern. For the previous seven years he had indulged Sinn Féin, giving the backing of the Irish government to the party every time there was a breakdown in the Northern political process. It seemed that no matter what the Provisional movement did—refusing to decommission weapons, persisting with punishment beatings and criminal activity and expanding its targeting and surveillance network on both sides of the border—Ahern was always prepared to make excuses for it. At Ahern's instigation, senior officials in his own

Department and in the Department of Foreign Affairs developed a close relationship with Sinn Féin, seeming to operate on the assumption that progressing the party's agenda was the core government policy on the North.

Although the rise of Sinn Féin in the local and European elections was facilitated by the indulgence shown to the party by Ahern, the scapegoat for Fianna Fáil's poor results was not the Taoiseach, but Charlie McCreevy. Fianna Fáil TDs blamed McCreevy for the ongoing controversy over spending cuts and for his blunt defence of government policy. Much of this grumbling had far more to do with image than substance: McCreevy may have refused to indulge in the 'compassionate and caring' language so beloved of his critics, but he did deliver a new agreement with the social partners in 2003 that delighted the trade union leadership.

Stung by the criticism, in the autumn of 2003, during a meeting with Ahern, McCreevy inquired if the Taoiseach had decided who he intended to appoint as Ireland's next European Commissioner the following summer. McCreevy intimated that he would like to take the job, if it were available. As the time for the appointment drew closer, however, he changed his mind and stated publicly that he wanted to remain on in the Department of Finance and complete his programme. But Ahern had now decided that McCreevy was a liability and was determined that he should move. The pressure on McCreevy was gradually ratcheted up by a series of well-placed leaks, which suggested that a majority of Fianna Fáil TDs wanted him out of the way so that the party could re-position itself to fight the next election. Ahern publicly declared himself to be a socialist, and although he had made the same statement many times previously, it was taken as a signal that a major shift in government policy was imminent. McCreevy eventually bowed to the considerable pressure and accepted Ahern's offer of the European Commissionership.

That cleared the way for a long overdue government reshuffle in the autumn of 2004. After a great deal of deliberation, Harney decided to move to the Department of Health—the most controversial and probably most stressful of all Departments. Her rationale for this high-risk strategy was that in Health she could demonstrate that the PDs could take tough decisions and achieve the kind of results Fianna Fáil was simply incapable of delivering because of that party's desire to appease all interest groups. The other side of the coin, of course, was that Health was a minefield of vested interests—famously dubbed 'Angola' by Brian Cowen when he was minister. Given the model of partnership that

Ahern and Fianna Fáil had installed across the public service, any attempt at reform in the health service was bound to provoke fury from a range of interest groups, starting with the powerful hospital consultants. As well as having to deal with these vested interests, Harney quickly walked into the middle of a major controversy over illegal nursing home charges imposed on public patients over the previous thirty years. A Supreme Court decision just a few months after her arrival left her with the headache of trying to find at least €500 million to repay some of the monies illegally deducted. It was a pertinent example of how Health could damage a minister's political health.

McDowell stayed where he was in the reshuffle; there was plenty more he wanted to achieve in the Department of Justice. By the spring of 2005 he had published thirty-five Bills and overseen the enactment into law of twenty-five of these. This represented 25 per cent of the entire legislative achievement of the government since the 2002 election. McDowell had also faced up to the complex issues raised by a loophole in Irish citizenship law, which allowed children born in Ireland and their families to become Irish citizens, even if they left the country immediately after the birth. There was intense criticism of McDowell by the Opposition parties and the media, but his referendum proposal to clarify the law on citizenship was carried, with almost 80 per cent of people voting Yes. After the government's referendum defeats on the Nice Treaty and abortion, that was no mean feat.

An even thornier political problem for McDowell was the ongoing saga of the peace process, which had turned into an endless propaganda campaign for Sinn Féin. In the autumn of 2004 McDowell became increasingly restive about the concessions being made to Sinn Féin. He was particularly anxious about his own involvement in what was coming to look more and more like a policy of appeasement towards republicans. In 2003, as the IRA was once more said to be on the verge of disarmament, Ahern agreed to the release of the killers of Garda Jerry McCabe as part of any final settlement. Four men had been jailed for the brutal killing of the garda and the wounding of his colleague, Ben O'Sullivan, in Adare, County Limerick, in 1996. They had been convicted of manslaughter rather than murder because witnesses were intimidated. The case had particular resonance for the PDs, not only because it represented the vicious side of Irish republicanism but because McCabe and O'Sullivan had had a close personal connection with Des O'Malley: during his period as Minister for Justice, from 1970 to 1973, and afterwards when he was still deemed to be at risk from the IRA, the two gardaí had been O'Malley's escort. During the negotiation of the Good Friday Agreement in 1998, O'Malley had insisted that the killers of Garda McCabe should not qualify for early release because they had committed the murder while the IRA was theoretically on ceasefire. The government had followed this line and the McCabe killers were specifically excluded from the deal.

Following the ratification of the Good Friday Agreement in 1998 and in subsequent referenda, the North had demanded an enormous amount of government time and energy. A power-sharing executive was established, but after a promising beginning it collapsed three times. The main reasons for these breakdowns was the failure of Sinn Féin and the IRA to deliver on their commitments to abandon paramilitary activity and decommission their weapons. However, the Irish and British governments made excuses for republicans and instead focused their attention on trying to squeeze further concessions out of David Trimble and the Ulster Unionist party.

In Assembly elections in November 2003 the unionist voters punished Trimble for his perceived weakness by giving a majority of seats to the more radical Democratic Unionist party, while nationalists rewarded Sinn Féin for its hardline stance by giving the party more seats than the moderate SDLP. Instead of establishing a greater level of trust between the two communities, the Agreement pushed each side into the embrace of extremists. In response the two governments spent most of 2004 trying to get Sinn Féin and the DUP to agree a deal that would see the Executive resurrected once more. As on the three previous occasions, an agreement appeared to be in the offing when all the parties and the two governments met at Leeds Castle in Kent in September, but that tantalising possibility slipped out of reach at the last minute. In the final months of 2004, Ahern and Tony Blair made a concerted effort to realise the potential presented by the Leeds Castle talks by urging Sinn Féin and the DUP to strike a deal.

There was a great deal of anguish in the PDs when Ahern, under pressure from Enda Kenny, told the Dáil in November that the release of the McCabe killers would be part of that deal. Fine Gael and Labour were outraged by the move and demanded to know how this had happened when the issue had been specifically excluded from the Good Friday Agreement. Most PDs were just as bewildered and angry at the decision. At this stage McDowell found himself in no-man's-land, tied into a policy that was anathema to his party and to a huge swathe of public opinion in the Republic. Since the 2002 election he had blown hot and cold on the subject of Sinn Féin. During the election campaign he had been devastating in his criticism of republican double-think and in his first year as minister he was blunt about the growing threat to society from IRA criminal activity on both sides of the border, drawing attention to the expansion of the IRA crime network in Dublin, as well as along the Border. McDowell received much media criticism for his pains, with naïve journalists demanding that he produce proof of IRA criminality.

Surprisingly, though, in 2004 McDowell appeared to back away from his initial claims and publicly accepted that IRA criminal activity was being wound down. As the prospects of a political deal got brighter in the summer and autumn of 2004, it seemed that he was happy to accept assurances from the republican leadership that they really were on the road to democracy. When the controversy over the McCabe killers blew up, McDowell said that it would be the happiest day of his life if he had to travel to Limerick to tell the garda's widow that her husband's killers were being released. What he clearly meant was that it would be the happiest day of his life if the IRA were wound up for good, but that is not what it sounded like. Ann McCabe struck a chord with the electorate when she appeared on television in early December and posed the simple question: 'Who is running this country, Bertie Ahern or the IRA?'[7]

Behind the scenes, McDowell was working hard to ensure that a new agreement, allowing Sinn Féin into government in the North and releasing the McCabe killers, would only come about if there were an absolute, unequivocal commitment by the IRA to end its criminal and paramilitary activities. Although the republican leadership expressed its willingness to engage in a massive act of decommissioning that would put the entire IRA arsenal of weapons beyond use, there was a marked reluctance to give a commitment to end criminal activity. Right through the autumn of 2004 Sinn Féin leaders refused to sign up to a formulation that would have committed the entire republican movement not to engage in criminality of any kind in the future. McDowell refused to let go of the issue, but Ahern and Blair gave the distinct impression that they did not regard it as a deal-breaker and the public was left in the dark as to its actual significance.

What did emerge as the deal-breaker was the DUP's demand for photographic evidence of decommissioning. When Ahern and Blair held a press conference in Belfast on 8 December to explain yet another failure to reach agreement, it was the photographs that featured as the only bone of contention; there was no mention of IRA criminality by either leader. The PDs, though, were holding their ground on the subject. Even as Ahern travelled to Belfast on the morning of 8 December, Harney told the Dáil that there were other issues apart from photographic evidence. That night the IRA issued the text of a statement that had been agreed with the two governments over the previous weeks. Crucially, the IRA left out the formulation on criminality that McDowell had requested. The clear message of their omission was that the Provisionals were not prepared to give up criminal activity—a measure that for McDowell was the bottom-line.

The following day McDowell had to endure a raw and stormy meeting of his own parliamentary party, whose members were furious at him for agreeing to the release of the McCabe killers. Most of his colleagues attacked him for allowing the issue onto the agenda at all. It took some time before he could explain to his colleagues that things had moved on and there would be no deal, and no release of the McCabe killers, as long as Sinn Féin and the IRA refused to give the required commitment on criminality. He pointed out the difference in the wording of the agreed statement to be issued by the IRA in the event of a deal and the actual statement issued by the IRA when the deal collapsed.[8]

The response of the British government to the collapse of the talks on 8 December was to immediately start a further round of talks with Sinn Féin, offering the party a deal that would enable it to out-flank the DUP. The Irish government declined to get involved in these talks, although Blair put pressure on Ahern to participate. Then everything was turned upside-down by the Northern Bank robbery on 20 December, especially when PSNI chief constable Hugh Orde confirmed ten days later that it had been carried out by the Provisional IRA. The Sinn Féin leadership repeatedly denied involvement, but almost no one believed them. In January 2005 came the brutal and much-publicised murder of Robert McCartney in Belfast. The campaign for justice by the dead man's sisters over the following months put Sinn Féin and the IRA under the kind of pressure it had not faced since the beginning of the peace process. In February 2005 the deal to release the McCabe killers was formally taken off the table by the Taoiseach.

There was even more anxiety about the corruption of democratic standards when soon thereafter it emerged that the Gardaí had uncovered a massive money-laundering operation in the Republic, which appeared to involve a number of prominent individuals. Some of the money from the Northern Bank raid was discovered by the Garda operation and their inquiries extended as far as Bulgaria and Libya. In a series of speeches and interviews in the first half of 2005, McDowell laid down the law to republicans. He went further than any other politician and named Gerry Adams, Martin McGuinness and Martin Ferris as members of the Army Council of the IRA. It had long been the convention not to name prominent Sinn Féin politicians as members of the Army Council, but McDowell decided that the Irish public had to know the truth – whatever the implications for the talks process.

At the PD annual conference in April, he bluntly told the Provisional movement of the government's bottom-line:

'There will be no armies, no arms dumps, no beatings, no extortion, no robbery, no breach of the electoral laws, no exiling, no smuggling, no protection rackets and no money-laundering by or on behalf of those who engage in politics.'

The minister went on to warn of the persistent threat to Irish democracy. 'The emerging web of money-laundering and asset-creation by the Provos reveals a frightening threat to our democratic institutions. IRA/Sinn Féin were well on the way to creating a state within a state. They were using well-placed sleepers and collaborators, some of them pillars of society, to achieve that end.' He added that until the IRA disbanded Sinn Féin could not be involved in government, North or South.[9]

As the twentieth anniversary of the PDs approached, the party's two ministers both occupied pivotal positions in Irish politics. Both Harney and McDowell attracted an enormous amount of publicity: some of it positive; much of it very hostile. Both ministers faced huge challenges in their Departments. Harney had staked her political reputation on reforming the health service, a gamble that worried even her strongest supporters. Des O'Malley described the Department of Health as 'a bed of nails, a crown of thorns' and expressed his concern for her: 'She vaguely asked my advice and I was not listened to, but her tenacity is such that she has succeeded at everything she has decided to do and I am sure it will be the same this time.'[10]

By taking such a clear line on IRA criminality McDowell effectively seized control of the Irish government's policy on the North in the first few months of 2005. He publicly named Gerry Adams and Martin

McGuinness as members of the IRA Army Council and made it clear there would be no more ambiguity in the government's dealings with republicans. The bottomline was that there could be no deal with Sinn Féin until the issue of IRA criminality was resolved. This, too, was a gamble, but there was a huge sigh of relief from a substantial section of public opinion that someone had finally taken a stand for democracy against republican Fascism. It was only appropriate that the first government politician to do that was the first PD Minister for Justice.

McDowell's tough stand ensured that republicans were put under unprecedented pressure to live up to the obligations of the Good Friday Agreement and wind up IRA activity for good.

Eventually, at the end of July 2005, the Provisional movement finally responded to all the pressure. Eleven years after the first IRA cessation, the movement publicly called off its campaign of violence. 'All IRA units have been ordered to dump arms. All volunteers have been instructed to assist the development of purely political and democratic programmes through exclusively peaceful means,' the organisation said in a statement. Much of the goodwill generated by the statement was dissipated a week later due to the highly publicised arrival in Ireland of the so-called Colombia Three. The return of the three republicans—who had absconded on bail before being convicted of training FARC guerrillas in Colombia—was yet another obstacle to a settlement in the North. It also embarrassed the Irish government, which was in a quandary about how to react.

McDowell's outspoken approach to republicans annoyed some elements in Fianna Fáil, who resented the PD influence over government policy on such a critical issue. That in turn provoked a number of spats between the parties, and the PDs suffered the public indignity of being seen to come off worst. The party's demand that a second terminal at Dublin Airport should be built and operated by the private sector was rebuffed at the Taoiseach's insistence. McDowell's plans to change the alcohol licensing laws by introducing continental-style café bars was also shot down after a revolt by Fianna Fáil back-benchers.

Harney had described McCreevy as the 'glue' that held the coalition together and by the time the first anniversary of his departure to Brussels came around, it was becoming increasingly obvious that the days of cordial partnership were over. The coalition was purely a business arrangement.

Chapter 20 ❧

PAST AND FUTURE

At a low-key celebration of the PDs' nineteenth birthday on 21 December 2004, Des O'Malley gave a short speech. Looking around the room in 25 South Frederick Street, in which were gathered most of the people who had founded the party almost two decades earlier, he started by saying:

> 'Tánaiste, Minister, ladies and gentlemen. Little did I know I would be starting the nineteenth party by uttering these words when I stood in this room in 1985.'

There was general laughter as those present looked at each other and wondered again at their success.

> 'I remember being in this room and being very apprehensive about the future. I couldn't have envisaged a future for the party that would have been so successful and so full of surprises. Contrast the economy then and now. Of all the changes we introduced, changing the tax system was the most important. It has contributed in a major way to the success of the party and the success of the Irish economy. It is a sign of success that we are now a country of immigration, not emigration.'

So, is O'Malley right? Examined simply in terms of the fortunes of political war, the PDs have been remarkably successful. The party has survived for two decades, and that is certainly far longer than almost anybody in political life in 1985 would have predicted. Although the party has suffered its share of disasters and come close to extinction more than once, it has always managed to bounce back. More remarkable than resilience is the fact that the party has been in government three times—spending more than half its lifespan in office. It forced Fianna Fáil to abandon its core principle of refusing to participate in coalition, which has had the unintended result of a profound and positive effect on the political fortunes of Fianna Fáil, as well as those of the PDs.

The comparison with other small Irish parties, both in terms of survival and participation in government, is instructive. The best-known of the previous small parties was Clann na Poblachta, led by Seán MacBride, which was founded in 1946. Like the PDs it enjoyed a successful first election, winning 13.2 per cent of the vote and 10 seats in 1948. After that election the party participated in the first Inter-Party Government, led by John A. Costello, but a rift between the party leader and one of his ministers, Noël Browne, led to a fatal split and it was reduced to 2 seats in 1951. The party lingered on until 1965, but it never had more than 2 seats after 1951 and did not participate in government again.

Another small party, Clann na Talmhan, which represented rural-dwellers, survived for longer, but had a somewhat similar experience. Founded in 1939 the party won 10.3 per cent of the vote and 13 seats in 1943. In a snap election the following year its vote increased, but the number of seats dropped to 11. In 1948 it dropped back further to 7 seats. The party participated in the first Inter-Party Government in 1948 and although its vote continued to decline, it also had a Cabinet post in the second Inter-Party Government, from 1954 to 1957. The party continued to contest elections until 1961, but had disappeared by 1965.

In the 1920s there was a strong Farmers' party, which lasted for more than a decade. Although it had some influence, it never achieved office. Two other small parties, the National League in the 1920s and the Centre party in the 1930s, also achieved short-term success, but did not survive for long. By contrast with all of those parties, the PDs have proved durable and far more successful in terms of winning office.

The PDs also managed the difficult feat of making coalition work, and work for them. Despite their history of deep animosity, O'Malley and Haughey managed the efficient operation of the first Fianna Fáil–PD coalition from 1989 to 1992. That coalition was strong enough to survive a series of crises and ministerial resignations, which put enormous strains on its cohesion. The O'Malley–Reynolds coalition was a very different animal. It came apart in less than a year, but that was because Reynolds wanted to end the relationship at the first opportunity. The Harney–Ahern coalitions of 1997 and 2002 have been remarkably stable and the

PDs have shown a capacity to make things work, even in challenging circumstances.

A comparison with the way the Labour party has operated in coalition in recent decades provides an interesting contrast in styles. Labour was in office with Fine Gael in the 1970s, 1980s and 1990s and with Fianna Fáil in the early 1990s. For most of its time in government, particularly in the 1980s, there was a great deal of tension between the coalition parties. It was not so much tension at ministerial level—although that did exist, particularly in the 1980s—as a huge internal strain within the Labour party, with a substantial section of its membership opposed to participation in coalition at all. This led Labour to undersell its achievements in office, while its partners resented the compromises they were forced to make to stay in government.

By contrast, at all levels—ministers, TDs and ordinary members—the PDs have all been more than happy to participate in government and are proud of the party's achievements in office. When the party was founded Des O'Malley maintained that one of his objectives was to convert Irish politics to the European model, where coalition was regarded as the norm and parties participated in government on the basis of negotiations on a specific programme. Judged on that basis, the PDs have achieved all that they set out to do.

Former Labour party Minister, Barry Desmond, maintains that it was by 'mining into a rich vein of political populism' that the PDs defied the fate of other small parties.

> 'They grabbed the easy ethos that minimal personal taxation, slashed public expenditure and the sale of State assets would, in a dog-eat-dog economy, bring about a prosperous and fair society in Ireland. They scorned the concept of a mixed social economy of vibrant public and private sectors with an electorate prepared to meet the cost of comprehensive social and public services.'

While critical of its economic policies, Desmond points to a characteristic that has helped to create the party's distinct identity: the courageous stance taken by leading individuals over the years on major issues that go to the heart of Irish democracy.

> 'Much as I do not share the PD philosophy, I would not wish to diminish their serious contributions at critical junctures in the past

few decades. Desmond O'Malley supported Jack Lynch, George Colley and Eoin Ryan, when the very dangerous political bully boys of Kevin Boland, Neil Blaney and Charles Haughey sought to dominate political democracy in Ireland. I was there during that turmoil. Mary Harney and Bobby Molloy also showed great courage in facing down the dictations of Haughey. Today, Michael McDowell, almost alone in government, has shown no equivocation in his dealings with Sinn Féin/IRA.'[1]

The underlying question is what influence have the PDs managed to exert on the course of Irish political, social and economic affairs? Has the party changed Ireland in the way its founders set out to do back in 1985? If the answer is yes, has the change been for the better? There is a deep reluctance, and not just on the part of its opponents but also in media and political circles, to concede the obvious influence the PDs have had on the course of Irish political and economic life over the past two decades.

One of Ireland's most distinguished economists, Professor Dermot McAleese, who retired from Trinity College, Dublin at the beginning of 2005, remarked on the general failure to give the PDs the credit the party deserves for the economic changes of the last decade-and-a-half. In an interview given shortly before he retired, the former member of the Central Bank board noted that the emergence of the PDs in 1985 had a more positive influence on the economy than many were prepared to recognise. He expressed his firm opinion that the low-tax, pro-business economy of 2005 was based in large part on PD policies. 'They proved that there was a constituency for this and they gave the intellectual power to it,' he said.[2]

An OECD report published in February 2005 bore out McAleese's point. The report showed that Irish workers paid the third lowest tax and social insurance contributions in the industrial world. They have also benefited from the largest reductions by far in tax and social insurance since 1996. The report also found that when child benefit payments were taken into account, the Irish tax and welfare system was the most generous in the world for single-income families on average industrial wages. Only the Mexicans and Koreans paid lower tax and PRSI rates than the Irish. According to the OECD, workers on average industrial wages in Ireland typically paid 10.6 per cent of their salary in income tax: the eleventh lowest out of thirty countries. They also paid an average of 5 per cent in PRSI contributions: the fifth lowest social insurance rate in the OECD. This meant the government was taking 15.7 per cent from the pay packets of average industrial workers, the third lowest percentage deduction in the industrialised world; rates are more than 40 per cent in Denmark, Germany and Belgium.

What was truly astonishing was the pace at which Irish labour taxes had been reduced. In 1996 the typical tax and PRSI bill for an Irish worker was as high as 28.5 per cent. Over the following seven years this was almost halved. These rates fell in twenty-three out of the thirty OECD countries, but nowhere else came anywhere near the Irish experience.[3]

So it is not an idle boast of the PDs to claim that its policies have caused a substantial reduction in the level of tax taken from ordinary workers. The other side of this coin is that the tax cuts and the resulting rise in living standards have fuelled a remarkable expansion in the number of jobs in the economy. The number of jobs has almost doubled since the PDs first took Office, from one million in 1990 to almost two million in 2005. This is something that nobody visualised in 1990, but it is the basis for Ireland's current prosperity.

While McAleese was one of the few independent observers to give the PDs credit for the economic transformation of Ireland, Michael McDowell was never shy about stating the claims of the party. In an important speech in the summer of 2004 he maintained that the liberal economic policies of the PDs were the basis for Irish prosperity in the first decade of the twenty-first century.

'In the 30-year period from 1 January 1973 to this year, Ireland was a full member of the EEC, which has since become the European Union. That 30-year period divides neatly into two halves. From 1973 to 1987, Ireland's economic performance was pitiful, abject, and disastrous. From 1987 onwards, Ireland has turned the path and clawed its way back from economic disaster to economic success. To the younger voter the first 15-year nightmare period of economic failure is at best a faint memory. But I think it is worthwhile to recall to mind some of its features and some of the policies which underpinned it.

It was a period in which the IMF were knocking at our door, where double-digit current Budget deficits were the norm, where mass emigration of our youngest and brightest was a constant feature of Irish social life and political discourse, where mass unemployment was endemic and apparently ineradicable, where entire urban and suburban communities suffered 80 per cent unemployment, where third generation unemployment was the lot of many families, where young Irish people had a fatalistic acceptance of failure, and where the flame of hope itself was low and guttering in a gale of political and economic despair.

It was also a period of massive state domination of the Irish economy. The state owned and ran banks, all energy generation companies, two shipping lines, all means of passenger transport, the only airline, a fertiliser business, a shipyard, a steel company, an insurance company, all telecommunications, all radio and TV, an oil refinery, and a seaweed factory. In fairness, I have to concede that there was some restraint—a proposal to nationalise Bewley's Oriental Cafés was turned down after careful scrutiny. Personal and other taxes were struck at suffocating rates. The lowest rate of tax was 35 per cent plus 7.75 per cent PRSI—a "low rate" of more than 42 per cent of the lowest taxable incomes of the most humble PAYE workers. The top rates of tax were reached by single workers earning below the average industrial wage—who faced marginal welfare and tax rates of two-thirds of income. So severe was taxation on the lower paid that I was told in a PQ in the late 80s that a man with four children and a wife working in the home was worse off working than on welfare at any wage lower than 90 per cent of the average industrial wage when the differential rent and cost of going to work was taken into account.

In the all-encompassing social democratic orthodoxy which then held sway, there were no political solutions on offer to the appalling malaise that we faced.'

McDowell went on to say that, starting with the MacSharry Budget of 1987, a different approach to a number of central policy issues had brought Ireland from the bottom to the top of the league of economic performance in the EU. While he conceded that there was no single explanation for this and that social partnership, generous financial assistance from the EU and direct foreign investment had all played a role, he maintained that a new approach to embracing liberal market economics had been a critical element in the turnaround.

'Those of us who from 1986 onwards challenged the horrific failures of the then orthodox theories of social democracy have seen our own policies emerge from heterodox to orthodox. Anyone who challenged state domination of the Irish economy was derided and attacked as "Thatcherite", "yuppie", "selfish" and "right-wing" by the élite that brought this country to its knees and kept it there between 1973 and 1987. It took some degree of courage to face down that blizzard of political invective and to insist that there was a better way—a way which involved radical tax reform, which involved the breaking up of monopolies, which viewed profit as healthy, which argued that entre-preneurs and risk-takers had to be rewarded, which argued that workers should and could be incentivised, which embraced competition, which was open to at least consider the option of privatisation. It still takes some degree of courage to stand up for those policies.'[4]

Labour leader Pat Rabbitte countered with a speech of his own two months later in which he challenged McDowell's claims. He claimed that the credit for getting the Celtic Tiger economy going belonged to the Rainbow government, of which he had been a member. He pointed out that since the 1950s successive governments had encouraged inward investment and that the generous assistance from the EU came from the social democratic instincts of Jacques Delors.

'Analysis of the historical record also shows that, contrary to the claims of the neo-liberal right, the major tax reduction packages of the 1990s were introduced after the boom began, rather than before it. No Minister came into the House to tell us that he was taking a punt on the future, by cutting taxes to initiate economic growth. On the contrary, tax reduction packages were part of a strategy worked out with the social partners to trade off tax reductions for wage restraint, and so add to the competitiveness of the economy. This strategy had its limits, but it was certainly not a neo-liberal one.'[5]

While there will always be debate about what exactly caused Ireland's turnaround from a basket economic case in the 1980s to one of the most prosperous countries in the world in the first decade of the twenty-first century, it is difficult to deny that the PDs played some role in that transformation. The extent of that role is a subject for discussion, but things would hardly have turned out as they have if the party had never existed. From the very outset the PDs set out with a liberal economic agenda, with a heavy stress on tax-cutting measures. This agenda was reviled by all of its opponents twenty years ago, yet in the intervening period most of its agenda has been successfully implemented. As well as realising its policies in government, the PDs also managed to shift the political centre of gravity. It has often been remarked that Margaret Thatcher's greatest achievement in Britain was not that she changed the policies of the Conservative party, but that she changed the policies of the Labour party. In Ireland, the policies of all the other mainstream parties have shifted decisively in the direction of the PDs and none would now dare to suggest an increase in personal taxation as a way of improving public services.

Of course, the PDs didn't shift the centre of gravity in Irish politics all on its own. The rest of the anglophone world was moving in the direction of more liberal economic policies in the 1980s, led by flag-bearers Ronald Reagan and Margaret Thatcher. At the very least the achievement of the PDs was to get in tune with the *zeitgeist*. Ireland would have had to change to some degree if it wanted to remain at the heart of an evolving European Union, but without the pioneering policies of the PDs, it might well have been too little, too late. The record of the late 1970s and 1980s indicates that the country would have been dragged screaming in the wake of EU reforms, rather than charging ahead of them as it did so impressively in the Celtic Tiger years.

The presence of the PDs in government allowed those in Fianna Fáil who recognised economic reality to get their party to accept policies it might never have implemented on its own. What was unique to the PDs was that the party placed so much emphasis on the need to cut taxes on labour in order to stimulate economic growth, job creation and pros-perity. However, it is probably fair to say that if the FitzGerald government had not wrestled with the country's debt problems and brought inflation under control (down from 21 per cent to 3 per cent by 1986) and if Haughey had not started to cut public spending drastically after 1987, tax cuts would simply have been impossible. The PDs were essentially in the right place at the right time, but to be fair to the party it took courage to propose and develop its agenda in the face of entrenched hostility from its political opponents, the majority of the media and the social partners.

Of course, tax rates and job numbers don't provide a full explanation of any economy. Critics of the PDs argue that while taxes on labour have come down, a range of other taxes, particularly taxes on consumption, have increased. Unlike tax on income, taxes on consumption are regres-sive because everybody pays the same rate, regardless of wealth. However, the nub of the issue for the PDs was that taxes on labour were at the root of the country's problems in the 1980s, so it was necessary to shift the tax burden off labour in order to generate economic activity and increase employment. There is no arguing with the success of this policy in increasing the numbers at work, which rose from 1.1 million to 1.9 million in a little over a decade. By helping to cut unemployment from close to 20 per cent to just 4 per cent the PDs have probably done more to ease poverty than any other political party. International studies have shown that the only way to eliminate poverty is through job creation and the PDs have certainly delivered on the jobs front.

There were hard choices along the way, which contributed to the image of the PDs as an 'uncaring' party. A key to job creation is to ensure that workers in paid employment receive better income than people on welfare. Economic incentives work at all levels of society and if it is economically more advantageous to claim welfare than to work, people will inevitably follow rational self-interest and stay out of the jobs market. That was one of the significant factors in the high unemployment that plagued Ireland during the 1980s. It is easy to accuse the PDs of being heartless for making it more financially rewarding to work than to claim the dole, but the economic litmus test is whether the policy has increased or reduced the absolute level of poverty in society. On that score, the PDs emerge as comfortable winners. Still, the characterisation of the PDs as a party of the rich and selfish, deeply suspicious of the public service and impervious to the plight of the poor in society has had a considerable impact.

In 2005 the Opposition parties focused the thrust of their policies on the need for a Fair Society as an alternative to the liberal model advocated by the PDs. Following Charlie McCreevy's departure to Brussels, Bertie Ahern attempted to re-position Fianna Fáil, at least in terms of public perception, as a 'socialist' party. What is striking about the record of the PDs and of their ally in government, Charlie McCreevy, is that they failed to convince the public of the importance of their role in the creation of the country's current prosperity. Most voters were happy to take the PD/McCreevy 'shilling', but few have been prepared to follow the PD drum.

Looking at it from a different perspective, the PDs are open to the criticism that the party failed to deliver on significant elements of its original agenda. Despite the public perception of the party as being hostile to the public service, the PDs have actively participated in a government that has presided over huge pay increases for public servants while failing to obtain any improvement in the quality of those services in return. Far from trying to slash numbers, as it suggested inadvertently and damagingly in 1997, the PDs in government have overseen a substantial expansion in public service numbers, particularly in the Health Service. The dubious benefits of this expansion are something the party should be embarrassed about. In terms of pay and conditions the Fianna Fáil–PD government has been very generous, indeed to the point of profligacy. Pay rates in the public sector comfortably exceeded those in the private sector between 1997 and 2005, thanks to a combination of national pay rounds and the questionable exercise of benchmarking.

The benchmarking process was a clear and successful attempt by the government to curry favour with public servants in advance of the 2002 general election. The astonishing awards, which were totally unsupported by any hard evidence that public service pay had fallen behind the private sector, were announced in the immediate aftermath of the election. All the evidence available at the time pointed to the fact that, far from lagging behind, public service pay was higher than comparable rates in the private sector. Instead of putting up a fight for some real transparency in the process, the PDs quietly acquiesced in this charade. It was an abuse of the public finances by the government, one that has the potential to seriously distort the labour market in the coming years.

Another serious error in the second term in government was PD involvement in the decentralisation of the public service. This half-baked and expensive scheme has the potential to wreak havoc in the public service in the long term, without achieving anything for planned regional development. By acquiescing in unwarranted pay rises for public servants through benchmarking and then supporting a decentralisation scheme that will undermine the efficiency of the public system, the PDs have opted for the worst of both worlds. Both are classic populist Fianna Fáil schemes, which the PDs should be in government to prevent rather than support.

Economic consultant Colm McCarthy argues that far from being radical and right-wing, as its opponents claim, the problem with the PDs is that the party has become too conservative and unadventurous:

'The PDs are now so up to their tonsils in social partnership they have actually become big government spenders. A whole side of the PD agenda—the need for competition, the elimination of waste in public spending and the abolition of unnecessary quangos—has all been forgotten about. They have been sucked into establishment values. I think the PDs have lost their radicalism.'[6]

Radicalism, of course, can be a double-edged sword. Michael McDowell coined the phrase that the PDs must be 'radical or redundant', but in the 1997 general election they almost managed to be both. The hard fact is that the PDs are engaged in a permanent struggle to get the attention of the electorate, or a least the segment of it that might vote for them. Stephen O'Byrnes is surprised by the party's inability to carve out a support-base for itself:

'I have always been puzzled at the inability of the party to establish deeper roots in the community, considering what it stands for and its record in delivering on its commitments. The party should have the potential to broaden its base. The paradox is that it has not really developed in Dublin or in the rapidly expanding suburban parts of Meath and Kildare, where its message has a direct relevance to voters.'[7]

This failure is a serious one for the PDs and in effect means that a simple case of bad luck could see the party being wiped out in a future election.

Like others in the PDs, O'Byrnes is struck by the success of the other parties in building and retaining tribal loyalties. Fianna Fáil has shown an incredible resilience in the face of all sorts of internal dissension, policy U-turns and disclosures about highly questionable behaviour. The party's ability to hold onto power through thick and thin is quite extraordinary. In its own way, too, Fine Gael's hold on the imagination of about one-quarter of voters is equally remarkable. Fianna Fáil has the great attraction of power and patronage to keep its followers happy. Fine Gael has been notably unsuccessful for the past two decades, with just one short interlude in power, and doesn't evoke the same tribal loyalty as Fianna Fáil, yet Fine Gael has both the organisation and a deep resonance with a significant proportion of the electorate to remain the leading Opposition party. For decades Labour has struggled in vain to break out of its third party status, but it too has shown an ability to survive against huge odds. The party can depend on staunch loyalty from its members during the dark days and to hold the votes of a segment of the electorate.

The paradox of the PDs is that the party has only managed to arouse this level of loyalty in places like Limerick and Galway—the stomping grounds of the original defectors from Fianna Fáil. In suburban Dublin, which should be its natural hinterland, the PDs have always lived on the edge and have never had even one safe seat. In fact, the PDs will hardly have one safe seat going into the next election. The party has always lived on the narrow hinterland between success and extinction, and the next election will be no exception. The PDs are capable of getting anything from no seats to 10 seats on a share of the vote that may range between 3 per cent and 5 per cent—it is that unpredictable. This is the fundamental problem for the party: after twenty years in politics, it still has not developed a PD vote. Voters will vote for individual PD candidates, but in the absence of a good candidate they will not respond to, or trust the PD brand.

This is a pressing dilemma for the PDs and there is no obvious solution. The party has managed to develop a clear and decisive image in the public mind (Michael McDowell and Mary Harney have seen to that), yet it can only win votes with very strong candidates. For instance, the PDs would not have won seats in Laois–Offaly or Longford–Roscommon in 2002 without Tom Parlon or Mae Sexton. More surprising, however, is that the same holds true for urban Dublin. Harney, McDowell, or a remarkable vote-winner like Liz O'Donnell can win seats, but relatively unknown PD candidates have not been able to break through, despite the relevance of the party's core philosophy to a significant segment of the electorate. While this is partly the result of the continuing pull of tribal political loyalties on Irish voters, the PDs must accept some share of the blame. The party has allowed the 'tattered flags' of the Civil War parties to fly far longer than anybody anticipated in the late 1980s.

PD general secretary John Higgins thinks that one of the reasons for the lack of a dependable support-base is that the party has taken up and discarded new candidates at every election, local and national:

'A lot of good people have run for the PDs and then been allowed to drift away when they were not instantly successful. The lesson of Irish politics is that candidates have to run again and again to establish themselves with the voters. That is something we are trying to address.'[8]

Another problem faced by the PDs is that the party has never generated the level of support within the business community that its commitment to free market economics might have been expected, given its policies.

Part of the explanation for this has emerged from the raft of inquiries and tribunals: a large segment of the business community did not care about the high tax rates in Ireland in the 1980s because they were not paying tax. They either flouted the law completely or operated tax-evasion schemes, like Ansbacher, to avoid paying their fair share of the taxes needed to keep vital services going. The business community had its own private deal with Fianna Fáil and, if anything, the PDs were a nuisance stirring up debate about the tax system. It suited the wealthy to let sleeping dogs lie—it meant the PAYE sector paid the exorbitant levels of tax. By challenging the status quo the PDs aroused the enmity of far more powerful forces in Irish society than the left-wing political parties.

Still, the PDs have survived for twenty years and have spent a majority of those years in government, implementing the policies they enunciated in response to the economic crisis of the 1980s. The challenge ahead is to devise a set of policies that will tackle the underlying problems in modern Irish society. Ireland's problems in 2005 are those of a wealthy country whose citizens are not getting the public services they need and deserve because of inefficiency or incompetence. Harney has attempted to strike out in that direction in her efforts to reform the Health Service. Her success or failure in that task will be crucial, as it will determine whether the PDs can project themselves as a party with a lot more to offer than a tax-cutting agenda. Other parties survive merely by being there. The PDs had to justify their existence at all times; to be radical or redundant is still the underlying imperative.

NOTES

Chapter 1. O'Malley leaves Fianna Fáil (PAGES 5–15)
1. Dick Walsh, *The Party* (1986), 29.
2. Stephen Collins, *The Power Game* (2001).
3. Interview with Barra Ó Tuama, 25 April 2005.
4. Interview with Des O'Malley, September 2004.
5. *Irish Press*, 7 October 1982.
6. *Irish Independent*, 7 October 1982.
7. Stephen Collins, *Spring and the Labour Story* (1993), 106/109.
8. Garret FitzGerald, *All in a Life* (1991), 435.
9. Private information.
10. FitzGerald, *ibid*, 435.
11. Bruce Arnold, *Haughey: His Life and Unlucky Deeds* (1994), 221.
12. Dick Walsh, *ibid*, 84.
13. O'Malley interview.
14. *Dáil Debates*, 20 February 1985.
15. *Irish Press*, 27 February 1985.
16. *ibid*.
17. Collins, *The Power Game*, 165.
18. O'Malley interview.

Chapter 2. Birth Pangs (PAGES 16–29)
1. Interview with Michael McDowell, 21 December 2004.
2. Niamh Brennan archive.
3. *ibid*.
4. *Sunday Tribune*, 23 August 1987.
5. Brennan archive.
6. PD archive.
7. Interview with Paul Mackay, November 2004.
8. Ó Tuama interview.
9. *Irish Press*, 20 April 1985.
10. Interview with Mary Harney, February 2005.
11. Ó Tuama interview.
12. Brennan archive.
13. *ibid*.
14. Mackay interview.
15. *ibid*.
16. PD archive.

17. *ibid.*
18. Paul Mackay diary.
19. Mackay interview.
20. Interview with Mairin Quill.
21. Harney interview.
22. Mackay diary.
23. *ibid.*
24. Mackay interview.
25. Harney interview.
26. *ibid.*
27. Mackay diary and interview.
28. Brennan archive.
29. PD archive.
30. Mackay interview.
31. *ibid.*
32. McDowell interview.

Chapter 3. Progressive Democrats (PAGES 30–39)
1. Mackay interview.
2. Harney interview.
3. PD archive.
4. *ibid.*
5. O'Malley interview.
6. Mackay interview.
7. Harney interview.
8. O'Malley interview.
9. Mackay interview.
10. *ibid.*
11. *ibid.*
12. *ibid.*
13. *Irish Press*, 21 December 1985.
14. Mackay interview.
15. Harney interview.
16. Mackay interview.
17. McDowell interview.
18. *Irish Independent*, 23 December 1985.
19. PD archive.
20. O'Malley interview.
21. Mackay and McDowell interviews.
22. *Irish Press*, 23 December 1985.
23. Gemma Hussey, *At the Cutting Edge* (1990), 184.

Chapter 4. The First Year (PAGES 40–53)
1. *Irish Press*, 1/2 January 1986.

2. Mackay interview.
3. O'Malley interview.
4. *Sunday Independent*, 20 January 1986.
5. Interview with John Dardis, 18 May 2005.
6. Stephen Collins, *The Haughey File* (1992), 81.
7. Interview with Bobby Molloy, March 2000.
8. RTÉ, 'The Week in Politics', 19 December 2004.
9. Quill interview.
10. Mackay interview.
11. Harney interview.
12. *Sunday Press*, 2 February 1986.
13. RTÉ, 'The Week in Politics', 19 December 2004.
14. PD archive.
15. Brennan archive.
16. Walsh, *The Party*, 93.
17. PD archive.
18. Brennan archive.
19. *ibid*.
20. *Irish Press*, 3 November 1986.
21. *ibid*., 28 October 1986.
22. Harney interview.
23. O'Byrnes interview.
24. *Sunday Independent*, 18 May 1986.
25. *Sunday Tribune*, 11 May 1986.
26. Interview with Pat Cox, 10 January 2005.
27. *Sunday Tribune*, 25 May 1986.
28. *Irish Press*, 26 May 1986.
29. *Irish Independent*, 26 May 1986.
30. Cox interview.
31. *Irish Press*, 24 May 1986.

Chapter 5. Preparing for Battle (PAGES 54–64)

1. *Dáil Debates*, 1985.
2. FitzGerald, *op. cit.*, 624/631.
3. PD archive.
4. Mansergh, Martin, ed., *The Spirit of the Nation: The Speeches of Charles J. Haughey* (1986), 1112.
5. *Dáil Debates*, 16 May 1986.
6. *ibid*.
7. McDowell interview.
8. PD National Executive minutes, 17 September 1986.
9. Cox interview.
10. *Sunday Press*, 1 June 1986.
11. PD archive.

12. *The Irish Times, Irish Independent, Irish Press*, 16 October 1986.
13. O'Byrnes interview.
14. Barry Desmond files.
15. *Irish Independent*, 16 October 1986.

Chapter 6. Election Triumph (PAGES 65–75)
1. Interview with John Kelly, 1990.
2. O'Malley interview.
3. David Farrell, *How Ireland Voted* (1987), 54.
4. Cox interview.
5. Interview with Geraldine Kennedy, 20 May 2005.
6. *Irish Press*, 19 January 1987.
7. Mackay interview.
8. PD archive.
9. Cox interview.
10. PD archive.
11. Cox interview.
12. *Sunday Tribune*, 8 February 1987.
13. *ibid*, 15 February 1987.
14. Girvin, Brian, *How Ireland Voted: 1987*, 19–20.
15. *The Irish Times*, 3 February 1987.
16. *Irish Press*, 20 January 1987.
17. *The Irish Times*, 28 January 1987.
18. *Irish Press*, 16 February 1987.
19. Collins, *The Haughey File*, 89.
20. McDowell interview.
21. *Irish Press*, 19 February 1987.
22. *The Irish Times*, 19 February 1987.
23. *Irish Press*, 5 March 1987.
24. McDowell interview.
25. O'Byrnes interview.

Chapter 7. The Morning After (PAGES 76–88)
1. O'Malley interview.
2. *Dáil Debates*, 31 March 1987.
3. *Irish Press*, 23 March 1987.
4. *Dáil Debates*, 31 March 1987.
5. O'Malley interview.
6. Collins, *The Power Game*, 179.
7. *Dáil Debates*, 9 March 1989.
8. Quill interview.
9. Dardis interview.
10. Kennedy interview.
11. Harney interview.

12. O'Byrnes interview.
13. Kennedy interview.
14. Harney interview.
15. McDowell interview.
16. O'Byrnes interview.
17. *The Irish Times*, 30 May 1988.
18. *ibid.*
19. *Irish Press*, 30 May 1987.
20. PD archive.
21. Government Procedure Instructions, fourth edition (1983).
22. *Flood Tribunal Report*, 2003.
23. *Irish Press*, 19 June 1989.
24. *Dáil Debates*, 10 May 1989.

Chapter 8. Election Disaster (PAGES 89–98)
1. Cox interview.
2. *ibid.*
3. David Farrell in *How Ireland Voted in 1989*, 29–30.
4. PD archive.
5. Collins, *The Power Game*, 191–2.
6. Interview with Peter White, December 2004.
7. *The Irish Times*, 28 May 1989.
8. PD archive.
9. *In Your Opinion* by Jack Jones (2001), 323–4.
10. *How Ireland Voted: 1989*, 57.
11. *ibid.*, 61.
12. RTÉ radio, 16 June 1989.
13. *The Irish Times*, 17 June 1989.
14. Harney interview.
15. O'Byrnes interview.
16. Quill interview.
17. O'Malley interview.
18. Collins, *The Haughey File*, 156.
19. Shane Kenny, *Go Dance on Somebody Else's Grave* (1990), 45.
20. Harney interview.
21. Kenny, *Go Dance on Somebody Else's Grave*, 47–9.
22. Harney interview.
23. McDowell interview.

Chapter 9. Into Office (PAGES 99–109)
1. Kenny, *Go Dance on Somebody Else's Grave*, 53.
2. O'Malley interview.
3. *ibid.*
4. Collins, *The Haughey File*, 160.

5. Cox interview.
6. *ibid*.
7. Kenny, *Go Dance on Somebody Else's Grave*, 74.
8. Cox interview.
9. Kenny, *Go Dance on Somebody Else's Grave*, 87.
10. *ibid*, 101.
11. McCreevy interview, 19 December 2004.
12. Collins, *The Haughey File*, 162.
13. Kenny, *Go Dance on Somebody Else's Grave*, 109.
14. Collins, *The Haughey File*, 163.
15. Cox interview.
16. Collins, *The Haughey File*, 167.
17. *Dáil Debates*, 12 July 1989.
18. Harney interview.

Chapter 10. Coalition Conscience (PAGES 110–121)

1. Interview with McCreevy, 19 December 2004.
2. O'Malley interview.
3. Harney interview.
4. Quill interview.
5. O'Malley interview.
6. *Dáil Debates*, 28 August 1990.
7. *Sunday Press*, 2 September 1990.
8. *Dáil Debates*, 31 January 1990.
9. O'Malley interview.
10. *The Irish Times, Irish Independent, Irish Press*, 1 February 1990.
11. Collins, *The Haughey File*, 182–195.
12. McCreevy interview.

Chapter 11. Radical or Redundant? (PAGES 122–133)

1. *Irish Press*, 17 February 1990.
2. Harney interview.
3. *ibid*.
4. *ibid*.
5. Harney interview.
6. McDowell interview.
7. *Dáil Debates*, 14 May 1991.
8. *Sunday Press*, 19 May 1991.
9. Interview with O'Donnell, 3 February 2005.
10. *The Irish Times*, 19 October 1991.
11. Collins, *The Haughey File*, 222.
12. *Dáil Debates*, 13 November 1991.
13. *The Irish Times*, 22 January 1992.
14. *Sunday Press*, 26 January 1992.

15. O'Malley interview.
16. *The Irish Times*, 23 January 1992.
17. *ibid.*
18. O'Malley interview.
19. Dardis interview.
20. *Dáil Debates*, 11 February 1992.

Chapter 12. If in Doubt, Leave Them Out (PAGES 134–145)
1. O'Malley interview.
2. Sean Duignan, *One Spin on the Merry-Go-Round* (1995), 20.
3. Harney interview.
4. *Sunday Press*, 8 March 1992.
5. O'Byrnes interview.
6. Duignan, *One Spin on the Merry-Go-Round*, 32.
7. Harney interview.
8. Duignan, *One Spin on the Merry-Go-Round*, 37.
9. *ibid.*, 33.
10. PD archive.
11. Duignan, *One Spin on the Merry-Go-Round*, 52.
12. *Dáil Debates*, 5 November 1992.
13. *ibid.*
14. *ibid.*
15. Duignan, *One Spin on the Merry-Go-Round*, 52.
16. Parker interview, 31 January 2005.
17. David Farrell in *How Ireland Voted: 1992*, Gallagher and Laver (eds), 29.
18. *ibid.*, 49.
19. Parker interview.
20. McDowell interview.

Chapter 13. Harney Takes the Helm (PAGES 146–156)
1. *Sunday Tribune*, 28 March 1993.
2. *ibid.*
3. *Dáil Debates*, 12 January 1993.
4. *Sunday Tribune*, 21 March 1993.
5. *Sunday Independent*, 28 March 1993.
6. *The Irish Times*, 29 March 1993.
7. RTÉ, Des O'Malley documentary.
8. O'Malley interview.
9. Harney interview.
10. *Sunday Press*, 10 October 1993.
11. Mackay interview.
12. Harney interview.
13. *Sunday Business Post*, 10 October 1993.
14. *ibid.*

15. *The Irish Times*, 6 October 1993.
16. Una Claffey, *The Women Who Won* (1993), 156.
17. O'Malley interview.
18. McDowell interview.
19. Mackay interview.
20. *Irish Independent*, 13 October 1993.
21. PD archive.
22. *The Irish Times*, 18 June 1994.
23. *Dáil Debates*, 12 October 1993.

Chapter 14. Civil War (PAGES 157–167)
1. Jack Jones, *In Your Opinion* (2001), 326.
2. Harney interview.
3. *Sunday Business Post*, 19 June 1994.
4. *The Irish Times*, 18 June 1994.
5. *ibid*.
6. Harney interview.
7. *Sunday Business Post*, 19 June 1994.
8. *ibid*.
9. McDowell interview.
10. O'Malley interview.
11. *Sunday Business Post*, 19 June 1994.
12. Interview with Brigid Teefy, 9 April 2005.
13. Quill interview.
14. O'Donnell interview.
15. Quill interview.
16. Dardis interview.
17. *The Irish Times*, 17 June 1994.
18. Parker interview.
19. *Irish Independent*, 13 June 1994.
20. *Sunday Business Post*, 3 July 1994.
21. O'Malley interview.
22. Harney interview.
23. O'Byrnes interview.
24. O'Donnell interview.
25. Harney interview.
26. *Irish Independent*, 6 September 1994.
27. *The Irish Times*, 21 May 1994.

Chapter 15. Shot Down in Flames (PAGES 168–180)
1. PD archive.
2. *ibid*.
3. *ibid*.
4. *Sunday Tribune*, 25 May 1997.

5.　*How Ireland Voted*, 1997, 43.
6.　'A New Deal', PD Manifesto, 1997, 15.
7.　*The Irish Times*, 22 May 1997.
8.　*Evening Herald*, 23 May 1997.
9.　*ibid.*
10. *The Irish Times*, 22 May 1997.
11. Harney interview.
12. McDowell interview.
13. O'Donnell interview.
14. O'Byrnes interview.
15. O'Donnell interview.
16. *The Irish Times*, 23 May 1997.
17. *ibid.*, 24 May 1997.
18. *ibid.*, 26 May 1997.
19. Michael Holmes in *How Ireland Voted*, 44.
20. *The Irish Times*, 22 and 31 May 1997.
21. Harney interview.
22. *The Irish Times*, 5 June 1997.
23. *Irish Independent*, 5 June 1997.
24. O'Donnell interview.
25. *The Irish Times*, 8 June 1997.
26. Harney interview.

Chapter 16.　Victory from Defeat (PAGES 181–192)

1.　*The Irish Times*, 10 June 1997.
2.　Collins, *The Power Game*, 308.
3.　*The Irish Times*, 20 June 1997.
4.　*ibid.*
5.　*Dáil Debates*, 26 June 1997.
6.　*ibid.*
7.　Harney interview.
8.　*The Irish Times*, 24 May 1997.
9.　*Sunday Tribune*, 21 September 1997.
10. McDowell interview.
11. Harney interview.
12. *Dáil Debates*, 10 September 1997.
13. Harney interview.
14. *The Irish Times*, 4 October 1997.
15. *The Irish Times*, 4 December 1997.
16. *Irish Independent*, 4 December 1997.
17. *The Irish Times*, 3 December 1998.
18. *Sunday Tribune*, 4 December 1999.
19. Harney interview.
20. PD website.

Chapter 17. The Prodigal Returns (PAGES 193–204)

1. *Dáil Debates*, 10 September 1997.
2. *ibid.*
3. O'Donnell interview.
4. *Magill*, June 1998.
5. *Dáil Debates*, 16 December 1998.
6. *Sunday Independent*, 24 January 1999.
7. *Dáil Debates*, 27 January 1999.
8. *Sunday Tribune*, 2 May 1999.
9. Mackay interview, 6 May 2005.
10. Harney interview.
11. *Dáil Debates*, 10 February 1999.
12. *Sunday Business Post*, 14 December 1997.
13. Mackay interview.
14. *The Irish Times*, 11 November 1998.
15. McDowell interview.
16. *ibid.*
17. Harney interview.
18. *The Irish Times*, 8 July 1999.
19. McDowell interview.
20. *The Irish Times*, October 2000.
21. *Sunday Tribune*, October 2000.
22. O'Donnell interview.
23. Harney interview.
24. 'The Week in Politics', 25 May 2001.
25. Harney interview.

Chapter 18. Up the Pole (PAGES 205–215)

1. *The Irish Times*, 11 February 2002.
2. Interview with Oliver O'Connor, 30 March 2005.
3. Interview with John Higgins, 18 May 2005.
4. Interview with Stephen O'Byrnes, 3 March 2005.
5. O'Byrnes article.
6. *How Ireland Voted* (2002), 72.
7. O'Connor interview.
8. O'Byrnes article.
9. *ibid.*
10. *ibid.*
11. O'Connor interview.
12. Harney interview.
13. O'Byrnes interview.
14. O'Connor interview.
15. *How Ireland Voted* (2002), 73.
16. Harney interview.

17. O'Connor interview.
18. Higgins interview.
19. Higgins interview.
20. Harney interview.

Chapter 19. The Party Goes On (PAGES 216–227)
1. Harney interview.
2. Fine Gael website.
3. *Sunday Tribune*, June and September 2002.
4. *The Irish Times*, 22 September 2002.
5. *How Ireland Voted, 2002*, March and Gallagher (eds) (2003).
6. Morris Tribunal website.
7. *Irish Independent*, 9 December 2004.
8. *Sunday Tribune*, 12 December 2004.
9. *Sunday Tribune*, 10 April 2005.
10. O'Malley interview.

Chapter 20. Past and Future (PAGES 228–240)
1. Barry Desmond interview, April 2005.
2. *The Irish Times*, 31 December 2004.
3. OECD Report, February 2005.
4. PD website.
5. Magill Summer School, August 2004.
6. McCarthy interview.
7. O'Byrnes interview.
8. Higgins interview.

APPENDIX 1

Organising the Party
Contents

May 1985

MICHAEL MCDOWELL

1. INTRODUCTION

1.1 The purpose of this memorandum is to survey the organisational problems establishing a new party and to establish a reasonable time-frame in which this can be done.

1.2 I assume that it is proposed to establish a single national party with local units in each Dail Constituency. While I appreciate that the decision as to whether or not every Constituency will be contested is yet to be made, there is no disadvantage in having an organisation in every Constituency. It may also be that the mere establishment of a Constituency Organisation will attract to the Party good prospective candidates. From the point of view of registering the Party for the purpose of the Electoral Act 1963 it is desirable to have a comprehensive coverage of Dail Constituencies.

1.3 Time is of the essence. If the Party is not established in the Autumn, there is the prospect that the impetus to get it going will flag all round. Likewise the chances of being forced into a bye-election or a general election while unprepared is increased.

1.4 If the Party is to be launched in the Autumn, it would be best to establish it to co-incide with the new Dail session. That means an early October launch. The first conference of the Party has to follow shortly (to establish any coherent sense of party and organisation among supporters). That conference can't be too near Christmas; ergo it has to be held no later than the third week of November.

1.5 The Party will not come into being by reason of an Autumn press conference; it has to be built. That means that the work of organisation, consultation, recruitment and appointment of officers has to start immediately. An organiser and a press officer need July, August and September to do their job professionally; they must be appointed within the next few weeks. The body which will supervise and assist them must also be appointed in the next few weeks. They have a lot of behind the scenes confidential preparatory work to do.

1.6 For these reasons, I feel that there is a great deal of urgency in this enterprise. To maintain momentum, to avoid unforeseen problems and to keep the political initiative, this Party must be functioning in late 1985. To achieve this, work must begin immediately.

2. TIMETABLE

2.1 In effect no overt activity can be undertaken until after the local elections and their immediate aftermath. This means that prior to the 1st of July only very basic and hidden preparatory work can be done.

2.2 The months of July and August are dead months for purposes such as calling meetings and attracting publicity. They can, however, be used for administrative preparation including appointment of officers, establishment of headquarters, listing and categorisation of supporters, fund raising and financial planning and preparing of a programme of support group foundation meetings.

2.3 The last three weeks of September will be available for holding inaugural foundation meetings of Constituency support groups. For reasons set out below, these meetings will best be co-ordinated on a regional basis.

2.4 Any prospect of a well organised start to the Party will be scotched if there is any substantial delay. <u>Everyone involved is taking a risk of sorts; those with established political links will be more exposed and less enthusiastic as each week goes by without any knowledge that the planning phase has commenced.</u>

2.5 As stated above, the optimal time for a party launch (i.e. an inaugural press conference) would be in the second week of October. A foundation National Conference might follow in the second week of November.

2.6 A National Membership drive to commence in mid January 1986 would be geared to "fill out" the skeleton body.

2.7 All the above is to put the Party on a footing to contest a general election at any time from spring 1986. While this might be an early date to predict a general election, it is a possible date. Unforeseen political events such as difficulties with the 1986 budget could precipitate such an election. Furthermore, it is fair to assume that:
(a) Labour and Fine Gael will <u>not</u> contest the next general election on a common platform.
(b) To try to keep the initiative, the Labour Party will choose an issue and a timing for a Dail dissolution best suited to their own interests and designed to rob Fine Gael of any chance of posturing as an overall majority party.

2.8 If opinion polls show a new party biting into Fine Gael support to a greater degree than expected, Fine Gael may also be tempted to call an early election, not to win the election but to kill the new party in its cot. Thus, the new party must establish itself with speed; the best way to achieve speed is to work to a time-table. That begs the question: <u>Who is to work to this time-table?</u>

3. A FOUNDATION COMMITTEE

3.1 I suggest that by June 15th, a foundation committee of 8 to 12 people be established. The composition of the committee is largely a matter for Desmond O'Malley. I would suggest the following criteria in deciding what the composition of the committee should be:
(a) balanced as to political origin of members
(b) biased towards organisation and finance

(c)   regionally balanced
(d)   totally confidential
(e)   composed of people who are willing to travel and consult with and report on potential support groups.

3.3 The Committee should have among its members at least two people who will be potential fund raisers for the Party.

3.4 The Committee should not be charged with preparing policy; that should be left to an informal group to be established by Desmond O'Malley. To motivate the Committee and to cross-fertilize policy formation, the Committee should be given regular briefings in progress on policy foundation and its general thrust.

3.5 Supporting T.D.s should not be members of the Committee. Those T.D.s (if they wish), the National Officers (to be appointed) and the Foundation Committee should be the steering group of the Party until the first conference. Supporting T.D.s will want to be kept abreast of progress in organising the Party.

3.6 Desmond O'Malley should be a member of the Committee and designated as its President. Whether he wishes to be Chairman as well is another matter; it might be better to have a Chairman other than the President in order to ensure continuity if Desmond O'Malley was unavailable. That should be decided in the light of who the available candidates are.

3.7 The Committee should meet weekly until the First Annual Conference. This may seem very frequent but there is a lot of work to be done and the only way to ensure punctual progress is to have very regular review.

3.8 The members of the Committee will have to travel the Country liaising with and convening Constituency Support Groups.
To avoid the danger of the whole committee being bogged down by one of two "talkers" and to ensure that more than one person is acquainted with vital aspects of the Party's activities there should be small informal sub-committees as follows:
(a)   a finance and fund-raising sub-committee
(b)   a rules subcommittee to draft the Party's rules for submission to the Foundation Conference
(c)   a Conference Organising Committee to make the arrangements for the Foundation Conference in November.

4. NATIONAL OFFICERS
4.1 The appointment of National Organiser will have to be a full time one. The job will be an organising and management one. The holder will also act as General Secretary and will have to :
(a)   establish a register of member supporters

(b) organise the party headquarters
(c) bring into being the party organisation
(d) control day to day spending
(e) supervise the administrative staff (initially a secretary)
(f) report to the Foundation Committee and do their bidding

The salary will be circa £20,000 per annum (interim until November). The position will be initially for a probationary period.

4.2 The position of National Press Officer is a crucial one. The holder will have to deal with the media generally and handle the publicity surrounding the formation of the Party. The holder will be:
(a) answerable to the committee for his/her publicity work
(b) answerable to the President for Party Press relations
(c) responsible for internal information and publicity
(d) required to liaise with publicity consultants in relation to image, P.R. and the like

4.3 If finances permit three regional organisers should also be appointed as follows:
(a) a Southern Organiser for Munster, except Clare
(b) a Western Organiser for Clare, Connacht and Donegal
(c) an Eastern Organiser for Leinster, Cavan and Monaghan

These officers would be answerable to the National Organiser and the President. The National Organiser would share Dublin with the Eastern Organiser.

4.4 At least one full-time secretary would be required. Supporting T.D.s might "lend" their secretaries on a part time basis.

5. HEADQUARTERS

5.1 A suitable headquarters will have to be rented with effect from 1st July. The premises will have to be in a reasonably prestigious location (not Mount Street). Accommodation will have to include:
(a) a reception area
(b) a secretarial area
(c) at least three offices
(d) a board room suitable for committee meetings, briefings and press conferences.

5.2 As buildings convey image, the premises will have to be modern, sophisticated and well furnished and decorated. Ample parking would be an advantage.

5.3 Good phone systems, a good photocopier and a small computer for word-processing and membership statistics will be required.

The Foundation Committee will have to take a short-term lease of these offices in late June.

6. FINANCES

6.1 I am ignorant of the extent of potential financial backing. I feel, however, that the business community would be anxious to help. An approach should be made to Allied Irish Banks or the Bank of Ireland to arrange for credit facilities and to ask for financial support. This will have to be done at the highest level.

6.2 Quiet, low key fund-raising will be required between June and November. The launch of the Party and the Foundation Conference will be expensive. These items as well as the costs of establishing the headquarters and paying wages will definitely require fund-raising efforts in the next few months.

6.3 A substantial annual subscription of at least £30 should be sought from members (with the exception of the unwaged). The initial enthusiasm for a new party should also attract financial support. A scaled-down version of Fianna Fail and Fine Gael lotteries should also be organised for 1986. Newspaper advertisements should be placed in November. These would have the effect of :
(a)   attracting funds
(b)   dispelling criticism that funding comes from vested interests

6.4 As stated above, finances should be handled by a sub-committee of the Foundation Committee.

7. PARTY STRUCTURE

7.1 I believe the main elements of the party structure should be:
(a)   a parliamentary party having the usual relationship to the rest of the party
(b)   a party organisation based on Constituency units and governed by a National Council

7.2 Constituency units will have to be flexibly defined in the early stages of the Party. Where a Constituency is strong enough to sub-divide into county areas or into polling areas, the Constituency Council will be like a comhairle Dail Cheanntair or Constituency Executive. In weaker areas, we may have to avoid excessive dilution of support by leaving the Constituency Council in charge of the whole area. As the Party develops, each Constituency council will have to submit an organisation plan for approval to the National Executive.

7.3 A National Council, consisting of representatives of the Parliamentary Party and persons elected at the annual conference to represent the Constituency bodies plus party officers, trustees and nominees of the President should be established at the Foundation Conference in November and then take over from the Foundation Committee.

7.4 As mentioned in paragraph 3.9 above, a rules sub-committee should be established to draw up an interim constitution and rules for approval by the Foundation Committee. These can be based in other bodies' rules (Fine Gael's rules are a very bad precedent). They can contain transitional provisions to be reconsidered at the next conference. Basic rules relating to the Electoral Acts and National Organisation are essential in case of an early election.

7.5 I feel it is important to attract young support to the Party and that a Regional Youth Movement should be established by each of the regional organisers. The Youth Groups should be represented on the National Council.

7.6 In addition to the National Conferences, regional conferences should be held annually. All conferences will have to be thematically organised and have discussion documents rather than simple resolutions as at Ard Fheiseanna.

7.7 Since women will be encouraged to play an equal role in the Party, I feel that no special women's groups should be established. Likewise, other organisations like trade union groups have been a failure and should not be attempted.

7.8 Overseas support groups might be useful allies and fund-raisers but they can wait.

8. PARTY NAME AND IMAGE
8.1 Distasteful though it may be, expert advice should be sought on image. While policy is not a matter for PR consultants, image is. Use of colour, symbols and suggestive associations are very important and will have to be decided on before the Party launch and the Foundation Conference. The help of professional visualisers and publicity men could be invaluable.

8.2 Names which occur to me for the Party include:
    NEW REPUBLIC
    THE NEW REPUBLIC PARTY
    NEW DEMOCRATS
    NATIONAL PARTY
    RADICAL PARTY
    DEMOCRATIC RADICAL PARTY
    CENTRE RADICAL PARTY
It would be a help if the name of the Party translated easily into Irish, e.g. "POBLACHT NUA" or "NUA-PHOBLACHT"

8.3 I feel that in name, style, image and substance the Party will have to and appear to be:
(a) new and not just a re-jig of assorted dissidents.
(b) challenging – not just resigned to more of the same.

(c)   dynamic – never pessimistic.
(d)   clean – no hint of Tammany Hall.
(e)   different – disdainful of FF and FG.
(f)   honest – but not naive.
(g)   competent – but not ruthless.
(h)   idealistic – not merely pragmatic.
(i)   business-like – a 'no-nonsense image'.
(j)   positive – not too critical.

8.4 I feel that the thrust of Party rhetoric and policy should be:
(a)   pro enterprise
(b)   in favour of economic participation by all
(c)   liberal and pluralist but not aggressively secularist
(d)   hostile to institutionalised dependency
(e)   favourable to incentives
(f)   pro self reliance
(g)   deregulating where possible
(h)   anti-monopoly and pro-competition but not overly into "privatising"
(i)   low-key on nationalism
(j)   stressing real republican values rather than nationalistic myths

8.5 Our image should be stamped on everything that we say, publish and do right from "day one"; name, logo, choices of venues etc. Names of positions and bodies in the Party should reflect a fresh business-like approach.

8.6 <u>Above all, any hint of amateurism must be avoided.</u> That is the label that Prendergast and Wall will most want to hang about our necks. It is a line that the media will be easily fed.

9. POLICY

9.1 I am not going to trespass on the area of policy in this paper save to make the suggestion that Desmond O'Malley and any other supporting T.D.s establish an informal policy group to prepare a 10 page general statement of policy subtended, if necessary, by detailed papers which would be reserved for discussion at the Foundation Conference.

9.2 The 10 page document should not be too cautious. It should be attractive to young people and activists. It should suggest novelty, optimism and, above all, that there is "more to come".

9.3 The Press Conference called to launch the Party should be well worked out and prepared for. Detailed questions on policy should be put back to the Foundation Conference. Carefully thought out responses should be ready for the more predictable questions which will [be] asked on issues such as personalities, prospects of success and attitudes to participation in Government.

9.4 I feel that any T.D. or Senator who wishes to join the Party should be encouraged to adopt a position for the remainder of the life of the Dail. He or she will vote in such a manner as not to precipitate a general election and so as to fulfill the mandate given him or her at the last election. Obviously they will have to resign from their respective parliamentary parties.

9.5 I feel that the presence of 6 to 8 members of the Oireachtas and the same number of non-Oireachtas personalities at the Launch Press Conference is essential. Desmond O'Malley and other supporting T.D.s should actively pursue such recruits over the summer months.

9.6 If the major parties get wind of the launch date, they will do their utmost to upstage it. A decoy date will be needed.

10. FOUNDATION CONFERENCE

10.1 The Foundation Conference to be held in November is of crucial importance. In order to organise it properly, each Constituency Council will have to have met twice in October, these meetings to be convened by the Founding Committee.

10.2 Delegates will have to be selected by the Councils. Voting rights will have to be established.

10.3 Liaison with the media will be of great importance. Clashing events will have to be avoided.

10.4 Discussion papers, designed to flesh out the paper issued at the launch press conference, will have to be circulated. The absence of 'spokesmen' may be a problem. The Foundation Committee may have to appoint a Session Chairman who will deliver key-note speeches and/or reply to and summarise debate much as a spokesman would. National personalities would be useful here.

10.5 The venue of the conference is of great importance; it cannot be too down market. Bussing of delegates to ensure a larger attendance and the avoidance of half-empty halls should be a priority.

11. CONSTITUENCY ORGANISATION

11.1 In order to provide a flexible but uniform Constituency organisation I suggest the following model:
(a) Each Constituency Party will consist of all the members of the Party in the Constituency

(b) The Constituency Party will elect the Constituency Council of, say, 30 members at an inaugural meeting

(c) If the Constituency Council considers it proper, it may divide the Constituency Party membership into areas based on the population or geography and allocate the membership accordingly.

(d) The Constituency Council will report to the National Council on its strength and will give the National Council a proposal for the establishment of area units, the voting entitlement of the units at the Constituency Council and the size of a new Council to be elected at an annual general meeting in February 1986.

(e) If the National Council approves the scheme, the Constituency Council will be re-elected in February 1986 with such officers as the rules may provide.

11.2 The question of Branch or Cummann structure will be a matter for agreement between the Constituency and the National Councils.

11.3 The Fine Gael system whereby Constituency organisers and PROs are debarred from being candidates works well and ensures that party headquarters has an impartial local agent to report on the Constituency. I think this system should be followed.

11.4 In September 1985, all sympathisers should be contacted to prepare them to form the Constituency party in October after the Party launch. The method of establishment should be explained to a few key people well in advance. Care should be taken in September to weed out undesirables and plants from the list of sympathisers. The inaugural meetings should be convened by the National Council or Regional Organisers.

11.5 A "veiled hint" type speech should be made by Desmond O'Malley in July or August to encourage more letters from potential supporters to ensure maximum attendance at the inaugural meetings.

APPENDIX 2

INTRODUCTION

There should be a preamble as to the reasons for setting up this new party and arising from agreement on these, the party is basing its fundamental principles and objectives.

This to be known as the Foundation Document or some other such name. My preamble and principles / objectives may need addition or replacement or refinement but I suggest it as an approach for the following reasons.

My thinking would envisage this message – the foundation document – in a short well presented booklet form.

I believe that there are considerable advantages in adopting such an approach.

1. If founding principles / objectives are published on their own, it may not necessarily concentrate the people's attention as to the reason why a new political party is needed.

2. The founding principles / objectives are a logical follow-on from our reasons for setting up a new political party.

3. It relieves the party of immediately having to produce detailed party positions on various economic and social issues.

4. By having the preamble and foundation principles adjoined in the foundation document, we tap the disillusioned vote in all parties and enlarge our constituency.

5. What we are really hoping for is a realignment in Irish politics and to break the traditional Fianna Fail / Fine Gael voting patterns. By having the preamble, we are putting down on paper something that nearly everyone realises, i.e. that the tweedledum / tweedledee political approach of these parties has failed.

6. By having the preamble and principles/objectives together in one booklet, we will attract the kind of people who want to join us but, more importantly will

automatically exclude persons who, while agreeing that something radical needs to be done and that the present party political structure is outdated and failed etc., <u>would not</u> feel happy re our objectives on liberal social legislation and / or the economic approach.

NOTE BOOK.

A. I consider it very necessary that the founding principles have at least one objective re women. However, as we have experts in that area, I leave that field open to them.

B. Having looked at my founding principles, I am sure that I have overlooked some obvious ones – but I am sure that we will cover and / or eliminate when all participants have put their views on the table.

From varied standpoints on the Irish political compass, the people initiating this new party, have already arrived at certain judgements on the present Irish political process;

1. We recognise that a large segment of Irish society are disillusioned and disenchanted with the present Irish party political system.

2. We believe that the Irish people will respond positively to an honest, clear thinking, enterprised based and socially progressive political party.

3. Due to the absence of brave, visionary, political leadership for some time, the Irish people have lost their enterprise, initiative and hope in the future.

4. We believe that barring some economic miracle, the viability of Ireland as an independent economic unit is threatened.

5. We believe that, as our economic problems are so massive and so rapidly deteriorating, that time is running out for the state to avoid a total breakdown of democratic institutions which will result in anarchy; and furthermore that the chaotic state of the public finances, will inevitably lead to interference from foreign lending institutions in the running of the Irish economy.

6. Increasing unemployment and emigration has led to a feeling of hopelessness in the Country.

7. The Irish people have lost faith in their politicians and political parties and they firmly believe that it is irrelevant as to the political grouping in power at any time in the future.

8. We believe that there is no difference between Fianna Fail and Fine Gael and that any difference is superficial and stems from Civil War positions, and such considerations have no place in the political consciousness of modern Ireland.

9. Normal political development has never evolved due to the Civil War and that a realignment in Irish politics is inevitable and desirable.

10. The main Irish political leaders and their parties are perceived, some to a greater or lesser degree, as power hungry, intolerant, and interested only in expedient short term political solutions to the exclusion of the overall long term good.

11. We believe that the populist, all things to all people approach of Fianna Fail and Fine Gael has resulted in the Irish people having no real alternative at elections.

12. Real social legislative changes are hindered by the absence of any clear philosophy of the major parties and especially because such initiations would be resisted by powerful interests groups, primarily the Catholic Church, and as such upset party voting patterns.

AND,

HAVING AGREED ON THE FOREGOING, WE BELIEVE IT
IS IMPERATIVE ON US TO EMBARK ON THE ESTABLISHMENT
OF THIS NEW POLITICAL PARTY – "ANOTHER"
WHICH IS FOUNDED ON THE FOLLOWING PRINCIPLES AND OBJECTIVES.

PRINCIPLES AND OBJECTIVES.

1. Our National aspiration is the unity of Ireland by consent and by peaceful means and our policy shall derive from the historic agreement of all the Irish nationalist parties in the report of the New Ireland Forum.

2. To give at all times honest, brave and courageous leadership and all policies to be for the benefit of all the people.

3. Our economic policies will be enterprised based and [based] on the need to restore initiative. [The word 'incentive' is handwritten here.]

4. To ensure that the principles of freedom of expression, civil and religious liberty and equal rights for all citizens are embodied in all policies.

5. Our social welfare policies will be biased in favour of the under privileged sections of Irish society.

6. To reduce the level of state involvement and interference in the economic life of the Country.

7. The State shall live within its means.

8. To reduce the level of national debt and to keep it at a level consistent with our state of economic development and thereby reducing taxation.

9. To create the conditions that all Irish people can live meaningful and worthwhile lives in Ireland.

10. To eliminate discrimination in all areas.

APPENDIX 3

September, 1985

NOTES AS COMPILED BY PAUL MACKAY

Ireland and the Irish people require positive, honest and dynamic leadership. This is particularly so in the area of politics.

The options presently available to the Electorate are not very attractive. A new party, with a new leader, untainted by the dishonesty of the past and removed from the politics of the Civil War may well be attractive to the Irish Electorate. Personality and politics will obviously play an important role in obtaining the confidence and support of the Electorate.

I list below a selection of the policies I would like to see a new party embrace and progress when the opportunities arise:-

(1) Enterprise. Emphasis on innovation, creativity and self help. Spotlight at all times placed on self reliance, pride in self and pride in the community – moving away from the politics of hand-outs and begging bowl mentality. For example, the Country cannot, at the present time, support the Social Welfare System. According to the Annual Reports for 1983 and 1984, as issued by the Department of Social Welfare, over 700,000 people received welfare payments each week. Adding to this figure their dependents the number benefiting from Social Welfare Receipts is 1¼ million people or 35% of the population. If the Country wishes to provide such a service then it must be in a position to earn same and not pay for same through borrowings and/or excessive taxation which only discourages enterprise.

(2) Tax Based Incentives for Creative Capital Investments. More emphasis should be placed on giving tax concessions/advantages for monies invested in certain projects that cannot be provided by the State. For example the building of industrial units and residential flat units were successfully provided by the private sector when attractive and real tax incentives were provided by the State. However, both these schemes were open-ended and eventually too many industrial units and recently too many residential flat units are chasing too few customers. Where tax concessions are to be granted in the future, they should be limited to a certain quantity and/or level.

The Irish roadwork system needs to be totally overhauled and in most places replaced and this is an area where the State could have the work completed by private enterprise with the aid of tax incentives.

Aer Lingus needs to replace its fleet but the cost is estimated at the prohibitive sum of £70m. Again, this is an area where private funds might be invested if the tax related benefits are made attractive.

(3) <u>Lifting of the Burden – Small and Medium Sized Firms.</u> It is important that the Government removes unnecessary regulations from small and medium sized firms. These firms are being bogged down by bureaucratic red tape. For Example the following should be considered:-

(a) Qualifying period for Unfair Dismissals.
(b) Company Law on accounting and audit requirements.
(c) Simplifying VAT procedures and raising the threshold from the present levels.
(d) Reduction of work load on employers arising from Income Tax deductions and Pay-Related Insurance Contributions.
(e) Abolition of restrictions on shop opening hours.

Managements and Companies need increased freedom of action against the growing Government intrusion and restrictions. There is a threat from the so called blue chip, risk free society that sees Government as having the responsibility to provide economic benefits rather than individuals facing their own obligations.

(4) <u>Banks</u>. Banks should be encouraged to take a more positive role in supporting new, small businesses. They should be encouraged to set aside a certain proportion of the reserves for equity investments in small enterprises, particularly those with export potential and/or high employment levels. Banks should also be encouraged to take advantage of tax based concessions as stated in (2) above.

(5) <u>Civil Service.</u> A total overhaul is required and in fairness to John Boland, the present Minister for the Public Service, he is making certain, positive moves in the right direction. What is required is an efficient, professional civil service that is properly motivated and responsible for its actions with all members being responsible for their actions and accountable for same. Administrative aids, machinery, etc. should be made available and utilised to the maximum by the Civil Service to make it a more cost effective and efficient Organisation.

(6) <u>Revenue Collection.</u> The Collector Generals Office of the Revenue Commissioners is in total disarray at the present time. The collection of revenue, unfortunately, is centralised and the system needs to be totally overhauled and

possibly decentralised so as to ensure that collection is properly exercised throughout the length and breadth of Country. By localising collection as, for example rates, the local officers will know the local circumstances and will be in a position to act accordingly.

(7) <u>Building Societies</u>. The proposals as set out in the recent Dail Sub-Committee Report should be fully investigated. These organisations need to be properly monitored, controlled and where necessary overhauled.

(8) <u>Drink and Absenteeism</u>. The E.M.S. Foundation shows that Ireland occupies 23rd place out of 28 countries in a survey of labour absenteeism in their report on International Competitiveness 1985. The C.I.I. commenting on the Report states that it is far too easy to blame employees, trade unions, Government and even the medical profession when it is ultimately the responsibility of management to ensure that an enterprise is managed effectively. The focus for this control they say must be part of an enlightened personnel management policy in each enterprise.

In a Country where manhood and even now womanhood appears to be achieved only in terms of the ability to get sloshed with the best I feel that management is up against it. No matter how effectively run, firms where half the employees are suffering from alcoholic poisoning every Monday are bound to suffer from a low G.D.P. per capita and account for Ireland coming last, but for Greece, on this score in the E.E.C. league.

(9) <u>Labour Laws</u>. The Labour Laws need to be reviewed, particularly trade union law and the law of Unfair Dismissals. The principle that every dismissal is deemed to be an unfair dismissal, unless the employer can prove otherwise, must be abolished. The main principle of law is that no one is deemed guilty unless he or she is proven guilty should be the main thrust of any new legislation. The Unfair Dismissals Act is presently a deterrent for employers taking on new employees.

Every effort must now be made to ensure that employers and employees are not restricted in carrying out their daily tasks. Bureaucratic and unwieldy laws and regulations must be reviewed with this objective in mind.

(10) <u>Hospital and Medical Services.</u> Far too much money is being spent and in a lot of cases wasted in providing hospital and medical services to the general public. These services should only be available to those who cannot afford to pay for same. Hospitals should be provided for the sick and not a play thing for the medical profession and a battle field for the trade unions. Far too much money and resources are now being squandered in these areas.

(11) <u>Childrens Allowances and Food Subsidies and Other Non Means Tested Benefits</u>. Persons should only obtain benefits from the State where they require same. Willy nilly cash payouts to all and sundry should not be the order of the day.

(12) <u>Clientilism</u>. Under the present P.R. System politicians breed contempt and bring themselves down to the level of the messenger boy looking for favours from those they should be directing and supervising, i.e. Civil Servants and Local Authorities. They give the impression to Constituents and to the public in general that they can interfere with the law of the land and get special favours and concessions that individual constituents could get for himself if he or she was properly directed/advised. Public representatives are elected to govern and ensure that State Offices and the whole State apparatus is properly and fairly operated for the benefit of the majority of the citizens of the State.

(13) <u>Northern Ireland</u>. Here I will make a brief and personal comment as how I consider the way the problem should be addressed. The Country requires less waving of the green flag and the playing of the so called green card by politicians and para militaries. What in my opinion is required is more emphasis on hammering out practical and realisable objectives. We need to build bridges, not walls. Instant and impractical solutions with short term political gain are not the answer. A United Ireland, if it is to be achieved, will not be achieved by violence – violence only begets violence and creates barriers for future generations. To alleviate the problem we in the South of Ireland have to make the Irish Republic an attractive proposition to the pragmatic and industrious Unionists who know a good thing when they see it.

The Republic of Ireland in its present form is not an attractive alternative to the Unionists at the present time. The nationalists and the Unionists will have to make peace within Northern Ireland and agree to live together within the province of Northern Ireland. Hopefully when this peace and living together has been established then and only then can the South of Ireland really think about working towards a united Ireland which means uniting and the merging of the various traditions and ideals of <u>all</u> peoples of the Island.

INDEX